The Scriptural Universe of Ancient Christianity

The

SCRIPTURAL UNIVERSE

of

ANCIENT CHRISTIANITY

Guy G. Stroumsa

Harvard University Press

Cambridge, Massachusetts
London, England
2016

Copyright © 2016 by the President and Fellows of Harvard College
All rights reserved

Second printing

Library of Congress Cataloging-in-Publication Data
Names: Stroumsa, Guy G., author.
Title: The scriptural universe of ancient Christianity / Guy G. Stroumsa.
Description: Cambridge : Harvard University Press, Massachusetts / 2016. |
Includes bibliographical references and index.
Identifiers: LCCN 2016015530 | ISBN 9780674545137 (cloth)
Subjects: LCSH: Sacred books—History and criticism. |
Church history—Primitive and early church, ca. 30—600. |
Christianity and other religions. | Books—Religious aspects—Christianity.
Classification: LCC BL71 .S77 2016 | DDC 208/.2—dc23
LC record available at https://lccn.loc.gov/2016015530

CONTENTS

Introduction: A Double Paradigm Shift	1
1. A Scriptural Galaxy	10
2. A Divine Palimpsest	29
3. Religious Revolution and Cultural Change	40
4. Scripture and Culture	55
5. The New Self and Reading Practices	71
6. Communities of Knowledge	83
7. Eastern Wisdoms	97
8. A World Full of Letters	108
9. Scriptural and Personal Authority	121
Conclusion: Alexandria, Jerusalem, Baghdad	132
Notes	*139*
Acknowledgments	*179*
Index	*181*

Ἰερουσαλήμ, ἀκυβέρνητη πολιτεία,
Ἰερουσαλήμ, πολιτεία τῆς προφυγιᾶς.

Jerusalem, drifting city,
Jerusalem, city of refugees.

—George Seferis, *Stratis Thalassinos
on the Dead Sea*

This book deals with the intricate relations between religion and culture in late antiquity. It was written in Jerusalem, a tragic city in which bigotry always lurks. I wish to dedicate it to my students in Jerusalem, in Oxford and elsewhere, who learn about the past in order to promote the values of humanism.

INTRODUCTION

A Double Paradigm Shift

Late antiquity saw a revolution in literate culture the consequences of which would be no less dramatic than that of the invention of the movable type in early modernity. I refer here not only to the transformation of the physical support of books but also, and more importantly, to the redaction of foundational texts of new religions, from Christianity to Islam, which perceived themselves as world religions (Manichaeism would be the first religion to define itself as such from the very start). These texts circulated almost freely between religious communities throughout the ecumene—and also across religious lines. In an age of religious empires, it was by the book, rather than by the sword, that the new world religions conquered, and that would remain true, to a great extent, for the Islamization of the Near East. In this early "global village," within and without the borders of the Roman Empire, it was often in translation that those texts circulated, and that commentaries were elaborated, usually in writing but also orally.

Such changes were radical, but in the Roman world the status of books underwent changes of an even more drastic nature. These pertained to their role in religion and religious education. Several religious trends developed in that period, for which various revealed, sacred scriptures were a cardinal element in their self-definition. Hence, we often speak of "religions of the book," and of "the scriptural movement" of the long late antiquity—from the redaction of the New Testament and of the Mishna, at the turn of the third century, to that of the Qur'an in the seventh.[1] This "scriptural movement," is considered typically by way of canon formation and hermeneutics. However, such investigation relegates to the shadows other aspects of books and their uses, such as patterns of reading. Rather than to a "scriptural movement," therefore, I refer here to the "scriptural universe" of ancient Christianity.

The notion of a "scriptural universe" offers a twofold advantage: first, it implies the vast dimensions and complex dynamics of the patterns involved, and second, it allows us to approach these patterns as indicative of a single, superordinate phenomenon. This phenomenon was that the transformation of religious life in late antiquity was to a great extent achieved through the dramatic success of Christianity. Traditional approaches to early Christianity (studied, almost, as if it had grown in a vacuum) are fraught with theological preconceptions and methodological misperceptions. The approach of the historian of religion cannot be that of the Church historian. Yet, it lies beyond the scope of this book to draw even a sketch of the scriptures of the different religious communities, or their hermeneutical literature. I shall not deal here separately with the scriptural systems (scriptures, canonization process, development of hermeneutical rules, etc.) within Rabbinic Judaism, Patristic Christianity, Sasanian Zoroastrianism or Manichaeism—or among the Neoplatonists. Many such descriptive studies, at once broad and detailed, can already be found.[2] This research, however, too frequently privileges the cognitive aspects of books, while neglecting the recently discovered performative and emotional aspects of books in late antique religions.

The Christianization of the Roman world promoted the growth of new modes of religiosity, in different cultural traditions and among various ethnic groups.[3] Books, including sacred books, had of course existed in archaic and ancient societies. Now, however, they were invested with a new status as they took the place previously held by sacrifice. The growth of Christianity also transformed attitudes toward Hellenic culture, just as it had offered a radical reinterpretation of the religion of Israel. Excepting Marcion and some Gnostic thinkers, the early Christian theologians did not strive to blot out the biblical tradition.[4] They sought, rather, to reinterpret and appropriate it. Likewise, most Church

Fathers never wished to eliminate the Greek cultural traditions, and were content to adopt them instead. More precisely, they took on those traditions that they deemed valuable and compatible with the new faith, such as philosophical *koinē*, mainly Platonic and Stoic thought, but not mythology and the Homeric epics. The new *cultura christiana* that was forming in late antiquity would eventually become the backbone of European cultural identity.

THE PRESENT study is thus a sequel of sorts to *The End of Sacrifice: Religious Transformations in Late Antiquity*. In that book I called attention to the disappearance of public blood sacrifices from the core of religious ritual, in various religious systems across the late antique Mediterranean basin and the Near East.[5] This disappearance, I argued, both reflected and reinforced an extraordinary modification in the very nature of religion, one so radical that we may speak of a real paradigm shift. I also set out a new approach to the "care of the self," and a fresh emphasis on the religious component of identity, usually expressed through participation in a community. These in turn led to a new relationship between public and private religion. Without question, the development of private cults in late antiquity stems from the new approach to religion that took shape around the fourth century.[6]

I pursue here the line of research initiated in that work on a new, central role played by revealed books or sacred texts in different religions. I shall do that by arguing that it reflects another paradigmatic shift, encompassing, beyond religion, other aspects of culture. More precisely, I seek to examine here the multifaceted transformation of the status and function of books and reading in the Christianized Roman world, asking how the new official belief in a revealed scripture impacted upon the attitude toward books in general. Essentially, one could say that in the ancient world, books were to literate culture what sacrifices were to religion. From the first to the fourth century C.E., the material support of the book underwent a dramatic change, in the passage from *volumen*, or roll, to *codex*. The implications of this passage were immense. While the benefits of *codex* over *volumen* have been well described, the religious impact of the change remains understudied. More than to any other single factor, the conversion of the Roman world may be traced to the codex. This book form advanced a dynamic, literate, and effective mode of religious mission and cultural transmission, one that took place across huge geographical areas. The paradigm shift in late antiquity thus is a double rather than a single one, affecting both religion and other aspects of culture.

THE FRENCH philosopher Rémi Brague has offered a new slant on the perennial problem of the relationship between religion and culture. For him, it was only through Christianity, from Paul on, that the idea of a Greek culture came into being.[7] What did exist until then was *paideia,* a broad term referring to a global life style. *Paideia* included what we call culture, but was not limited to it, as Greek religion was also part of it. In a sense, Brague sums up, Greek culture is *paideia* minus religion. Particularly intriguing in Brague's formulation is the parallel he draws between Christianity's double derivativeness, vis-à-vis both Judaism and Hellenism. According to him, only the first, its derivativeness vis-à-vis Judaism, permitted the second. Brague's insight echoes Harold Bloom's claim about poetry: creativity should be understood as "a map of misreading."

The religious revolution of late antiquity, then, having (more or less) eliminated sacrifice as a central element of religious ritual, put the book in its place.[8] First, the canonized Book (or Books) of God's revelation, and, beyond that, a whole hermeneutical literature, continually growing and reorganizing itself in circles of secondary (and tertiary) hermeneutical canons. This is true in Rabbinic Judaism and in Sasanian Zoroastrianism as well as in Patristic Christianity. The Rabbis, however, required a more complex structure to inherit and reinterpret Greek philosophy as they had inherited and reinterpreted Israelite religion. Appropriation was the touchstone for early Christian thinkers with regard to Jewish and Greek books.

The salvaging of the Greek cultural tradition (or at least those parts of it—mainly philosophy—deemed worthy) in the Christianized Roman Empire demonstrated a historical paradox. Among the late antique Christian religious elites, bishops and monks, in different ways, functioned as carriers of a culture they despised (let us not forget that "Greek" for Christian authors writing in Greek, usually meant "pagan"). In like manner, these persons were also the carriers of Jewish texts, while despising contemporary Jews, whom they deemed incapable of grasping the words of their own prophets. The early monks, in particular, were strikingly negative toward Greek culture. For them, Hellenism was at once cognitively false and ethically wrong. That these revolutionaries transmitted cultural patterns and texts that they vigorously repudiated is quite intriguing. Precisely here lies the historical paradox in the transmission of *paideia* in early Christianity: it was effected by marginal groups of "outsiders" rather than by the mainstream intellectual elites. Indeed it was precisely their alienation from Greco-Roman *paideia* that made it possible for the monks to introduce hitherto unknown forms of reading and writing.[9]

We are groping here for a grammar of cultural transmission. Salvaging pagan culture meant, in a sense, its sacralization, just as the Christianization of the Empire entailed the acculturation of religion. To a great extent, both religious and cultural transmission in late antiquity are directly linked to mobility.[10] Different webs connected people and communities, throughout the Roman Empire, and also across political boundaries, as Syriac and Talmudic literatures abundantly show. It is through the travel of persons that ideas and behavioral patterns circulated: merchants, soldiers, prisoners, teachers, students, and missionaries all contributed to the flow of information about different forms of culture and structures of religion.

THE LATE ancient transformation of modes of culture parallels such transformation in the modes of religion. Religion transformed the status of cultural heritage, just as cultural heritage left a deep imprint on religious identities. Books would now move to the front and center of the religious stage. This is true both for ritual and theology—the latter term being defined at once as an intellectual reflection on religion and as a hermeneutical effort to interpret the scriptures. Judaism and Christianity, on the one hand, and the "pagan" religions, on the other, are typically considered to diverge at the point of monotheism.[11] Yet, I propose that it is the one Book, at least as much as the one God, that distinguishes Judaism and Christianity from their competitors in the ancient world. This book, starting with Abraham, was translated and interpreted to the extent that it created a whole new field of knowledge.

One may say that the hermeneutical mind is the *forma mentis* specific of the Abrahamic religions. In such a mindset, knowledge is a major dimension of religion, on a par with ritual and religious experience.

The consequences of the double paradigm shift of late antiquity were dramatic enough for one to even speak, tentatively, of a new "axial age." The German philosopher Karl Jaspers coined the term *Achsenzeit* to describe dramatic transformations in approaches to thought and salvation in archaic societies, from Greece to China, around the middle of the first millennium B.C.E. Despite its evocative powers, Jaspers' conception has come under serious criticism.[12] For our purposes, the term "axial age" seems to fit late antiquity better than the period suggested by Jaspers.[13] It is also along a special axis that the double paradigm change reflected in the religious and cultural transformations of late antiquity took place. It permitted the intersocietal transmission of religious and cultural trends and ideas, crossing the East-West divide on the Eastern *limes* of the Roman Empire. The early modern historian Sanjay Subrahmanyam suggested the term "connected history" to describe the complex interchange between East and West in the age of the great discoveries.[14] A similar approach might be fruitfully applied to late antiquity. The age of religious empires was also the age of great missionary movements: Christianity, Buddhism, and Manichaeism before Islam, which helped, each in its own way, to carry and transform theologoumena and rituals across Asia, along the Silk Road. The *limes* culture was a cultural *koinē* shared by people with different linguistic, ethnic, and religious identities, as well as political allegiances. It is in this *limes* culture that what I propose to call "connected religious history" (and which in German is referred to as *Transkuturalität*) can be best studied.

THE EXTENSIVE imbrication of religion and culture in early Christianity, throughout late antiquity, is laid out in the following nine chapters, which follow neither a chronological nor a strictly thematic order. Perhaps they might be thought of as so many variations on the themes delineated in this introduction.

Chapter 1, dealing with questions of communication and language and with canonization processes, presents a panorama of the late antique "textual communities." Building on Subrahmanyam, it also introduces the idea of connected religious history and assesses the idea of a "scriptural movement" in late antiquity.

The consideration of religious memory links us to a theme that will be developed in Chapter 2, where I analyze different kinds of religious memory, implicit and explicit, in various modes of religiosity. I also take up the memory aspect of the paradigm shift in ancient Christianity.

From there, Chapter 3 tackles questions of historiography of the Roman Empire and its Christianization. It asks about the implications of cultural and religious change on the concept of *paideia,* and how this was perceived by a number of leading twentieth-century religious historians. The main purpose of this chapter is to understand the conceptual genealogy of the dynamics between religious revolution and cultural change in late antiquity.

Only then do I deal directly, in Chapter 4, with Scripture and *paideia,* with hermeneutical communities in late antiquity; that is, with what I call secondary canons and with hermeneutical writings. My emphasis on Augustine, a central witness to the new *cultura christiana* in the making, foregrounds the fresh approach to books in Patristic culture.

In Chapter 5, I argue that the new status of books, as well as the immediate popularity of the codex among Christians, permitted the development of new reading practices, in particular within the monastic movement. I further claim that these new reading practices transformed the reading system altogether.

This new reading system is best exemplified in the monastic communities of knowledge, dealt with in Chapter 6. In the emerging *cultura Dei,* the new relationship between religion and knowledge is demonstrated by the privileging of *epistēmē* (discursive knowledge) over *gnōsis* (soteriological knowledge).

In Chapter 7, I deal with the fascination, even infatuation, with the East and its traditions of wisdom. This fascination did not start with Nietzsche's *Also sprach Zarathustra.* In the late antique Near East, the phenomenon of *"limes* intellectuals" showed the porousness of political boundaries and their permeability to cultural traditions. Barbarian scriptures and barbarian cultures reached a distinct and distinguished status among late antique *literati,* both pagans and Christians.

Chapter 8 pursues further the question of contacts and exchanges between Eastern and Western cultural traditions. Spotlighting a striking document stemming from Palestinian monasticism, it seeks to highlight the mystical and magical power of the letters of the alphabet in late antiquity. The text called *On the Mystery of the Greek Letters* is particularly topical for our quest, as it reflects the Christian entwining of Greek and Jewish traditions.

Finally, Chapter 9 attempts to delineate the relationship between scriptural and personal authority. These two types of authority relate to the written and oral transmission of scripture. The taxonomy underscores the dialectics between texts and teachers, and between the authority of the establishment and that of the charismatic leader. It also lays bare the complex, perennial relationship of the One and the Many, of revelation and education in Christianity.

The limitations of this book are quite obvious to me. Although I sought to cast my net wide (probably much too wide for the taste of many) and tackle a number of related problems, I was obliged by considerations of space to leave some important issues outside the scope of my inquiry. For instance, I could not deal with topics such as scriptures as objects, the performative uses of books, the roles of books in prayer, or spirituality and magic.

TOO OFTEN, the late ancient world is declined in a dual mode: Jews and Christians, pagans and Christians, pagans and Jews, Christians, and Manichaeans. This binary approach is somewhat misleading: religious identities should not be granted an ontic, static character that they did not possess.[15] Moreover, as should now be obvious, only by subtle and dynamic recourse to the antique world can we hope to have any grasp at all on its reality. Late antiquity saw the passage from the "theological triangle" of pagans, Jews, and Christians—to another "theological triangle," that of Christians, Muslims, and Jews—the "Abrahamic triangle." The civilizations that issued from the Abrahamic triangle would remain in contact and conflict for more than a millennium in both Europe and Asia.[16] It is in late antiquity, before the rise of Islam, that the hearts and minds in the Near East were prepared to receive the message of the new prophet from Arabia. In a strong sense, late antiquity is the crucible of the Abrahamic religions. In the Near East, there would be in the early Islamic centuries a dramatic new Arabic chapter in the transmission of Greek thought that had started in Greek, Latin, and Syriac in late antiquity. Although this major chapter in the history of Western thought falls beyond the scope of our investigation, the following pages study aspects of what may be called *praeparatio coranica*.[17]

IN NO way does this book attempt to present a synthetic view of the scriptural universe of early Christianity. Like any universe, it was patently variable, responding continually to other scriptural universes. I do hope, however, to give the reader a sense of the dazzling complexity, of the turbulence created by the whirlpool of texts, oral traditions and behavioral patterns stemming from varied religious and cultural backgrounds in the Mediterranean and Near East.[18] But if it is no synthetic work, neither does it represent the analytical exposition of a clearly delineated problem, drawing directly from a limited corpus of primary sources. The present book, rather, based upon my work in the past few decades, was purposefully written as a historiographical essay. As a second-order reflection, it argues that the creation of a Christian culture in late antiquity stemmed from a network of communities, with their practices, their stories, and their books.[19] Like any essay, this one will take shortcuts, so to speak, from time to time.[20] For instance, I resort to traditional terms such as "Judaism," "Christianity," or "Gnosticism" without always indicating that they do not necessarily reflect historical or social realities adequately. Of course, concepts such as "Judaism," "Christianity," or "Gnosticism," possessed as they are with a rather questionable ontology, are somewhat problematic. Yet, the current fashion of referring to the plural ("Judaisms," "Christianities"), of casting doubts as to the heuristic usefulness of "Gnosticism" in order to refer to various dualist trends in early Christianity, strikes me as raising as many questions as it purports to answer.

Let us then start our brisk circuit, through which we shall be able to glimpse some of the most brilliant stars in the scriptural universe of ancient Christianity.

1

A SCRIPTURAL GALAXY

Introduction

A traditional taxonomy differentiates between scriptural and nonscriptural religions. Scriptures are revealed texts, whose authorship is believed to be divine. While certain books (we may speak of "foundational texts") did play a significant role in nonscriptural religions (such as Greek or Roman religion) it is generally assumed that this role was fundamentally different from that played by revealed scriptures. This assumption has been convincingly questioned.[1] The concept of "sacred scriptures" was introduced in the context of nineteenth-century Romanticism and Orientalism, where it facilitated a Western examination of Hinduism and Buddhism.[2] The notion of sacred scriptures, however, does not add a great deal to our understanding of ancient religions. While the development of writing impacted enormously on religion, "sacred scriptures" were in no way an inevitable result of this development. Rather, they remain a particular case in history. Unquestionably, religions that made use of script (and hence, books) had a major advantage over those that did not do so, or those that did so only minimally.[3] In that sense, what has been called the "scriptural turn" of the first millennium B.C.E. was also highly instrumental in the emergence of a religion of the book in ancient Israel.[4]

Scriptural religions (or "religions of the Book") such as Judaism, Christianity and Islam are frequently counterposed to archaic religions like those of Greece and Rome.[5] Yet, sacred books were also known in late antique Hellenic religion; one may recall for instance the *hieroi nomoi* or the *Orphic Hymns* in Greece.[6] The Sybilline Oracles in Rome are a further example. Even the ritual-centered Roman religion was transformed by books[7] and could also be called, to a certain extent, a "religion of the Book."

In this chapter, I reflect on the complex role of writing and books in the late ancient mutation of religion. In doing so, I shall make some preliminary forays into what I propose to call, borrowing from Marshall McLuhan, "the scriptural galaxy" of late antiquity.[8] Until fairly recently, both the material side of holy books and their importance in magical and divinatory practices was downplayed.[9] Hence, scholarly discussions of scriptures in late antiquity tend to be based on a rather static perception of religion. Scriptures, indeed, are one pole, among others, of religious life, related at once to a series of hermeneutical writings (in different genres), oral traditions of interpretation, rituals, and nonritual actions such as divination or magical practices. Moreover, texts do not act in history by themselves, and the question of agency cannot be ignored. Human beings redact, copy, memorize, read, study, teach, and transmit scripture.[10] In the scriptural galaxy, then, scripture is best contextualized as one important element in an acutely dynamic system. Moreover, scripture should be read against the backdrop of the exegetical polemics of heretical groups, as well as in light of its polemical relationship with the scriptural systems of other religious communities. Such an approach is quite labor intensive, but it may help us grasp the dramatic scriptural turn of late antique religion.

Alongside those of Jews, Christians, and Zoroastrians, the sacred texts of a number of heretical trends in the Abrahamic system deserve consideration. Both as they emerged and later, these texts were censored by mainstream theologians, and designated as "apocryphal"—the antithesis, so to speak, of the "legitimate" scriptures. Such books, perceived as dangerous precisely because of their similarity to official scriptures, frequently were set for public destruction, usually by fire. The burning of religious books was a known practice in late antiquity.[11] A large number of apocryphal texts (in particular Gospels and Acts attributed to the various Apostles) redacted among early Christians soon became prized among the various Gnostic and other dualist trends of early Christianity. Similarly, the Manichaeans and Mandaeans produced a large number of new texts, both scriptural and hermeneutical, which they made use of alongside existing literature. Some other groups, on the borderline between religion and philosophy, such as the Hermetists or the Neo-Pythagoreans, also generated numerous religious writings.

I SHALL now make some brief remarks on the status of books and reading in Roman society. The first centuries of the common era saw a surge in literacy rates and a revolution in the material support of books, from roll to codex.[12] Together with literacy, the number of readers seems to have grown steadily in the Empire. Nonetheless, literacy in Roman society, while significant, remained limited. As such, written and oral expressions of culture intermingled constantly, creating a singular late-ancient hybrid. This hybrid, which we might call "limited literacy," is a particular phenomenon, with a specific set of consequences. One of them is an intense interplay between the private and public use of books. In Rome, books were written to be read in public (*recitatio*) as much as enjoyed in private. Another consequence concerns the powers attached to literacy: in a world where even prayers were recited aloud, silent reading was associated with sorcery. Books, then, stood at the intersection of author, reader, and public. The balance of this triadic relationship would be upset by the new status of the Bible, God's revealed text, in Christianized Roman society.

Books could be bought in Rome, although they were expensive. *Tabernae librariae,* bookstores, were found in many cities. Although its dimensions are unknown, a Roman book trade definitely existed.[13] The public taste for reading was whetted by a new form of book, complete with new editorial devices. These included separations between texts, which helped new categories of readers (referred to as *uulgus, plebs, media plebs,* and *plebeia manus,* in which Ovid includes women) to read.

It is probably more accurate to speak of the circulation than of the publication of books in the Roman world. Books were usually kept in libraries.[14] Indeed, libraries and Latin books emerged at approximately the same time. The first Roman libraries were born of conquests—events that also caused the destruction of libraries—for instance, that of Alexandria by Julius Caesar (in 47 B.C.E.). Similarly, books could be stolen from libraries: for example, Antony confiscates those of Pergamon and gives them to Cleopatra. Like the *recitatio,* the public reading of literary works, Roman patronage encouraged the establishment of private libraries. Lucullus, who builds an impressive library in his Tusculum villa, is one example. In the absence of copyright laws and the presence of limited copyist accuracy, it is thanks to public libraries that a modicum of stability was achieved in the transmission and conservation of literature. Indeed, to deny a book reception at a public library was to condemn it to death. Further, literary books were read in public, sometimes in cenacles. Literary prizes, together with these public lectures, strengthened the chances of a book's survival. As well, the author himself (almost invariably a male) might hand out free copies of his book.

Some studies have stressed the sociological dimensions of ancient literacy. William Johnson, for instance, in a published collection of articles on the culture of reading in Greece and Rome, has treated elite reading communities in the high empire.[15] Such studies, typically authored by classical scholars, pay scant attention to the history of religions in late antiquity. It seems that there is room for fresh efforts to better understand the *religious* dimensions of book culture in the "textual communities" of late antiquity.[16]

Across premodern societies, cultures retained important oral dimensions, and literacy remained, even in the best of times, a privilege of very few. In such cultures, books were used primarily as instruments for the authentication of texts rather than as a means of communication. Among the responses provoked a decade ago by William Harris's important book on literacy in the ancient world[17] was that of Mary Beard. She noted that Roman paganism, far from being a "text-free" religion, granted considerable significance to writing.[18] For his part, Keith Hopkins has identified what he called "sub-elite" literacy among late-antique Christians and the pivotal part this literacy played in the Christian "conquest" of the Roman Empire. Hopkins contended, for instance, that the Coptic language may have been used, early on, as a "script of protest." He adduced as proof of this notion that Coptic was the language of many preserved manuscripts stemming from Gnostic, Manichaean, or monastic circles—all of them, in different ways and varying degrees, marginal movements. Discussing the incessant interweaving of the written and the oral, Hopkins concluded that it was Christianity's peculiar attitude toward its scriptures that enabled it to develop the coherence necessary for its eventual victory over the Roman Empire.

As noted above, books were transformed in the Empire. First and foremost was the change in the material support of books in their form.

Books, which had traditionally been written on scrolls, from the first to the fourth centuries increasingly took the form of codices—although these codices, like the scrolls, were usually written on papyrus rather than on parchment. In this regard, Guglielmo Cavallo, perhaps the leading scholar on books in the Roman world in general and in early Christianity in particular, has described the passage of scroll to codex as nothing less than a revolution.[19] Indeed, this passage represents the most dramatic transformation in the history of the book prior to Gutenberg.

In the religious world of late antiquity, form and function of books were inextricably tied. By the end of the fourth century, the codex had definitively won the battle of form. Much has been written in the past few decades on the transition from scroll, or *volumen*, to codex, and this move can hardly be overemphasized. Since the pioneering studies of Colin H. Roberts and T. C. Skeat, and up to recent reevaluation of the evidence, we have learned a great deal about this passage. Codices were cheaper to produce than scrolls, since the text was written on both sides of the papyrus or parchment, and they were more compact and thus easier to carry. As well, codices had the advantage of ease of use; reference from section to section was made much simpler. In short, the circulation of ideas was transformed radically. During the fourth and fifth centuries, different works began to be placed within a single codex, and various editorial aids, such as "incipit" or "explicit," were inserted at the start or end of each work. These large books required the use of only one hand (unlike the scroll, for which two hands were needed). Moreover, the wide margins offered room for jotting down notes on the text itself. In sixth-century Italy, Cassiodorus used this technique. His glosses on the Psalter, which were heavily influenced by Augustine, had a major impact on the making of medieval monastic culture.[20]

Religious Transformations and Textual Communities

In the first four centuries of the Common Era, the passage from scroll to codex occurred faster among Christians than among other religious communities. The consequences of this well-known phenomenon for religion warrant serious scrutiny, as they were both diverse and deep: besides being cheaper to produce and easier to carry than the scroll, the codex permitted easier intertextual cross-references, thus encouraging the development of new hermeneutical patterns. From now on, books would play a central role in all religions, not only in the so-called religions of the book.[21] And religions without scriptures, such as the Oriental and Mystery cults, would not survive.

The shift in religion from sacrifice-centeredness to book-centeredness has been called a move from cult religion to book religion: *Kultreligion* to *Buchreligion*.[22] Despite its heuristic attraction, I consider such a neat categorization misleading, as books did not actually replace religious ritual. Rather, alongside their multiple cognitive roles (i.e., in theology, hermeneutics, or polemics) scriptures (as scroll or codex) also become directly associated with some of the core rituals of religion. I would suggest an alternative theorization: book as cult, or *Buch als Kult*. In the religious culture of late antiquity, books had important performative aspects, such as their role in public ritual, both in the synagogue and in the church. One can speak of a ritualized reading as well as writing, in particular of the Bible, among Jews and Christians alike. Moreover, the emotional component of books is a major and underrecognized aspect of their function. Unlike literary reading in Rome, which might be described as extensive, the reading of scripture is best described as intensive. This is true for both Christians and Jews, although for the latter, things are further complicated since much of the late antique hermeneutical tradition remained oral (i.e., the Oral Torah). Intensive reading, in particular the Psalms, becomes a real bibliotherapy: reading in the book of God, one deciphers one's own soul.[23]

One point is clear: henceforth, religion and books would be eternal bedfellows. Liturgy, hermeneutics, theology, polemics: books were now part and parcel of religious life and identity. Religious education could also become a scholarly venture, rather than a praxis-oriented skill acquisition alone. Becoming religiously mature might require significant literacy skills: an adult male Jew was now expected to be able to read the Torah scroll. Religion had also become a matter of learned interpretation, which followed clearly established hermeneutical rules.[24]

The Christians soon produced an impressive body of work, which went much beyond the texts later canonized in the New Testament, from the vast apocryphal literature to the early apostolic and apologetic texts, and the whole theological library of Patristic writings. In this context, a "media revolution" of early Christianity has been proposed.[25] Strikingly, however, after the Christianization of the Roman Empire, this literature did not become the core of Christian education. Only a minute proportion of Christian writings was translated and disseminated throughout the Christian *oikoumenē*.

Literacy rates, of course, had far from skyrocketed. Although such things are extremely difficult to measure, there is no reason to believe that many Christian males were highly literate (the only exception to the low rate of literacy seems to have been among the Jews).[26] However, across communities, the religious leadership was now highly literate, enriching without pause the world of scriptural hermeneutics as well as the life of ordinary persons.[27]

B RIAN STOCK coined the term "textual communities" to describe medieval communities in which the scriptural text was at the very core of daily life: the scriptural text was read, copied, chanted, commented, or meditated upon (in translation).[28] The members of a textual community, be it a monastery or a *beit midrash* are active participants in the life of the text. The phrase has better descriptive value in this context than that of another, somewhat related term, "reading communities," which works best among small privileged groups of highly educated people.[29] Scriptures and the interpretive literature that grew around them, whether commentaries or theological, legal, or polemical treatises, as well as meditative or midrashic texts became so central to the life of religious communities that one may even speak of "hermeneutic communities." The cognitive aspects of the book were rooted in religious education: full religious personhood demanded literacy.

It is tempting to apply Stock's useful term to late antiquity. However, the two sociological realities, that of late antiquity and of Western medieval Christendom, are so distinct from one another that such an effort would be intellectually questionable. Late antiquity was characterized still by extreme religious multiplicity. The period saw increasing complexity in the network of religious communities, which since Hellenistic times had gradually acquired their independence from ethnic traditional bonds, and even cultural milieus and linguistic environments. Religious communities of very different persuasions existed side by side, either in competition with or apparent ignorance of one another. Rivalry and ignorance, of course, never impeded the exchange of ideas or osmosis of religious practices. Little would remain of this religious plurality in the medieval period, both in the Latin West and in Byzantium, where all religious otherness would have long been branded as heretical or pagan.

Communication and Language

The world of late antiquity witnessed the birth of what we now call "world religions," that is, mass religions of salvation that can be adopted independently of one's ethnic, linguistic, and cultural identity. Christianity, then Manichaeism, and eventually Islam, are the main examples of world religions within the scope of our current purview. (Buddhism, which is a global religious movement, started earlier, and lies outside our present scope.) These religions traveled by and with books. Within an imperial context, and even more so when crossing imperial borders, books drove the engine of religion.

From Paul to Mani and beyond, religious leaders leveraged writings, which announced and advanced their mission to remote locales. These writings did not replace scriptures; rather, they affirmed them. Naturally, it was not only ecclesiastical persons who put books to use, but also, among many others, missionaries, holy men, merchants, and prisoners of war. While books traveled in many ways, however, they did not travel by themselves. The authority of a book highlights that of its carrier, who, in its turn, reinforces the book's status. Scriptures, copied by holy men, may be said to reflect, like them, the divine presence in the world. In late antique Christianity, the codex of the Gospels, the Logos incarnating the presence of Christ, is often the vestibule to contemplation. The scriptural codex and the holy man represent the two most striking icons of religious authority in late antiquity.[30] It is in the Valentinian *Gospel of Truth* that we find, perhaps, the most striking representation of scriptural strength: Christ on the cross is covered not by a tunic, but by a scroll of the scriptures.[31]

Thus, as books permitted a breadth of contact that would have been otherwise impossible in late antiquity, they constitute the key to the religious transformations of this period. Books were the vehicle of communication between like-minded communities as well as across religious boundaries. Here, the advantage of Christianity, Manichaeism, and eventually Islam over other religions and the Oriental cults in the Roman Empire (excepting Judaism) was quite clear: through their books, those missionary religions held the upper hand over their competitors.[32]

The linguistic reality in late antiquity compounded an already complicated web of religious communities. Greek or Aramaic, in its various garbs (and in particular Syriac) as a *lingua franca* permitted easy communication between areas separated by political, though not necessarily by linguistic and cultural, borders. Latin, Greek, and Aramaic were known across large areas, allowing for a broad interface of beliefs, stories, and even rituals across boundaries of religious identity.

By tradition, a sacred text was written in "high," or hieratic, rather than in "low," or demotic, language. Like Jews and Christians, pagans also eventually learned to refer to their own sacred texts. For Emperor Julian, the fact that the New Testament was written in the more popular Greek proved that it could not seriously be considered to be a sacred text. Yet this was proof of the very opposite for others. The New Testament reflects a revolutionary attitude to scriptural language, now meant to be accessible to all, even to those with a very modest level of literacy. The same attitude would permit the early translation of the Christian scriptures to various vernaculars of Christian communities, such as Coptic, Syriac, Armenian, or Gothic.

Here, as elsewhere, the case of the Jews is rather special: although Jewish communities were dispersed even beyond the boundaries of the Roman and the Sasanian empires, Judaism was in no way a "world religion" of universalist pretentions. Hebrew, for the Jews the hallowed language of the Bible, remained for the Jewish educated class a *lingua franca,* alongside the Aramaic vernacular. Although the Bible could be translated, the original text was endowed with a special status: it is only in the Hebrew scrolls that the Torah was read in the synagogue ritual, in striking contradistinction with the Christian approach to the Biblical text, which was as valid in translation as it was in the original. In a sense, the language of the Torah for the Rabbis was similar to Qur'anic Arabic in the (later) Islamic doctrine of *i'gaz al-Qur'an:* the Scripture's language remains inimitable.

The sacred character of the language of revelation encompassed its very elements: words, and even the letters themselves, were granted an ontological status that surpassed anything known before. Divine power in books, but also in words—pronounced, read, or written—and letters, represent an alternative world, parallel to that of the material, created world. The ontological power of words reaches its acme in divine names, as well as in magical texts. Religious diglossia, undergirded by the coexistence of scriptures in both the vernacular and the original language, strengthened the perceived power of scripture in its entirety, including the individual characters. A number of late antique texts reflect this heightened power of the letters (*stoicheia*) of the alphabet, which are considered elements (*stoicheia*) of the whole universe. In this paradigm, it is not only that the scriptures represent the divine revelation. Rather, the divine body itself is constituted of those letters.[33]

Canonization Processes and Religious Memory

In its early stages, a new religion typically releases a wave of literary creativity: prophecies are revealed, commentaries are published, ritual texts are redacted. This was certainly true of the two heirs to Second Temple Judaism, early Christianity and early Rabbinic Judaism. A portion of these writings, considered to be inspired, would soon become integral parts of a new canon of scriptures, through a process of selection by the nascent religious authorities. Writings included in the canon are thought of as part of the divine revelation, and thus subject to a hermeneutical system that allows drawing from them an infinite number of spiritual and legal lessons. All other texts, even those quite similar in tone and structure to those now canonized, were either attributed a lesser value or are identified as apocryphal—that is, false: impure, dangerous, and marked for destruction. The history of early Christianity, for instance, shows the degree to which canonization is a selection process, and how such a process, over time, parallels the conflict of orthodoxy and heresy. The texts most appealing to various Gnostic and dualist groups, for example, are defined as apocryphal and Satanic.

Yet apocryphal writings were not the only unsettling texts. Many scriptural verses and passages could create discomfort for the believer. There are two main methods of dealing with such verses and passages. The first is the way of interpretation: the problematic verses are lifted from their literal sense, through established hermeneutical rules, and understood metaphorically. This is, by far, the most common tactic across religious traditions. The other, more radical, option is to expurgate such passages from the scriptural text, explaining that they had been appended to the original, usually by Satan (hence the Qur'anic

"Satanic verses"). While Marcion applied this method of textual trimming to various books of the New Testament, the Ebionites (a leading Jewish-Christian group of the first centuries of the common era) applied it to several books from the Hebrew Bible.

Despite the increasing presence and heightened status of books in late antiquity, oral traditions still reigned. In that world, the attitude toward scriptures, which often carried the founding prophet's *ipsissima verba*, remained as ambivalent as it had been in Plato's time. The abiding question was: Was it safer for truth to be transmitted orally, or should one trust only written texts? This question received no definitive answer. An important Manichaean text reveals to us that Mani sought to avoid the "error" of the Buddha, Zarathustra, and Jesus, who had satisfied themselves with oral teaching, trusting their disciples to transcribe their words accurately. Mani would make sure that he himself would redact his own teaching, in his own words.[34]

Shaul Shaked, to whom we owe so many incisive studies about religion and magic in the late ancient Near East, has remarked that two paradigms can be discerned in the transmission of sacred scriptures. These two paradigms hinge on the presence or absence of an acknowledged period of orality within the tradition. For Shaked, the Indian and Iranian traditions, predominantly oral, can be juxtaposed to the Jewish and Christian ones, which make heavy use of writing. He further notes that the decision, within a tradition, to shift from orality to textuality tends to threaten the delicate balance of power between these two modes of transmission.[35] However, a sort of synthesis does exist in the "oral book," which was an important feature of the ancient world. There, the deep ambivalence vis-à-vis written texts was such that some books were memorized, and remained unrecorded, sometimes for a very long time. The Avesta, which was not committed to writing for about one millennium, stands as a striking instance. It was memorized, usually quite adequately, by people who no longer understood the original language of the work.

We can identify two main strategies regarding books (and their language) in late antiquity. These were the "low" and the "high" levels; that is, the *demos* versus the elite as primary cultural transmitter. Both the philosophers and the Jews opted for the latter, though each did so in a distinct way. The Christians, in contrast, were strong supporters of the "demotization" of scriptures. The translation of the scriptures—that of the Septuagint, then the *Peshitta* or Jerome's *Vulgata*—was declared to have been inspired, short-circuiting, as it were, the original Hebrew text. Hence my suggestion, long ago, to see in early Christianity a "religion of the Book" only in a limited sense, and to speak instead of the Christianity of this period as "a religion of the paperback."[36]

FROM THE second-century Jewish *Tannaim*, who learned by rote their assigned chapters of the Mishnah, to fifth-century Church Fathers such as Augustine, who quoted Biblical texts verbatim, it was memory that made the scriptures the overwhelming presence that it was in the daily life of religious elites. Some scriptural texts, however, were more present than others. The book of Genesis, with the *hexaemeron* and the sagas of the patriarchs, the life, passion, and teachings of Christ, as told in the Gospels, and the 150 Psalms of David, which were chanted, both aloud and inaudibly, by Christian monks and simple Jews alike, were probably the best known among all scriptural texts.

An intriguing case is that of the *Books of Mysteries*. These texts were written by Jews (already at Qumran) and Christians throughout late antiquity and in the Middle Ages, and later also by Muslims. The books purport to reveal cosmological secrets. Similar writings were also written by pagans, but did not create problems among them. The monotheistic, but not the polytheistic milieu looks askance at such works, as revealed scriptures are presumed to encompass all aspects of life, when viewed through the appropriate hermeneutical lens. The *Books of Mysteries* offers to the elect a shortcut, evading the control of the religious authorities and revealing secrets. It is no surprise that these writings stand at the root of the mystical traditions in the Abrahamic religions.[37]

Interconnected Religious History

Late antiquity witnessed a further religious transformation: intergroup curiosity about scripture.[38] This interest was typically manifested in polemics: Jews, Christians, Gnostics, Manichaeans, and Zoroastrians (not to mention pagans and philosophers) debated one another, but each had as well a genuine interest in the scriptures of the other. And, while polemics implies opposition, the reality was far from simple. Religious writings are not always what they purport to be. Not infrequently in polemics, straw men are set up, with the argument actually aiming at self-definition.

The scriptural galaxy of the late antique period was characterized by multiple interfaces. The first of these was between webs of texts and stories (e.g., midrash, commentary, liturgical poetry). Texts are typically written, and stories are typically oral, although this is not an absolute rule: sometimes, the text is oral (although very precisely transmitted, from generation to generation), while the stories may be set down in writing. But this interface is joined by others, as these texts and tales circulate among different communities sharing a religious identity, and also between communities belonging to different religious groups, including those that are rather inimical to one another. These groups can be said to have intertwined histories.

The "intertwined histories" approach helps us to see things at once from various perspectives, but it remains marred by several problems inherent to the traditional approach to the history of religions. Although I cannot elaborate here, I shall mention, at least, the lack of contextual background from which many of these studies suffer. More helpful, perhaps, is a notion of a "connected religious history"; this idea recalls the fundamental unity of the late ancient scriptural galaxy. And it is precisely this unity that constitutes the religious ethos of the period.

Scriptural hermeneutics were based on written texts, but they also received various oral developments. The new interest in scriptures and books aside, late antique society was not, as such, a literate society. Communication remained essentially oral in late antiquity. Stories circulated between religious groups and communities and were transformed, sometimes slightly, sometimes considerably.[39] In this sense, one may speak of a hybrid society, where orality and script functioned as twin engines of the formation and transformation of collective, cultural, and religious memory.

The Scriptural Movement

By late antiquity, literacy had ceased to be the privilege of scribes, and had become the woof and warp of general society. The reliance on texts, in particular on revealed scriptures, as well as on a rich body of hermeneutical works on these scriptures, was growing apace. This reality has given rise to the idea of a late ancient "scriptural movement." Implicit to this proposal is that more than in other periods, there was in the long late antiquity (roughly from the New Testament to the Qur'an) a preoccupation with heavenly or revealed texts offering the foundation or legitimation of new religious communities.[40]

On first sight, the notion of a "scriptural movement" is quite appealing, as it provides a vector in the religious history of the Mediterranean and the Near East that would highlight the trajectory from Jesus to Muhammad, from the New Testament to the Qur'an. However, its heuristic validity appears to be severely limited. First and foremost, in some cases the notion simply does not seem to apply. In Judaism and Zoroastrianism, for instance, we can observe almost the opposite phenomenon, namely a dramatic turn toward oral transmission within traditions that already had developed significant written literatures. How can one account for this? It seems that at some point, people became reluctant to commit religious traditions to writing. While we do not know precisely why this happened, a desire to maintain the singularity of existing scriptures might have played a crucial role here. The Jews developed a copious literature during the Second Temple period, using Greek as well as Hebrew and Aramaic. Like the Jews, the Zoroastrians were heirs to a very old religious literature (which their priests had kept oral). In late antiquity, the Rabbis, who had become for all practical purposes the sole representatives of Judaism, proudly presented their discussions as "Oral Torah," in contradistinction to Moses' "Written Torah." For them, the revealed scripture was considered to be so singular that there was, alongside the Torah, no room for any other book. For the Rabbis, then, there could be only one Book, the divine and revealed one. The heuristic usefulness of a "scriptural movement" is also limited in a second way. During our period, the movement of intensive codification was by no means restricted to religious texts. Thus, we see the sustained effort on the part of the Roman authorities to integrate legal codification, as reflected first in the Theodosian Codex and then, in the sixth century, in the Justinian Codex, or *Corpus Iuris Civilis*. A further example is the compilation of the Talmud (both the Babylonian and the Palestinian versions of the Talmud date approximately from the late fifth or early sixth century).[41]

This second limitation, that it was not only religious texts that were subject to intensive codification, brings us to the next point. Up to the end of the Middle Ages, religion and law were still quite fused, much more so than they are in the modern world. In other words, there was a very broad interface between these two fields. It was the Reformation that wedded religion with faith, in the process excluding from the marriage the sphere of law. With the accumulation of available texts, and as the religious communities interacted (even though this contact remained more often than not polemical), the urge increased to collect, organize, and summarize the ever-growing number of texts. Thus arose the idea of a religious or legal *summa*, reflected for instance in the two versions of the Talmud, the Roman legal codices, and even the Christian heresiological treatises. All such major theological and exegetical corpora constitute secondary scriptural canons.

Self-Definition

A popular expression runs: "Tell me what you read and I'll tell you who you are." This dictum was as true for late antiquity as it is for modernity. Indeed, during this period books became a crucial, if not a cardinal element of self-definition. This process occurred on both an individual and a group level. With regard to the former, one was defined, to a significant extent, by the book he considered to be divinely revealed. With regard to the latter, this book (or set of books) belonged to the members of a particular community, and only to them, setting the members apart from all others.

That scriptures were becoming fundamental to both individual and group identity is underscored by how different religions, not only those of revelation, relied on their holy books. Emperor Julian, who had rejected the Christian faith of his youth for the traditional Hellenic (polytheistic) tradition of his ancestors, was unable to free himself from the Christian attitude to such books. Similarly, late antique Platonic circles revered almost as divine some of Plato's texts, such as the *Timaeus*, which dealt, like *Genesis*, with the creation of the world. Among the late Neoplatonists, the *Chaldean Oracles*, to which their mysterious language gave a hieratic echo, were also considered to be a holy text of sorts—something that may well reflect a Christian influence.[42] From a Hellenic, non-Christian perspective, Polymnia Athanassiadi has asserted vigorously the striking importance of the idea of a holy book in late antiquity.[43]

Indeed, having a holy book became a must for any religious group. The Qur'anic expression: "the People of the Book" (*ahl al-kitāb*) clues us in to a widespread phenomenological perception: these groups vied with one another, each one taking pride in its own book, or *kitāb*. This late antique view of scriptures as constituting the core of religious identity would have a powerful echo in the modern study of religion. The phrase "Religions of the Book" was introduced in 1873 by Max Müller in his *Introduction to the Science of Religion*.[44] Müller may well have had in mind the Qur'anic phrase.[45]

We know of no clear antecedent to the term *ahl al-kitāb*, whether in Greek, Syriac, or Hebrew. Indeed, "People of the Book," whatever its original meaning, cannot have been a self-designation. As far as we know, the Jews never referred to themselves by this sobriquet. Their holy scripture had a name: the Torah. And the Hebrew expression *'am ha-sefer* appears only much later.[46] Similarly, as we shall see, late antique Christians did not define themselves as "Possessors of the Book." They could perhaps mention the Gospels, or the New Testament, or even the whole Bible as the sacred text of God's revelation, but there is no indication that they ever called themselves "People of the Book." For the Manichaeans, the Christians' competitors in aggressive proselytizing throughout the ecumene, holy books were highly significant artifacts. Among them as well, however, one fails to encounter any self-definition as "People of the Book."[47] The expression, then, seems rather to represent the common baseline of various communities bound by similar, though not identical religious beliefs and practices. Within the ethnic and religious web of the Near East, the Qur'an was able to observe the existence of different claims with respect to various books containing God's prophecies.

This web was comprised of literary texts, but also of much more than that. It was also, for example, a web of stories. These stories circulated throughout the ecumene, mainly orally, between communities of faith, both those sharing the same religious background, and those divided by theological beliefs. The tales complemented or replaced written texts, often commenting on those texts in a mode we may call midrashic. Kaleidoscopic in nature, the stories offered a limited number of elements (or mythologoumena) that at each turn of the system would be rearranged in what seemed to be an infinite number of different reflections. It is this web of texts, stories, communities, and religions that constitutes the scriptural galaxy.

Scripture and Books

At this point, we turn to a broader question: To what extent was the ancient attitude to books in general, and education in particular, transformed in late antiquity, from the Christianization of the Roman Empire to the emergence of the Islamic Caliphate? In other words, did the fact that the state was now established upon one revealed book—that is, as political power was held by believers in a divinely revealed book—change the attitude to books in general, and if so, how? Books remained rather rare in the ancient world. Even in the Eastern provinces of the Roman Empire, it is likely that no more than fifteen or twenty percent of people were literate (in the West, the numbers are closer to five to ten percent). And yet, the new religious coherence of the Christians was informed not only by their scriptures, but also by how they viewed books.

As is well known, the newly Christianized elites of the Roman Empire decided to retain traditional educational patterns, despite their deep ambivalence regarding texts of Hellenic and Greco-Roman *paideia*. In the retention of the *paideia*, however, two types of adjustments were made. First, some of the classical Greek texts, judged immoral, were downplayed. Second, and more significantly, traditional education was supplemented, at all levels, with religious education, that is, the study of scriptures. For many years, this religious education was perceived as external to *paideia*. Thus we read in Basil the Great's famous pamphlet, *Discourse to the young, and how they might benefit from Greek literature*. Basil here offers no hint of an educational system directly or solely inspired by Christianity. Similarly, Augustine, who stated (e.g., in his *De Doctrina Christiana*) that philosophical culture is not the only conceivable culture, ignores the institutional aspect of culture.[48] There were indeed in late antiquity very few attempts to create a Christian educational canon. Instead, there was a highly successful attempt to read together, as if on parallel tracks, the texts of the Biblical canon and those of the Greek literary canon.[49]

The intricate rules of Greek scriptural hermeneutics, as we know them among Jews and Christians, were first developed in Alexandria in order to interpret Homer. These rules were then applied by Alexandrian Jews to the Bible, eventually reaching the Church Fathers through Philo. But while the hermeneutical rules were applied to the Homeric epics in the Hellenic educational tradition (*paideia*), the Christians, following the Jews, had two textual traditions at work. This cultural diglossia, as it were, stands at the root of both Jewish and Christian culture, reflecting, in both cases, the *aporia* of Athens and Jerusalem. There are some important connections between Alexandrian book culture and the history of the biblical text.[50] The biblical scriptural canon did not replace the Greek cultural canon. It is upon this double footing that *cultura christiana*, which became the basis of European culture, eventually was established. The foundation and early development of *cultura christiana* represents the major cultural shift of late antiquity, and this cultural shift is exemplified better than anywhere else in the establishment of the monasteries. There were of course several different cenobitic forms of monasticism, in the West as well as in the East. Of particular note in our context is the study aspect, as some of the monasteries (e.g., Nisibis in the East and Cassiodorus's Vivarium in the West) became full-fledged academies of higher learning. This fact strongly influenced knowledge exchange in the Arabic and Latin medieval worlds.[51]

At this point, then, books and various writings formed the fulcrum of highly diverse religions, including those that privileged deeds over words. Once again we see the deep impact of the new presence of literacy on different levels of religious life. In turn, perceptions of culture were recrafted. In the Greco-Roman world, Greek *paideia* (which was intended of course primarily for the higher—and male—layers of society) was a significant component of cultural self-perception, but not of religious identity. *Paideia* had been based upon those texts codified in Alexandria in the third century B.C.E. Ironically, it was only in Judaism that this *paideia* was to show itself in full flower. *Talmud Torah* (i.e., "the study of the Torah") came to be considered by the Jews the greatest possible religious duty, or *mizwah*.[52] Hence the insightful remark of the ancient historian Elias Bickerman, made almost in passing, according to which the Jews inherited from the Greeks their intense interest in books and learning, placing these at the core of their daily lives. It is a true irony of late antique Judaism that it took no part in "the scriptural movement." Indeed, it would almost seem that Rabbinic Judaism retreated into a world from which all but one book—the Torah—had disappeared.

Yet it was not a holy book that Emperor Julian lacked. Rather, it was a mechanism of holy book use. Unlike the Christian bishops, pagan priests did not have at their disposal a system of religious education. While the Christians did not reject wholesale Hellenic *paideia*, they supplemented it by religious education, which basically amounted to commenting upon the Holy Writ. Where Judaism and Christianity (and later Islam) really diverge from the Greco-Roman religions was not in the presence or absence of "sacred scriptures" but rather in the presence or absence of a system of scriptural interpretation.

2

A DIVINE PALIMPSEST

After Thomas De Quincey's the *Confessions of an English Opium-Eater* (1821), Baudelaire referred to memory as to a "divine palimpsest" in *Les paradis artificiels:* "Qu'est-ce que le cerveau humain, sinon un palimpseste immense et naturel? Mon cerveau est un palimpseste et le vôtre aussi, lecteur. . . . Et le palimpseste divin créé par Dieu, qui est notre incommensurable mémoire. . . ."[1] The scriptural galaxy set out in Chapter 1 is a further candidate for this term. The traditional philological approach to the canonization of the (Jewish or Christian) scriptures, sophisticated as it may be, does not do justice to a number of important elements in the process of canonization broadly conceived. Included in this process is the fluidity of texts in their oral and written versions, the censorship (and heretical designation) that is the flip side of the canonization process, as well as the reworking of the biblical stories and their interpretation in commentaries, liturgical poetry and iconography. All of these are part of what one may also call a "palimpsest," a parchment in which new stories (or rather new versions) are written upon old ones, replacing but not effacing them. Through the new version, we may glimpse the old. It is to this divine palimpsest of religious memory that the present chapter is devoted.

Individual and Collective Memory

Memory, a topic of intense current inquiry, is often considered as either individual or collective. The prevailing view in neuroscience is that memory can be discussed only within the context of the individual mind—although some new studies seriously challenge this stance.[2] The dynamism of memory, however, is now a truism in memory studies: memory is in no wise a static conservatory of things past. Rather, memory actively reconstructs the past, and even engages with the future by providing guidelines for action. Memory's plasticity permits it to remodel itself continually. This reconstruction is ongoing, and, as we shall learn below, undergirds the interplay between oral and written traditions in religion.

Unlike their neuroscientific colleagues, for nearly a century now sociologists and historians have spoken of the "collective memory" of a society,[3] sometimes referring to its "social" or "cultural" memory.[4] While collective memory has prompted a great deal of scholarly effort, the *relationship* between the personal and the collective dimensions of memory has been quite neglected.

While "religious memory" is generally conceived as a special case of collective memory, in matters of religion as in all other spheres, collective memory starts with the individual. After reviewing some of the main scholarly attitudes toward religious memory, I shall offer several suggestions on the relationship between individual and collective memory in the religious field. Deeply divergent attitudes toward memory are played out in both in oral and written traditions. As we shall see, these attitudes have a profound impact on the scriptural universe of late ancient Christianity.

Religious Memory, from Halbwachs to Assmann

The French sociologist Maurice Halbwachs referred to "religious memory" as those aspects of collective memory that deal with religious practice as well as with religious beliefs.[5]

We shall consider religious memory first through the lens of Christianity in late antiquity. This approach permits us to reflect on the birth of a new religious tradition, proclaimed to be a reinterpretation of an older one, and this in times of dramatic change in the relationship between oral and written literatures in the Near East and the Mediterranean. I shall propose the existence of two kinds of religious memory, and, further, that this double-pronged memory clearly parallels the semantic and episodic (i.e., long-term, declarative—or explicit) memory discussed by contemporary researchers, who theorize two (and sometimes more than two) systems of memory, used simultaneously.[6] In this, modernity has little on the ancients: a dual conception of memory is found in Greek, where *mnēmē* refers to continuous memory and *anamnēsis* to recollection. I shall seek to show that these two kinds of religious memory function in a simultaneous and complementary way.

As noted, religious memory can be considered a special case of collective memory. Halbwachs introduced the notion of "[collective] religious memory" (*mémoire [collective] religieuse*) in *Les cadres sociaux de la mémoire*, originally published in 1925. There, he wrote of how religion retains intact the memory of the past. For Halbwachs, the transformation, through time, of both dogma and ritual, enriches this memory. Further, religious memory follows the same laws as collective memory, reconstructing rather than conserving the past. Rituals, texts, and traditions do the work of reconstruction.[7]

An intrinsically social phenomenon, collective memory is related to the invention and use of writing and to the ability to archive knowledge outside a single mind. Yadin Dudai has noted rightly that little is known about the acquisition of collective memory.[8] Halbwachs, for his part, posits a parallel between the passage from personal to collective memory and that from collective memory to history.

Among all aspects of culture, religion, in both its tale-telling (*mythos*) and ritual action (*praxis*), is the one most conspicuously marked by memory. Across societies, religion functions as a conservative social mechanism, which seeks to preserve the memory of an ancient time.[9] Hence, it insists on remembering the past and on cultivating tradition. For Halbwachs, who was influenced early on by both Henri Bergson and Émile Durkheim, memory is at once private and public, personal and political. Like any collective memory, religious memory does not preserve the past but reconstructs it, through texts, traditions, and the present.

In Halbwachs's Bergsonian taxonomy, individual (or interior) and social (or exterior) memories are not wholly distinct entities. Individual memory, never completely self-enclosed, always has a social dimension.[10] Halbwachs holds that memories are always collective, as a person is reminded by others even of events which one alone experienced, and of things that one alone saw.[11] Individual memory, then, is far from a thing apart.[12] The question of definitions figures here very strongly. For Halbwachs, religion can be equated with tradition, and the process of "traditionalization" is directly related to memory. Hence, a "Halbwachsian reduction of religion to memory" has been discussed.[13] If, however, individual memory is not indeed fully "individual" then one may speak of "memory" as a collective phenomenon in a nonmetaphorical way. Dealing with religion, the French sociologist Danielle Hervieu-Léger describes it as a "chain of memory."[14] This is true in nonliterate as well as in literate societies, although it is expressed in very different ways in each of these.

La topographie légendaire des évangiles, Halbwachs's last work, remains to this day the classic study of memory in early Christianity. Here, Halbwachs showed that it was only in Jewish memory that Christian memory could find its roots, but that early Christian memory transformed the Jewish memory on which it was grounded. One might say that late antique Christianity aimed to appropriate Jewish memory.[15]

Jan Assmann has done much in the past twenty years or so to deepen our reflection on the religious dimensions of cultural memory. Assmann holds that only after perhaps three generations are personal memories transformed into cultural memory. During that period, he proposes to speak of "communicative memory" (*kommunikative Gedächtnis*), when memories are transmitted by witnesses of an event to their children and grandchildren.[16] For Assmann, religious memory is stabilized through institutions and rituals are the medium of reproduction of religious memory.[17] Below, I build on Assman's notion of communicative memory for three generations, but offer a slightly different suggestion: for religions of the book, scriptural hermeneutics play a role at least as important as that of rituals in the stabilization process.[18]

Modes of Religiosity and Paradigm Shift in Early Christianity

The Oxford social anthropologist Harvey Whitehouse has proposed a theory of religion that distinguishes between two basic modes of religiosity, which he calls "doctrinal" and "imagistic." The former, which is highly routinized (in the Weberian sense of the word), is characterized by high frequency and low arousal, while the opposite is true of the latter. These two modes are found across societies.[19] Of interest for our purposes are the different kinds of memory Whitehouse associates with these two modes of religiosity. He proposes to follow the distinction, broadly accepted among memory scientists, between explicit (or declarative and conscious) and implicit (or nondeclarative and unconscious) memory, and between two kinds of explicit memory, short- and long-term memory, the latter in turn divided between semantic and episodic memory. In Whitehouse's view, the doctrinal mode of religiosity makes use of semantic memory, while episodic memory is mainly activated in the imagistic mode. Moreover, Whitehouse contends that different admixtures of the two modes can be discerned in all patterns of religious life.

Several attempts have been made to apply the categories developed by Whitehouse to the anthropology and history of religion. One dealt with major religious trends in the Roman Empire.[20] Another one, edited by Whitehouse and James Laidlaw, was entitled *Ritual and Memory*.[21] In one of his many studies of oral and written cultures, the anthropologist Jack Goody compares image and doctrine (in Whitehouse's parlance) to speech and writing, and notes that in the interface between religions of oral cultures and religions of the book, the latter have an advantage, and tend to absorb the former.[22]

Goody argues that it is possible to speak of collective memory in the absence of literacy. This claim must be qualified, as in preliterate societies, where religious memory was perforce oral, there were no written archives.[23] Without those, collective memory can only assume the contours of oral traditions and myths. One possibility, then, is to consider the organization of memory in both nonliterate and in literate societies. The written archives and literary texts of literate societies drew less upon memory to recall the past as well as other elements of collective identity. Nonliterate societies, in contrast, made much use of generative memorizing (which is based on repetition and variation). Enigmas, proverbs, myths, fables, and stories, are all dependent on social memory, a memory more or less shared by the whole public.[24] Historians of ancient religions have pointed to the different ways in which ancient societies present different articulations of oral and written memory. The existence of two types of religious memory, related to orality and to writing, can be detected in various archaic societies, in Greece as well as in Mesopotamia.[25]

In ancient and premodern societies that we may call semiliterate, oral and written memory functioned together, as literacy was the privilege of a small number of elites. Such societies were characterized by an interface between oral and written culture.[26] In the history of religion, the most important distinction in this respect is the appearance of scriptural religions, such as Israelite religion and Zoroastrianism. The revealed nature of these texts (which were mostly written, but sometimes remained oral, as in the case of the Iranian Avesta) situated them at the very core of both religious thought and ritual. Hence, we may speak of a real paradigm change in religious memory with the rise of the scriptural religions. The emergence of writing prompted a similar shift in the cultural field.

BY CONSIDERING the development of religious memory in early Christianity, I hope to shed light on the general topic of collective memory. The first centuries of Christianity represent a pivotal chapter in the history of religions. Christianity stands as a particularly illustrative case of the birth of a new religion and the invention of a new religious memory. Here we see a drastic reformulation of an earlier religious memory, that of Israel (for the Church Fathers, Christianity was *verus Israel*), thanks to a series of new hermeneutical thought patterns. In the following pages, we shall explore how this new system of religious memory was closely linked to momentous changes in the relationship between orality and literacy, to attitudes toward reading, and to the blossoming of scriptural religions in late antiquity. We shall examine each of the various elements involved in the formation of early Christian memory, with the goal of thereafter treating them in a synthetic fashion.

In the Christianized Roman Empire, the literary heritage of the Greco-Roman culture was subsumed within the scriptures; that is, within the book of divine revelation. The parallel hermeneutics of these two literary corpora would heretofore constitute the core of Christian cultural memory. This memory was entwined with a complicated conception of scriptures: two main levels (Old and New Testaments), each to be read in relation to the other, the first announcing the second, the second interpreting the first. This interplay holds true as well with regard to Jewish scripture and Greco-Roman cultural tradition (*paideia*), whose literary corpuses each needed to be read in light of the other.[27]

The transformation of memory in early Christianity was conditioned by the new split between religious memory (essentially, the reinterpretation and appropriation of that of Israel) and cultural memory (essentially, the reinterpretation and appropriation of that of Greco-Roman civilization). Hence, in early Christianity one finds the emergence of a complete novelty in the context of ancient societies: a clear delineation between the sacred and the secular.

THE CHRISTIAN scriptures themselves being a two-tiered corpus, encompassing both the Old and the New Testaments, made for a very complicated exegetical situation. The New Testament provided the key to the correct understanding of the Old Testament, which represented a *typos,* or *figura,* of the momentous events described in the Gospels: under the Christian text, the Jewish subtext.[28] Like Greco-Roman culture, the ancient history of Israel was to be deciphered as the hidden text in the divine palimpsest, under the fresher ink of the deeds of Jesus and of the early Church, *verus Israel.* Notably, the Christian attitude toward the Hebrew Bible (which was always read in translation) entailed a new approach to *historia sacra* itself, and hence a new pattern of historical memory. Memory, in such a system, became less the remembrance of things past than the uncovering of things hidden, and retrieving secret truth under lies apparent, the work of the devil. Gnosis, in that sense, and the dualist, esoteric movement that it represented, sought to retrieve the hidden memory of the divine message of salvation.[29] In the hermeneutical system of early Christianity, religious memory meant actualization, and transformation, rather than conservation. Some key texts, such as *Psalms,* were memorized, and recited both in public ritual and in individual prayer and meditation—in particular by "religious virtuosi" (i.e., the monks), to borrow a term from Max Weber. This type of "reading" can be characterized as "intensive" or meditative, rather than as "extensive" or discursive, as reading had been in the pagan world.[30] Silent reading, which began only in late antiquity, advanced the privatization and internalization of reading, and facilitated the memorization of selected texts.[31] Codices improved intertextuality by permitting easy movement between passages distant from one another in the text. The entire body of religious texts, comprised of both revealed scriptures and their interpretive texts (e.g., commentaries, theological tractates, spiritual works) is the object of what we may call "explicit religious memory."

Implicit and Explicit Religious Memory

Religious memory was multidetermined, of course. The alternative system was based on oral traditions and rituals rather than on written texts. In a world of limited literacy, oral and written religious traditions functioned simultaneously, in different registers, as it were. While oral religious traditions had been the modus operandi in preliterate societies, a blend of oral traditions and written texts was the treasure stored in "explicit religious memory."[32] Moreover, since preliterate times, rituals have been performed through a memory of a tradition as it was actuated in previous generations. We might call this second system of religious memory "implicit religious memory."

The two systems of religious memory, the implicit and the explicit, complement one another. Ritual patterns are reinforced by thought patterns, while theological conceptions are reinforced by ritual behavior. These systems echo the two systems of declarative memory, the explicit corresponding to episodic memory, the implicit corresponding to semantic memory.

Throughout late antiquity, the two systems of religious memory operated in tandem. Moreover, in the first Christian generations, we can observe the passage from personal to collective memory—in particular, of the life and death of Jesus as well as his teachings, which until then had remained oral. Jesus's first disciples had personal memories of their hero, and these memories soon became the kernel of the religious memory of the embryonic religion.[33] As told orally, the kernel memory was put to writing in the various Gospels, those that became canonical and the many more that were rejected by the orthodox tradition as apocryphal. Following Assmann, we might say that the memory of Jesus was for two or three generations "communicative memory," thereafter becoming cultural (or religious) memory.

LATE antiquity, and in particular the birth and development of both Christianity and Rabbinic Judaism, saw a transformation of religious memory.[34] As has been investigated amply, beginning with the biblical injunction: *"zachor!"* ("Remember!") and down through the centuries, memory has been a salient feature of Judaism.³⁵ As is also well known, the Eucharist, the central Christian ritual and a representation of Christ's sacrifice, was referred to as *anamnēsis* (memory, in the sense of "recollection") in the ancient Church. Thus we see hints of the power invested in memory during antiquity.³⁶

We may note a distinct parallelism. While the first generations of Christians were learning to turn their oral memories into texts,³⁷ the Jews were accomplishing a no-less-alchemical transformation of their own religious memory. With the Second Temple in ruins, the Jews reverted to oral teachings in order to preserve the uniqueness of their sacred scripture, the Torah. Moreover, as Christian late antique intellectuals, whom we call the Church Fathers, were busy redacting the huge corpus of Patristic literature, in a number of languages (Greek first, then, mainly, Latin and Syriac), the Rabbis were redacting orally and memorizing their oral commentary on the Torah, the Mishna, and then their legal discussions and other hermeneutical interpretations on the Mishna over a few centuries, the Gemara (both texts constituting the Talmud, the Oral Torah). Working in some ways in parallel, then, the two sister religions wound up forming two very different conceptions of religious memory. For the Christians, memory is essentially the "memory of God" (*mnēmē theou*), while for the Jews it remains, fundamentally, that of God's "great deeds" in history, since the creation of the world. In the Christian worldview, Jewish memory was all storage, no recollection, and was therefore frozen, irremediably stuck in the past. From the point of view of the Jews, Christians could not have any "storage" memory of Israelite history; hence, their "recollection" was pure imagination. In actuality, both the Jews and the Christians of late antiquity generated a complex system of religious memory, though one looked hardly anything like the other.

I have argued that there exist, concomitantly, two distinct kinds of religious memory, implicit and explicit, and that these types have a parallel in the two types of declarative memory (semantic and episodic) discussed above. Further, these two kinds of religious memory seem to correspond to Whitehouse's two modes of religiosity (imagistic and doctrinal). In these different couplings, the two systems of memory function together, the one "consolidating" (i.e., fixing in the mind) the other.³⁸ In late antiquity, the development of the religions of the Book demanded that religious memory shift from ritual and orality to hermeneutics and textuality. This move constitutes the major transformation of religious memory in late antiquity. Religious memory, from being ritualistic, or imagistic, and intuitive, became theological, or doctrinal, and discursive. This transformation took different shapes in Judaism and in Christianity, as in Rabbinic Judaism hermeneutics remained to a great extent oral, while the Church Fathers generated a huge literary production, dubbed, by one scholar, as early Christian "logorrhea."[39]

Freud's Contribution

The study of memory is deeply indebted to Freud and his groundbreaking work on the unconscious. As Eric Kandel's fascinating autobiography reveals, a clear path has been beaten between Freudian psychoanalysis and the contemporary biological study of memory.[40] Freud knew very well that nothing is ever fully erased in the psyche. What becomes illegible always leaves traces, and only their decipherment, the work of memory (*Erinnerungsarbeit*), can reconstitute the original text under the palimpsest.[41] For Freud, neurosis might even be synonymous with the human condition. The human condition also manages the functions of remembering and forgetting, and perhaps in the sphere of religious memory as well there is unavoidable dysfunction: too little memory and we have amnesia, too much memory and we have cancer, an overgrowth that impedes forgetting and renewal. As noted earlier in this chapter, perhaps it boils down to the elasticity of the system. The elasticity of religious memory in scriptural religions is determined by their system of hermeneutics and by the interaction between the two systems of memory, explicit and implicit. The ever-changing balance between remembering and forgetting, between the old and the new, is the secret motor of transformation in religious history.

In this dialectical account of individual and collective memory, the history of religions might be read, like the psyche, as a divine palimpsest retaining traces of the whole past. The early Christians, who thought of themselves as *verus Israel* and claimed to replace *vetus Israel* on the divine parchment, never fully effaced the ancient text. Indeed, late antiquity saw many religious groups that sought to define their identity through intense polemics with one another.[42] Islam is surely one of the more influential of these: the Qur'an is a palimpsest written over the (partially) erased texts of both the Old and the New Testament.

I have aimed in this chapter to demonstrate the intricate role of memory in a religious movement such as early Christianity (seen, to a great extent, in the context of its sister religion, Rabbinic Judaism), in which oral traditions and scriptures were utterly inseparable. This consideration was a prerequisite to further forays into aspects of cultural practice. The double paradigm shift discussed in the Introduction juxtaposed the two generic fields of religion and culture. In the Chapter 3, we shall tackle the main arguments in the scholarly debate of the past half-century on the relationship between religious revolution and cultural change in the Roman Empire.

3

RELIGIOUS REVOLUTION AND CULTURAL CHANGE

Religious memory, we recall from Chapter 2, may be considered a kind of palimpsest, on which traces of older, erased texts can be discerned beyond the letters of the newer inscriptions. This chapter extends that notion, engaging with the precise content of such a palimpsest: what will be revealed when religion and culture are written anew? We thus turn to a historiographical approach, reflecting on the radical religious and cultural changes that took hold in the Roman world, and how these have been theorized by recent scholarship.

Paideia *and Cultural Change*

Saint Jerome reveals in a famous letter how he became tormented by his love of the classics. Once, during Lent, a fever seized him, and he felt caught up in the spirit and dragged before a Judge. Jerome presented himself as a Christian, but the Judge retorted: "You are lying. You are a disciple of Cicero, not of Christ. For your heart is where your treasure is." Sentenced to be flogged, Jerome groaned and swore an oath: "Lord, if I ever again possess worldly books, if I ever read them, I shall have denied You."[1]

Jerome's nightmare lays bare the posture taken by the new religion of the Book to books themselves in late antiquity. The sense is that the revealed status of one literary corpus had effected the utter delegitimation of all others. What was to be the fate of worldly books, once those containing God's revelations became available? The religious shifts that swept the late ancient Mediterranean amounted to nothing less than a revolution, manifested perhaps most clearly in the radical character of the early monastic movement. This transformation had deep cultural implications.[2]

This chapter offers a prolegomenon of sorts to the historical problem of the impact of religious revolution on culture and education in the Roman Empire. The current literature offers excellent investigations of both educational patterns and bookish culture in the later Roman world, a world in which education was primarily book-based. Nonetheless, a slight—but crucial—modification in frame of reference seems to be called for. Thus, we shall now consider, from the perspective of religious history, continuity and rupture (in all their permutations) in the transmittal of culture. In other words, we seek to understand the impact of religious mutation on the ethos of a culture.

Ethos of a Society

The ethos of a society, its essential character, guides its beliefs and ideals and constitutes the foundation of its ethics. This ethos evolves alongside cultural and religious change. Christianity affected the ethics as well as the culture of the Roman Empire, deeply impacting on the ethos of Roman society. In a well-known—but poorly understood—move, the Jews retreated after the first Christian century from any serious negotiation of Hellenistic culture. The early modern intellectual giant Joseph Julius Scaliger famously viewed this fact as a real problem for historians of antiquity. And yet, the Christianization of classical culture cannot be properly understood without the Jewish contribution. The Swiss historian of religion Philippe Borgeaud has articulated a "theological triangle" comprised of Greece, Egypt, and Israel in the Hellenistic world.[3] A similar triangle can be shown to be made up of Christianity, Judaism, and Greco-Roman culture under the Roman Empire; a third one, that of the Abrahamic religions, would shape the medieval worlds from Oxford and Cordoba to Baghdad.[4]

Both Christianity and Islam are signal instances of religious revolutions. The early Christians rejected at first, together with paganism, the literary culture of the ancient world. Similarly, earliest Islam defined itself, in Arabia and beyond, through its utter opposition to ambient paganism. Yet Christianity, at first alone and later together with Islam, eventually became the cultural broker of Greco-Roman culture and permitted the transmission of the classical heritage from pagan antiquity to the medieval world, both in Greek and Latin, either directly or through Arabic (and often Hebrew) translations. This paradox of a religious revolution becoming the cultural broker of a rejected culture stands at the heart of our inquiry.

Henri-Irénée Marrou's seminal work shows that *paideia* constituted in late antiquity a kind of civil society, a cultural *koinē* of sorts, in which both pagans and Christians could participate.[5] This reading of *paideia* formulates anew the question of the Hellenization of early Christianity.[6] *Mutatis mutandis,* as Peter Brown has pointed out, *adab* would function in a similar way in medieval Islamicate societies, permitting some kind of cultural integration between Muslims and *dhimmis,* both Christians and Jews.[7] The dialectical relationship between religious revolution and cultural transmission within a single culture as well as between different societies represents a crucial problem of late antique history, still insufficiently understood. Religion in the ancient world was transformed by the success of Christianity in late antiquity. Together with the disappearance of public blood sacrifices came to the fore a distinction between "true" and "false" religion. Moreover, religion was coming into its own, more and more distinguished from other spheres of life. A new relationship between religion and culture would be born of this development.

From the first century on, the Christians were both great producers and consumers of books. The early Christian gusto for books went well beyond the works that later became canonized, which were referred to, in abbreviated fashion, as "the books," *ta biblia.* The Christians' deep respect for books, inherited from Second Temple Jews, paved the way for increased access to education among them.

The early development of a vibrant Christian literature in the Roman world, first in Greek, then in other languages, such as Latin, Syriac, and Coptic, brings us to the question of Christian approaches to Greco-Roman literature. One can discern two main Christian attitudes toward pagan (or Hellenic) culture. In the second and third centuries, the rejection *en bloc* of Greek culture as being fatally tainted with the false pagan gods and the distorted values of their believers is a major feature of apologetic writings. Tatian, in the second century, went further, propounding a radical asceticism, or encratism. Tatian's encratism, the early martyrs, and the first Christian monks have been linked decisively.[8] The wholesale rejection of classical culture and of worldly values would be carried yet further in the early Christian monastic movement of the fourth and fifth centuries. The monks promoted a counterculture, a "new philosophy," that was worlds apart from the literary culture of Greco-Roman *paideia*. Classical education reinforced social rankings: the haves and have-nots of *paideia*.[9] Outside the monasteries, there were in late antiquity very few attempts to create a Christian educational canon.[10] In this sense, Origen's Christian Academy in Caesarea Maritima in third-century Palestine represents a highly original achievement.[11] The philosophical schools too had sought to run against the grain of traditional *paideia,* but the ingrained social divisions had proved too much for them. Christian monasticism would succeed where they had failed.

Yet, the tout court rejection of Greek literature by the monastic camp was by no means the sole response. Another soon appeared, also in the second century, reaching its peak in the golden age of Greek Patristic literature in the fourth century. Christian writers following this path sought a way to demote pagan writings without relinquishing *paideia*. It would be difficult to overestimate the decision of the newly Christianized elites to hold on to the traditional educational pattern, tinkering with it only enough to Christianize some content.[12] Indeed, this move would eventually permit the formation of a European culture established upon the dual system of the Hebraeo-Christian writings and the classical corpus.

From Cumont and Marrou to Veyne and Brown

Although Marrou was both a Patristics scholar and a devout Christian, his magisterial *History of Education in Antiquity* barely gave a nod to the Christianized Empire.[13] In the two generations that have elapsed since Marrou's book, much research has been done both on education and on the status of books in late antiquity among pagans, Christians, and Jews. Yet we still do not understand fully the transformation patterns of Greek *paideia* in societies established upon religions of the book, Islam as well as Christianity. This knowledge gap is serious, as it is upon this transformation that the infrastructure of medieval Christian cultures was built, in the Greek East as well as in the Latin West. Moreover, the addition of the Islamic Caliphate to the Medieval West and to Byzantium would afford us a synoptic view of what I propose to call the social ecology, or "ecosystem" of medieval cultures. It is no longer possible to discuss the transformation of *paideia* as if it were simply a passage from pagan Greece and Rome to the Christian West. Now, differences between East and West can be articulated. For instance, in the West, the disappearance of schools at the end of late antiquity placed the monasteries in the front seat of classical culture transmission. Monks in Byzantium, while also involved in this endeavor, seem to have taken more of a back seat in this regard.

In his *Interpretatio Christiana*, the French historian Hervé Inglebert offered a remarkable take on the transformations of knowledge in Christian antiquity.[14] Taking up the different fields of cosmography, ethnography, and history, Inglebert engaged with issues ignored by Marrou, notably the fate of classical culture as it passes through the "Biblical filter." He describes four different vectors in the evolution of Greek *paideia* in late antiquity: (1) The rejection of some aspects of classical culture, deemed incompatible with Christianity[15]; (2) The creation of new cultural approaches to traditional genres such as historiography and heresiology, or attitudes toward death; (3) The survival of some elements (such as techniques), which remained essentially unchanged in the Christianized Roman Empire; and (4) The synthesis between classical culture and Christian approaches of this culture. These four tendencies in the evolution of classical culture in Late Antiquity are quite documentable.

As we saw in Chapter 1, holy books are not exclusive to religions of revelation. Emperor Julian, in his desire to fight the wretched Galileans, felt the need for the Hellenes to possess, like the Galileans, their own sacred scriptures. What his attempt to reverse the wheel of history seems to have lacked is the idea of religious education, rather than a holy book. Unlike the Christian bishops (and the Rabbis), pagan priests did not have at their disposal such a system, one which engaged mainly with scriptural commentary.

The ethos of a society, mentioned above, has a bearing on how modes of thought and behavioral patterns interact. This point, philosophical as much as historical, concerns the power of ideas and the impact of theology on society. To an extent, theological conceptions shape political decisions as well as social structures. It is in these terms that the relationship between the religious transformation of the Empire and its changing ethos must be understood. Ethos, of course, is not synonymous with moral behavior. Nowhere, and never, do men and women live as they know they should live. Hence, ethos is not equivalent to moral *praxis*, but rather represents the ideal life, as a society imagines it. Although the Roman Empire, labyrinthine in social nature, may never fully yield its ethos to us, we may know more about ethical attitudes than about concrete human relations in it, as Peter Garnsey and Caroline Humfress have noted.[16] Patristic literature, for instance, offers instructive discussions of theatre and spectacles, activities condemned for their depravation of morals.[17]

How does the ethos of a given society evolve? More than twenty years ago, I argued that early Christian attitudes to the body transformed anthropological conceptions in the Roman Empire.[18] In this vein, we might consider what happens when a religious idea formerly unheard of, a new approach to the divine, suddenly becomes the core of common discourse. What is called today the "Christianization" of the Roman world (a phenomenon previously referred to as "conversion to Christianity") has been explained in various ways. Ramsey MacMullen, for instance, distinguishes between religious and nonreligious factors in the conversion process in order to highlight the complexity of Christianization and its impact upon society.[19] Inglebert, for his part, discusses the "triple complexity" of the concept of Christianization, a polyvalent term, which designates the conversion of individuals and the modification of social items, as well as both the process and its result.[20]

Christianity succeeded in reappropriating Greco-Roman culture, or more precisely the marginal or even counterculture represented by philosophy, in quite subtle ways. The new religion presented itself as more than a new philosophical school; it self-identified as "philosophy in a new key," to use Susanne Langer's classic metaphor.[21] We know now, since the seminal studies of Pierre Hadot, that the ancient philosophical schools were schools of life as well as schools of thought.[22] Philosophical life, established upon "spiritual exercises," remained that of a very small minority, but one with great prestige. Indeed, it was thought to represent the ethos of the Greco-Roman cultural elites and to promote an ideal equilibrium between life and thought.

The vexing question of the transformation of the ethos in the Roman Empire has been approached, more or less successfully, by a number of scholars in the twentieth century. Their inquiries have centered around the encounter of foreign cultures with Hellenized Roman culture. On the very first pages of his *Oriental Religions in Roman Paganism,* for instance, Franz Cumont laid out the capital importance of the East in understanding the Mediterranean world under the Roman Empire.[23] Since archaic times, the Greeks and the peoples of the Near East sustained a complicated relationship, economic and cultural as much as military. More than other classicists of his generation, Cumont recognized the artificial and pernicious character of the cognitive boundaries established by the traditional disciplines between the Mediterranean and the Near East. More precisely, Cumont affirmed the significance of "the East," and he identified in that East the religious values that had permitted, under the Empire, a lively spiritual renewal, of which Christianity represented the acme. In the domain of religions, contended Cumont, the contribution of the East to Greco-Roman culture was essentially positive. Cumont's contribution is best appreciated in context: for most classical scholars of his generation, the cultural interchange between East and West reflected a *mixis* of Greek (or Greco-Roman) culture with the lower cultures of the Near East.

To Cumont's inclusive approach, one might counter, for instance, that of the Dominican André-Jean Festugière. Like Cumont, Festugière put particular emphasis on religious life, on the meeting of religions and cults. For him, however, the decline of rationalism observable in the second century was in large part due to the "Oriental *fata morgana*."[24] Despite their differences, both Cumont and Festugière affirmed that the religious transformation that occurred under the Empire can be accounted for only by recognizing the impact of a number of traditions coming from the East. Trained as a classicist, Cumont was fascinated by the East. He echoes here the classical philologist Richard Reitzenstein, although Cumont always remained in a sober register, at a significant remove from his German colleague's often far-fetched speculations. For him, the study of the "Oriental religions" should shed light on the Christian conquest of Rome: Christianity, too, was a religion that came from the East. Festugière, for his part, expressed interest only in the Hellenic side of the *praeparatio evangelica,* not in the Jewish origin of Christianity.[25] Indeed, the European mind has never perceived Christianity as an "Oriental religion," but rather, together with Greco-Roman culture, as the root of European identity.²⁶ It is a truism that the religious transformation of the Roman world is epitomized in its Christianization. Before the end of the fourth century, more than half the inhabitants of the Empire had become Christian.²⁷

Only in 1961, the year of his death, did Werner Jaeger publish his *Early Christianity and Greek Paideia*.²⁸ This work, based on a series of lectures, was for Jaeger a prolegomenon to a "more comprehensive book on the historical continuity and transformation of the tradition of Greek *paideia* in the Christian centuries of late antiquity." This was the book he had already planned by 1933, the publication year of his *magnum opus*, *Paideia*. In Jaeger's view, the early Christian thinkers adopted the approach of Greek philosophers when writing about religion and the divine. For him, "that was the decisive moment in the encounter of Greeks and Christians." Jaeger speaks of *synkrasis*, as Christian intellectuals present Christianity as a philosophical school, with Christ as the teacher, and the Scriptures as the single textbook.

The Church Fathers' intellectual success bore some ironic fruit. We see this in Julian's attempt to formulate Greek *paideia* as Hellenic theological education, while Hellenism was now identified as a religion, along the model of the despised Galileans. One should note here that Jaeger counterposed Christian *paideia* to Jewish *paideia*, as he identified the latter with the Law.²⁹ For him, the Jewish view resembled that of the philosophers, for whom *paideia* was embodied in the law (*nomos*) of the city (*polis*). Jaeger, who considered carefully the educational aspects of early Christianity, called attention to the fact that for Origen, God is the "teacher of the world" (*ho theos paidagogei ton kosmon*).

Jaeger saw in early Christianity the encounter of Greek philosophy and Judaism. Hellenistic Judaism, however, had met philosophy before the birth of Christianity, a meeting witnessed, in particular, by the writings of Philo of Alexandria, a contemporary of Paul who was the last in a long list of Jewish authors writing in Greek. Since the Jews gave up Greek as a language of culture after the first century, it is to the Church Fathers that we owe the preservation of Philo's writings. Jaeger rightly identified the masterpieces of Patristic literature as the decisive moment of confrontation between Greek conceptions of wisdom and Jewish conceptions of the divine. The first Christian thinkers learned to use the intellectual tools developed by the philosophical schools when addressing themselves to non-Christians. In doing so, they were reformulating the Jewish approach to the divine in Greek philosophical concepts.[30]

In Chapter 7 we shall more fully consider the late antique avatar of the Greek intellectual curiosity about the wisdom traditions of ancient peoples, such as the Egyptians, the Babylonians, the Hebrews, the Persians and the Indians.[31] The fact that they were unable to understand the languages of these peoples, or even to read their scripts, added to their curiosity, of course, and to their conviction that such wisdom was a profound one. Porphyry, for instance, argued that the philosophers of those nations reflected on the divine just like the Greek philosophers. Under the cover of various mythologies of their different cultures, the sages of all nations were partaking in essentially the same ideas about the divine. In the second century, Numenius went further, claiming that Plato was a "Hellenizing Moses," (*Moyses attikizans*), thus setting up the Greek philosophers to be students of the Hebrews. Like Numenius before him, Porphyry, in the third century, was in search of a *via universalis,* and hoped to establish the foundations of a truly universal thought.[32] Thus, the Greek philosophical approach was confronted in the second century with the Christian one. Jaeger wrote of this as a meeting of two universalist systems. Both, for him, were countercultures—obvious in terms of early Christianity, but also applicable to the *askesis* typical of the philosophic life style.[33]

It was precisely this encounter between Greek philosophy and Christianity that permitted the transformation of the ethos in the Roman world and the birth of Christian humanism. The religious ethos of Judaism and Christianity insisted upon the common origin of humankind through God's *fiat*—a far cry from the first principles and the nature of man as perceived by the Greek philosophers. Prior to the fourth century, however, the Christians, who lacked an ethnic identity, were considered to belong to an outlawed religion. They thought of themselves as belonging to a school functioning in Greek but according to the principles of Hebrew—in other words, barbarian wisdom. For them, *hellenismos* was no longer a cultural ideal. Rather, it referred to polytheism alone, indicating a perverted religious attitude, forever overturned by the divine revelation to Israel.

The first Christian theologians and apologetic writers thus succeeded in expressing religiosity in a novel way. Some Greco-Roman intellectuals had been struggling, less successfully, to express a similar interest in traditions of wisdom emerging from the Orient. This is true in particular for those from the Empire's Eastern provinces, such as Numenius or Iamblichus, both from Apamea; these intellectuals came from the cultural *limes,* at the confluence of cultures. In order to find among the barbarian nations the principles of wisdom, the Christian thinkers and Hellenic philosophers practiced different sorts of mental acrobatics. Justin Martyr, for instance, spoke about a spiritual seed (*sperma pneumatikon*) implanted by God in all peoples of the world, even if the revelation to Israel alone had been at once complete and pure from pagan conceptions. The Patristic downgrading of Greek thought was accompanied by an upgrading of "barbarian wisdoms" of all kinds. Universalism thus appeared to be more natural among Christian than among pagan thinkers in the Roman Empire. This was the case precisely because Christian universalism was established upon the religious idea of prophetic monotheism, and because this monotheism demanded the establishment of a universal ethical system. As we now know, monotheism was rather widespread in the Roman Empire, even among "pagans."[34] While the apparently oxymoronic term "pagan monotheism" certainly reflected a reality, it was a soulless one, so to speak, devoid of myths or rituals. As such, it proved unable to lay the foundations for a new universal system of ethics. Mani, a contemporary of Porphyry, succeeded in creating the first truly universal religion. The foundational texts of Mani's religion of light made room for the various great religious traditions of the world, integrating the Buddha, Zarathustra, and Jesus in the cosmic history of salvation.[35]

Paul Veyne belongs to a later generation than Jaeger, and his intellectual development and cultural milieu could not have been more different from that of the German refugee scholar. No direct influence of the latter on the former can be discerned, yet some of Veyne's works, including some of the most recent ones, seem to be the flowering of Jaeger's ideas. For instance, Veyne's *When Our World became Christian* (first published in French in 2007) seeks to explain early Christianity and the Christian conquest of Rome by way of instances drawn from twentieth-century political history.[36] With more than a bit of intellectual coquetry, Veyne expounds from his position as a former Communist why religion ought to be taken seriously—religious ideas as well as religious practice, monotheism as well as polytheism. Veyne, first and foremost an important historian of pagan Rome, also wishes to understand the transformation of the dominant ethos in the Empire. In a chapter in the *History of Private Life*, a collaborative project the first volume of which he edited, Veyne analyzes the passage from Rome to Byzantium.[37] He starts by noting that after an entire century of cultural sociology, historians have begun to acknowledge their inability to explain cultural mutations. As against common perception, noted Veyne, the new ethics in the Empire owed no debt to the Stoics. Stoic philosophy, of course, had already affirmed the tight ties between religion and ethics. But the religious zeal of the Christians (comparable to that of the Jews), their strength and determination to fight for their ideas until martyrdom, was totally alien to Stoic philosophers such as Seneca or Marcus Aurelius. Like his late friend Michel Foucault, Veyne seeks to understand the transformation of the "care of the self" in Imperial Rome through the privatization of religion.

In an important article titled "Cult, piety and morals in Greco-Roman paganism," Veyne discusses the different concepts of morality among pagans and Christians.[38] Without falling into the error of caricaturing pagan religiosity as fundamentally frigid (a caricature originally attributed to Christian religiosity), Veyne points out that paganism could not offer the love of a living God, as it was unable to conceive of what he calls "internal relations of consciousness" between gods and men. The early Christians were indeed a marginal group in Roman society, as they belonged to the Empire without sharing its mores. Yet their "ethical warmth" permitted them, once they used philosophical tools, to effect a "decisive reversal of religious thought." They could accomplish this reversal with the help of the Hebrew Bible and its perception of God as the source of ethics and the "foundation of the Good." It was through Christian thinkers, then, who took a wholly different approach from that of the philosophers, that both religion and ethics were universalized.

Thus, Veyne came to understand the end of gladiator games under the Christian emperors. "It is, indeed, Christianity which put the end to gladiator games, but it did so through complex circuits, in convoluted ways."[39] For Veyne, the Christians' ethical universalism, established upon a religious basis, "drills an abyss between Christian morals and the ethics of pagan philosophical sects. . . ." Ethics at the core of religion: this was certainly a *novum*, of Jewish origin, in the ancient world. The ideal of a sincere heart oriented toward God and the care of the poor (and hence the duty to hand out alms): these are for Veyne the revolutionary novelties of Christianity. Slavery, and its transformation, was considered similarly by Veyne: while Christianity did not directly change the mores, it was able to transform their foundation, that is, the underlying ethos. It is in this way that the mores themselves eventually evolved. In the Christianized Empire, the extreme social conformism that had characterized ethics and religion in pagan society would gradually weaken.[40]

In the past generation, Peter Brown revolutionized the study of late antiquity in general and of the period's religious history in particular.[41] He has resurrected late antique men and women, Christians for the most part, but also pagans and Jews, and reinserted them into the fluid historical milieus in which they evolved. Together with his erstwhile student Robin Lane Fox, Brown reminds us that in late antiquity Christianization was an endless effort, one which succeeded largely thanks to the enthusiasm of innumerable persons.[42] Some of them, such as Augustine and Shenute, exemplified a deeply engaged life, and revealed the implications of a deeply significant existential choice between two modes of life and two cultures, that of the *mundus* and that of the Church.[43]

Christianity remains for Brown, as it was for Marrou, the most fascinating phenomenon of Roman religious history. Like Jaeger, Brown acknowledges the Jewish sources of Christian ethics and the fateful encounter of Christianity and Greek philosophy. Like Veyne, he reckons the irresistible power of emotions in religious history.

Brown set out definitively that the transformation of culture was fundamental to the religious revolution of late antiquity. In his chapter on late antiquity in the *History of Private Life*, he explained that the Christians moved swiftly to democratize the counterculture of the philosophical schools.[44] The new school of "barbarian philosophy" was open to all, from all social classes. The Christians added the care of the poor—and that meant an exceptional level of solidarity within the group—to the care of the self and to anguish about the soul's destiny. The Christians, wrote Brown, did not preach a totally new moral code; rather, they took more pains than the pagans to live up to their own standards. Moreover, the Christians proposed a new approach to education, which would be mainly implemented within the monastic milieus. Brown further asserted a "sexual revolution of late antiquity" as the most dramatic consequence of the cultural revolution of the period antiquity. Here, too, the monastic movement served as a spearhead, with the refusal of many young men and women in the Empire to marry and procreate, and by doing so, rejecting the traditional order of society.[45]

The Double Helix: Athens and Jerusalem

Unlike their pagan counterparts, Christian priests were obliged to interpret the Scriptures of their sacred doctrines.[46] Since the anonymous *Epistle to Diognetes,* in the second century, Patristic literature conceived of Christianity as a school of thought, comparable in its structures to the Greek philosophical schools, but diverging markedly from them with regard to teachings. Thus, we have a paradox: as Christianity adapted itself, intellectually, to the Greco-Roman world, the concept of *hellenismos* became identified, for Christian authors, with polytheism—a fact highlighted by Glen Bowersock.[47] The Christians felt more deeply alienated from traditional *paideia*—it was established, after all, upon the gods of the Homeric epics—than from philosophy. In 361 C.E., Julian prohibited Christians from teaching Greek literature. Like the Christians, then, the pagans also recognized the gulf that lay between the two worldviews. Julian's decree reflects the triangular relationship between political power, religious ideology, and education. Similarly, almost two centuries later, Emperor Julian's decision, in 529, to close the Academy in Athens—and the subsequent exile of the Platonic philosophers to the Sasanian Empire—was a political decision informed by religious ideology.

A single educational system could hardly be imagined for such a society. And yet, the great Christian patrician families, like those of the Cappadocian Fathers, (the two brothers, Basil of Caesarea and Gregory of Nyssa, as well as their cousin, Gregory Nazianzen) decided to develop just that. In the process, they retained much of the extant classical education, adding to it a supplementary education, based upon the Holy Scriptures.[48] This decision, which might not have been made in full consciousness of its consequences, and in any case was probably not fully implemented, figured strongly in the formation of Western culture. Until the fall of the Eastern Roman Empire in 1453, Byzantine education would be established as much upon Homer as upon the Bible.[49] Only in monastic schools (usually attracting the poorer students) would Homer disappear from the curriculum.

The roots of the European educational systems, then, plunge deeply into the cultural interaction of Greece and Israel. As we know, the Rabbis of the Talmud had made the study of the Torah the Archimedean point of the practice of the commandments (*Talmud Torah ke-neged kulam*).⁵⁰ Long ago, Elias Bickerman noted insightfully that such a conception of learning, of *scholē*, as reflecting the acme of ritual retains the deep mark of Hellenistic impact on Judaism.⁵¹

The meeting of the wisdom traditions of Greece and of Israel in Patristic literature was the most powerful and enduring interface between East and West. Its historical impact was even stronger than that of the interface between Greek thought and the Islamic Near East from the tenth to the twelfth centuries. The Fathers of the Church made it clear that the Christian "school" was a new type, unknown to the Greek philosophers. Indeed, Christian wisdom had nothing in common with Greek "wisdom," or rather with Greek "wisdoms," since each philosophical school had its own conception of truth. The precedence given to ethics in early Christian thought distinguished it from the philosophical schools. Hellenic intellectuals, while appalled by the irrationality of their opponents' metaphysics, were deeply impressed by the strength of their moral convictions.⁵² For the Patristic authors, the real difference between themselves and the Greek philosophers was that the Christians practiced what they preached. Indeed, nothing similar to what I call the "sapiential activism" of the Christian theologians can be found among the Greek philosophers. Sapiential activism is the Patristic response—with roots in Jewish Hellenistic literature—to the Hellenic philosophers' "care of the self."⁵³ Both messianism and eschatology imply the salvation of both the individual and the world as the final accomplishment of God's promises and of human repentance. The ecclesiastical historian Theodoret of Cyrrhus (whose *floruit* dates from the first half of the fifth century) writes in his *Therapeutics of the Hellenic Illnesses* that in the monks' "true philosophy" one needs less to understand the world than to transform it. Such a Marxist conception, as it were, reflects a Jewish atavism: the idea of the "establishment of the world in the divine kingdom" (*tikkun 'olam be-malkhut Shaddai*),⁵⁴ the work demanded from everyone before the coming of the messiah. Christianity inherited from Judaism, among other things, a link between personal reform, spiritual and moral, on the one hand, and the redemption of humankind on the other.⁵⁵ Sapiential activism (*paideia tou Kyriou*) in Christianity constitutes a major feature of the religious revolution of late antiquity.[56] To this activism was appended a completely new type of education that foregrounded religious instruction.

Let us return to the transformation of ethos mentioned at the start of this chapter: how is it possible to explain the great religious transformation in the Roman Empire, and the relationship between this religious change and the transformation of the ethos? Such mutation can be accounted for, but only by affirming the interaction of different cultural and religious systems. The Christianization of the Roman Empire owes a tremendous debt to the Jewish view of religion, which had as its epicenter theological reflection. This view, deeply informed by the idea that a single scriptural corpus constituted the core of the new religious education, and that this education was essentially implemented in ethical action, explains the basic Christian attitude to pagan books and to traditional *paideia*.

We now turn to the transformations of Greco-Roman *paideia* in the Christianized Empire, at a time when the Divine wisdom of the revealed scripture surpassed fully the worldly wisdom found in books written by humans.

4

SCRIPTURE AND CULTURE

> An old man has said: "The prophets produced books; then came our Fathers, who put them into practice; those who came after them applied them; those who came after them put them into practice; those who came after them learned them by heart; then came this generation, which copied them and put them into cupboard, without doing anything."
>
> *Apophtegmata Patrum,* Anonymous Collection, 228

Surveying the main historiographical approaches in the past half-century, Chapter 3 dealt with some major cultural implications of the religious revolution launched by Christianity. Moving a little deeper, we shall now investigate the mechanisms through which the idea of a Christian culture took root.

In the Roman Empire, both Judaism and Christianity singularized themselves as what came to be known later as "religions of the book." The numerous religious writings and the multiple communities organized around these writings throughout the Near East, from the birth of Christianity to that of Islam, indeed represent a striking phenomenon. To be sure, similar texts had also been redacted earlier, from the Avesta to the Orphic Hymns. What is unusual about the late ancient Near East is the high intensity, or level of activity of communities organized around a sacred book. In these communities, the sacred book holds a central place in the ritual, and it must be continually interpreted and reinterpreted against competing texts, as well as against heretical interpretations of this book. Speaking of the proliferation of "religions of the book" in the Roman and late antique Near East, the historian of religions Wilfred Cantwell Smith described a "scriptural movement."[1] Along similar lines, in his groundbreaking study of the sectarian milieu within which the Qur'an took shape the Semitist John Wansbrough proposed the term "midrashic communities."[2]

Hermeneutical Communities

Jews and Christians, more than most late antique religious communities, organized their entire religious life, including their cult, around reading, chanting, and studying their holy books. As has been pointed out by the historian of antiquity Keith Hopkins, pagan priests did not interpret books.[3] The fundamental importance of Torah study among the Jews spurred an educational pattern unique in antiquity, established upon the oral discussion of the legal system drawn from the Pentateuch. Such pattern was part and parcel of a deep intellectual religiosity. From the Talmudic point of view, "the ignoramus cannot be pious" (*ein 'am ha-aretz hassid*).[4]

The level of literacy among the Jews was likely higher than among other nations in the Empire.[5] The Rabbis, who acquired—and transformed—priestly religious power after the destruction of the Temple, were defined by their knowledge, a knowledge that could be inculcated, in principle, to all male children—hence the central importance of education in Rabbinic Judaism.

In an obvious sense, early Christianity was a "religion of the Book," since for the Christian (as well as for the Jewish) communities there was a canon of authoritative texts that stood at the core of their identity. Indeed, it has been said that "Christianity is the only religion born with a Bible in its cradle."[6] The abundant literature produced by the early Christians was soon classified, for instance by Eusebius, into books "acknowledged, disputed, and heretical."[7] It is certainly the case that Christianity was thus perceived by Greek and Roman polytheist authors who engaged in polemics against it. The Christian devotion to holy texts was widely acknowledged in the Roman Empire, as shown by Lucian's *Peregrinus* (11–12), for example. Nonetheless, pagan philosophers were known to reproach Christians for what they perceived as disrespect toward their own scriptures (i.e., the Septuagint): the pagans were honing in on the Christians' metaphorical interpretation of their commandments.⁸ It is as the true followers of the Jewish scriptures that the early Christian intellectuals perceived themselves, and wished to be perceived—as *verus Israel*.

We do not yet understand precisely how Christians and Jews, as well as Zoroastrians, Manichaeans or Mandaeans perceived their holy books. More specifically, we do not know much about the status and role of such books in the daily life of communities claiming officially to live according to them. The study of scriptures was for many years highly literary, concentrating almost exclusively on texts and canonization processes. In recent years this has changed, and the interface between scriptures and life as well as between written scriptures and oral traditions in late antique communities has become a topic of scholarly scrutiny.

Let us take the Manichaeans as a first case. Mani himself established a set of scriptures, to which his followers attached great importance. Their canon included a Pentateuch of Mani's books, and they are known to have written their holy books with particular care. They are even known to have illustrated them—a fact not attested elsewhere in the religions of late antiquity.⁹ About the Mandaeans, in contrast, our knowledge is scanty, and it is not even clear that one can speak of a scriptural canon in their case.¹⁰

In a study on literacy and power, Alan Bowman and Greg Woolf have proposed to speak of "textual communities," and they refer to the "sacral graphocentrism" of the early Christians. Robin Lane Fox, for his part, writes of "sacred literacy." Similarly, Moshe Halbertal discusses "text-oriented communities" in his work on the canonization of classical texts in the Jewish tradition.¹¹ In late antiquity, perhaps more than in any other observable period, communities were defined by their attitude to their holy book (or books) and its (or their) place in the *Weltanschauung*, in cult, as well as in daily hermeneutics.

THANKS to the Christian spiritual conception of sacrifice, the role of priesthood regained in early Christianity the significance it had lost among the Jews following the destruction of the Temple in Jerusalem. The rise of the Rabbis, coincided with the end of the traditional priestly elites among the Jews after 70 C.E. As a direct consequence of this priestly attitude, early Christian bishops were able to cultivate a profound knowledge of the biblical text and of its hermeneutical rules. Hence, early Christian thinkers developed the idea of a two-tiered religion, in which the higher level, meant for the religious (and intellectual) elites, required *gnosis*, a deep knowledge of the divine message. The lower level, open to all, was based on *pistis*, faith. Such a double theology, at once exoteric and esoteric, is found in other religious systems in antiquity. It was developed most explicitly, however, by Clement of Alexandria, toward the end of the second century.[12] Notably, among both Christians and Jews, intellectual progress, like moral progress, remained closely linked to spiritual progress: religiosity in its fullest sense hinged on a thorough grasp of divine revelation.

Such a discursive approach was common among early Christian writers, but it was not shared by all. In monastic literature, but also elsewhere, for instance in the letters of Anthony and the writings of Evagrius Ponticus and Basil the Great, one finds an anti-intellectualism that adopts fideism, rejecting *gnosis* and discursive wisdom. For such theologians, faith alone opens the door to God.

Lactantius's *Divine Institutions* is the first systematic work of Christian theology to have been written in Latin, in the first decade of the fourth century. Lactantius (ca. 240–ca. 320) was a teacher of rhetoric, a disciple of the African Arnobius of Sicca, and in his old age an adviser to Constantine. Rational argument was his chosen tool of pagan persuasion. *The Epitome of the Divine Institutions*, perhaps a pseudepigraph, articulates Lactantius's program well. For the author, the pagans' false religion (*falsa religio*) is comparable to the false wisdom (*falsa sapientia*) of the philosophers, who remained alien to truth despite their intellectual gifts and knowledge, "since they knew neither God nor God's wisdom."[13] Philosophers can come to no agreement, in Lactantius's view, as they lack wisdom:

> In philosophy, there is no cult, and there is no philosophy in cults. Religion is false when it is without wisdom, and wisdom is false when it is without religion.
>
> But where both are together, there must necessarily be truth, so that if one looks for what is truth itself, one can rightly say that it is a wise religion or a religious wisdom.[14]

Such crisp remarks demonstrate a reflexive conception of religion, as well as that of an internalized ritual and of an activist wisdom. Here we see the encounter, in early Christian thought, of a religious conception of wisdom with an intellectualist conception of religion, producing a Christian humanism along lines already formulated by Hellenistic Jewish thinkers. For the early Christian thinkers, wisdom no longer had the autonomy vis-à-vis religion it had held in Greek philosophy.[15] In Basil of Caesarea's *Discourse to the Young*, written in 370–374, and arguably the earliest formulation of Christian humanism, the classics are confronted with the evangelical doctrines (3.1), and the study of pagan literature is conceived as a propaedeutic to knowledge of the Christian mysteries (3.7).[16]

IN THE fourth book of his *De Doctrina Christiana*, written in 426, Augustine writes that the canonical writings (i.e., those considered to be authoritative) are notable not only for their wisdom, but also for their eloquence. He goes on to discuss a particular sort of eloquence that is typical of those authors who are the most authoritative and of those who receive the fullest divine inspiration,[17] an idea with a powerful future.[18]

By spotlighting the literary qualities of sacred texts, Augustine foregrounds their place in Christian education, an education that instructs not so much to shine in this world as to move from it to a world of pure happiness.[19] Such an education diverged markedly from traditional *paideia*, which mined as sources the classical authors and *artes liberales*. Thus, Augustine's ambivalence toward *paideia* showed through his entire literary corpus.[20]

For Augustine, as for Jerome, traditional *paideia* inculcated in children precisely the wrong values. As we saw in Chapter 3, a new educational pattern, adding biblical culture to traditional Greco-Roman literature, appeared in late antiquity, both in the Greek East and in the Latin West. This new educational program set the sacred texts and their commentaries alongside Greco-Roman *paideia*, not in opposition to it. This Christianized *paideia* represents a central aspect of the great cultural transformation of late antiquity, which went hand in hand with the gradual adoption of Christianity as the state religion in the fourth century.[21] Below, I reflect on the preconditions of this new *paideia* as well as on its implications for the late antique transformation of the concept of the authority of both sacred and literary texts.

Paideia *and Christian Culture*

Christian *paideia* would eventually constitute the kernel of medieval culture, in Byzantium as well as in the Latin West. It intersected two complex and utterly distinct corpora. On one side stood the scriptures, defined as the Septuagint with the addition of the texts constituting the New Testament, and regarded as the culmination of the biblical prophecies. On the other side stood the Greek (and, later, the Latin) literary corpus, especially those texts that came from the philosophical tradition, and above all those of the Platonic and Stoic schools. It was harder for Christians to accept this latter corpus rather than the former as authoritative: it was less clearly defined than the first, and it never acquired the authority that the revealed books of Christians and Jews enjoyed. In late antiquity, these two textual corpora called for strikingly different educational and cultural practices. They would also identify the social and political issues of authority and power at stake in each one of the formative scenarios: for instance, what sort of education did one need to become a bishop, a rhetor, or a functionary of the Roman Empire?[22] The ill-defined Greco-Roman corpus included texts, such as the Homeric epics, which would retain a highly ambivalent status in early Christian literature. Up to the very last days of Byzantium, children learned to read by studying the Homeric verses.[23] But these writings were also the foundational texts of ancient Hellenic (i.e., pagan) culture. Of course, the Homeric texts do not present themselves as having been in any sense "revealed," and play no part in Greek religion—although they certainly reflect religious practice and tradition of the Mycenaean age. Nevertheless, they were viewed by Christian intellectuals as the pagan counterpart of their own sacred books. As the "Bible" of the pagan pantheon, Homer was not well received in ancient Christianity. Nonetheless, Christian scholars overcame their ethical distaste of the texts by making use of the hermeneutical traditions that had been developed by Greek grammarians since the sixth century B.C.E. In this, they were following in the footsteps of a long list of Jewish Hellenistic authors, of whom Philo is only the last known representative. Some Christians were thus able to find some food for thought in the works of Homer, despite their instinctive mistrust of them.[24]

Patristic literature exhibits two competing attitudes toward "pagan" or Hellenic literature. The first attitude demands the total rejection of all texts other than those that have been revealed or canonized. Thus, in the third century, the *Didaskalia Apostolorum* forbade Christians from reading any "foreign" (i.e., pagan) literature. Similarly, at the start of his *Oratio ad Graecos* Tatian (died ca.185) distinguishes between the wisdom of the barbarian peoples (a concept to be discussed in Chapter 7) and Greek philosophy, whose elegance belies false ideas. This attitude, to use Tertullian's pungent formulation, rejects any compromise between Athens and Jerusalem.[25] It did not disappear with the Christianization of the Empire, and we can follow its traces in the literary output of late antique monasticism.[26]

However, this fideist attitude, which retained the radical character of earliest Christianity and its opposition to surrounding culture, remained in the minority. The bulk of Patristic authors proposed various solutions to the problem of the relationship between divine wisdom, revealed in the sacred books, and human wisdom, neatly preserved on the shelves of libraries. Clement of Alexandria and Origen were deeply ambivalent about Greek culture, yet they did not strive to achieve a complete break with knowledge as it was perceived in that culture, or with the old pedagogical methods through which this knowledge had traditionally been imparted.[27] The Church Fathers used two main strategies in their attempt to avoid such wholesale rejection of Greek *paideia*. The strategies, detailed below, were premised on the idea that as one God is the ultimate source of both the Bible and of the traditions of folklore and wisdom of each nation, there should be some sort of correspondence between these two corpuses.

As far as Christian scholars were concerned, the new religion was to be presented as a philosophical school, one that was in possession of a wisdom superior to that of the philosophers precisely because, *qua* barbarian, it was expressed in a different conceptual language.[28] For Clement of Alexandria, Christians were able to philosophize without learning (*Strom.* 4.8); similarly, Justin Martyr had spoken of a "knowledge of the unlearned." This is exactly what Eusebius does in his *Praeparatio Evangelica*. By and large, Christian theologians were very keen to present themselves as being part of a wisdom movement. As part of such a movement, Christian revelation could be seen as the culmination of the universal search for truth, the last piece in the jigsaw puzzle of divine aspects in the history of cultures: even before the incarnation of Jesus Christ, God had found various ways to partially reveal himself, for instance in Platonic philosophy. In such an approach, Christ's message could be seen as fully complementary: it did not replace the knowledge transmitted by traditional education, but rather supplemented it.

The early Christian writers dealt with the commonalities between scripture and the foundational texts of the Hellenic tradition by conceiving of the latter as a copy of the former. A term was coined to describe this: "the theft of the Greeks."[29] This idea appeared rather frequently from the second century onward, in the writings of Tatian, and then of Clement. Hence, the teachings of the Greek philosophers that appeared in line with those of the scripture were accounted for by the idea of pagan philosophers pilfering ideas from the sacred texts. From a practical point of view, this notion allowed Christian authors to avoid having to reject out-of-hand any teachings common to scripture and the philosophers.[30]

Augustine

A second strategy was developed by some Patristic authors, which made use of a very different, Biblical metaphor, referring to the Egyptians' riches, stolen by the Israelites during their flight from Egypt.[31] According to Christian as well as to Jewish tradition, the children of Israel had good moral grounds for this action. In contradistinction to the Greek theft, which had resulted in the dispersion of Hebrew wisdom into a pagan culture, the theft of Egypt's riches by the Hebrews allowed them to decorate their own teachings with elements of elegance taken from a pagan culture. To beautify their wisdom texts, Christians used the intellectual (and scientific) traditions as well as the rules of literary sophistication that they had found in Greek literature: one could thus talk of "the beauty of Japheth in the tents of Sem" (Gen 9: 27).

It is against this backdrop that we read Augustine's *De Doctrina Christiana*. For Augustine, Christian wisdom must be judged according to the criteria of pagan culture. Hence, Christian literature, no more than Greek literature, can evade evaluation on the basis of aesthetic principles. The two theft metaphors help to account for the "mixing of genres" between the Hebrew Scriptures and Greek culture, with their respective attention to either form (the Israelites' theft from the Egyptians) or content (the Greeks' theft from the Hebrews).

The Church Fathers approached Greek literature in much the same manner as they approached the Hebrew Bible. Both these literary corpora, written before the coming of the Lord, were in a sense Christian *avant la lettre*. More precisely, they both announced below-ground Christian truth. Christian scholars read between the lines of their texts, something that the Jews, they thought, were unable to do (a handicap that prevented them from reading their own Holy Scriptures properly). In this way, the Church Fathers placed Jews and Greeks in opposition to one another, not simply appropriating their writings but also stripping them of their respective identities. Neither group was considered able to discover the truth concealed at the core of its own spiritual and cultural history.

For Christian thinkers, "Greek literature" referred, first of all, to the writings of the philosophers. This included the metaphysics of Plato, of course, and also the ethics of the Stoics. Although the Aristotelian and Pythagorean schools did not have a direct impact upon Patristic thought, Aristotelian and Pythagorean traces are easily discerned in later Platonic and Stoic works, written in the Roman Empire. Some texts were thus relatively easily incorporated. If Christians were to manage Greek *paideia*, they could not avoid confrontation with the Homeric epics, with the embarrassing behavior displayed not only by the mortals but also by the gods who littered the pages of these tales. There was, however, a solution: since the time of the grammarians of old, as we have seen, the Greek hermeneutical tradition had guided Christians in a method of interpreting Homer that was both metaphorical and spiritual. Thus, the Christians accepted the whole system of Greek *paideia*, yet modified it through a religious teaching based on the scriptures. In their fashioning of Christian identity, early Christian intellectuals, from the second to the fourth centuries, displaced the culturally authoritative Greek texts with the Christian Bible. The basic principles of Greek education were retained, but they were modified as they were subsumed to the scriptures: the Homeric texts were examined through reference to the Bible. Such a major transformation of the structure of education reflected an equally major transformation of its goals. While classical education created or enforced a difference in social rank, as Tim Whitmarsh has proposed, Christian education aimed at encouraging *imitatio Christi*, if not through martyrdom, then through ascetic practices and monastic life.[32]

Secondary Canons

Elsewhere, I have applied to the dual system of foundational texts developed by the Church Fathers the metaphor of the "double helix" introduced by Francis Crick and James Watson to describe the structure of DNA.[33] The double helix of late antique Christian culture, upon which European culture was established, presents Homer and the Bible as two parallel helices with an infinite number of correlations between them.[34] Moreover, since the conversion of Greco-Roman culture, the cross-pollination between Athens and Jerusalem has remained the very essence of Christian culture.

Late antique Christian thinkers, in the main, neither wished to efface Greek culture nor to replace it with the Jewish scriptures. This conservative instinct impacted on the formation of a Christian culture. Christianity presents itself not only as a school of thought, but also as a religion based on a revealed book (or a series of revealed books, that is, a canon). Such a self-perception invites the question of the relationship between the sacred books and all other books. The Church Fathers seem to have made a concerted effort to mix genres: they established their new Christian culture on the bedrock of classical culture. In other words, we may ask what effects a religion of the book would have on an already bookish culture.[35] Referring to Christianity as a "religion of the Book," implies that the Bible, a book with a special, revealed status, would soon become in itself a cultic artifact. While the ritual aspects of the holy book (both among Jews and Christians, as well as among Muslims) are only now receiving intensive attention, these aspects are situated at the very core of these religions. Put differently, "religions of the Book" are at the same time "cultic religions," but ones in which holy books play a central role.

Thus, the double helix of Homer and the Bible reveals the new Christian culture of late antiquity as at once a *sacralization of culture* and an *acculturation of religion*.[36] In other words, a bidirectional movement took place in the new symbiosis: Greco-Roman culture was Christianized while Christianity underwent Romanization. Self-identifying as an intellectual and spiritual school, Christianity paradoxically presented itself as reflecting and transforming a major aspect of Greco-Roman culture. By claiming to launch a new kind of philosophical school, Christian theologians sought to reclaim a legitimacy that Roman philosophers were denying them. In the very measure that those Christians hoped, beyond the mere legalization of their religion, to become the new intellectual and spiritual Roman elite, they were bound to present (and eventually to conceive) their religion as one intrinsically linked to *Romanitas*.

We now move to a brief consideration of the radical complexity of the New Testament.[37] Christianity has the Bible read on different levels, each fitting a specific kind of human intelligence. Moreover, the Christian Bible is a kind of twofold text, as the Old and the New Testaments are understood to echo one another constantly. The Old Testament, from this point of view, reflects the divine promise made explicit in the New Testament: it is called, in Patristic terms, *sacramentum futuri*. Thus, the Christian thinkers, even before they took on *paideia* and paganism, engaged in a battle with the Jews. Only one of the two "sister" religions could read the Biblical texts correctly. Ancient Christianity, then, defined itself in opposition to both Judaism and Hellenism. Indeed, it denied to both the authority to interpret the founding texts of their own cultures.

Yet a canon a scriptural system doesn't make. Rather, a canon constitutes the bones, the skeleton, as it were, of the body of a religious community. The "flesh" of this body is the hermeneutical life of these texts, and the cultural practice that ensured their production and circulation, as well as their reproduction in hermeneutic communities. However, how such scriptural systems operate within the life of a community is a complex question. The Christian community defines itself both through and in the scriptures, by the correct interpretation of these texts, and orthodoxy is reached progressively, through argumentation with heretics of all stripes.

Strikingly, the concept of a "New Testament" in the last decades of the second century emerged in parallel to the redaction of the Mishna.[38] By the end of the second century, Jews and Christians had already split into two distinct communities, each defining itself largely in opposition to the other. Each strove to find the key to the correct reading of their common literary inheritance, the biblical text. For the Christians, this key was the New Testament; for the Jews, it was the Mishna—*deuterosis* in Greek. Just as this new canon had been established, however, another series of texts emerged, instituting the hermeneutical rules by which this initial canon had to be read (the Talmud among the Jews, the writings of the Church Fathers among the Christians). Robert Travers Herford noted long ago the significance of the Theodosian Codex and the Babylonian Talmud being redacted in the same period. He argued that this editorial coincidence was pivotal to the formation of medieval culture, which also saw the crystallization of Church law and the blossoming of Patristic literature.[39]

One canon is followed perforce by a commentary, which soon receives canonical status, becoming another canon. The latter, in its turn, is eventually supplemented by a commentary (or several commentaries), which are also eventually canonized. This cycle is broken only by a revolt within the community, demanding a "return to the sources"—*ad fontes*. Thus, a canon is much more than a list of sacred texts, considered against apocryphal books. In fact, a canon is nothing less than the engine of the hermeneutical life of a religion, its principle of authority. This authority belongs to the community, which invents, transforms, and preserves the rules according to which holy writings should be read. As the scriptures are invested with an infinite number of meanings, their divine author is divested of the authority of the author of a literary text. It is the community of readers that gives sacred writings their meaning.[40] The *regula fidei* becomes, then, a *regula legendi*.[41]

Augustine and Books

After Origen, Augustine takes pride of place in the ancient world with regard to intensive preoccupation with books.[42] In his *Confessions*, Books One to Eight, the bishop of Hippo tells how, as a young man, he investigated three types of book cultures, from philosophy through Manichaeism to Paul's letters, in a search for truth.[43] Yet, whether this "bookishness" is truly Augustinian, or whether it reflects, rather, the theologian's Christian identity, is unclear.[44] Of all ancient authors, Augustine is easily the most prolific. His written corpus outstrips that of any other Latin (or Greek) author. Augustine may also be the most reflexive of all ancient writers, having written *Retractationes*, critical summaries and evaluations of his views in each of his writings.[45] Augustine spent his life reading, writing about, and meditating upon the corpus of biblical texts. Despite his immersion in the world of scripture, however, Augustine never forgot that the divine source of its authority remained beyond the text, even beyond language itself. Thus, the human relationship with God could be expressed fully only in a *visio Dei*, a revelation of divine glory. What links, we may then ask, did Augustine conceive between God's Book and those written by His creations?

Augustine's works tell us a great deal about books in the late Roman world.[46] For Augustine, *uolumen* is rather a concept, while *liber*, or *codex* is a reality of everyday life. Oddly, however, Augustine never refers to the *uolumina* of the Jews, who are the Christians' "book keepers" (*custodies librorum nostrorum*), and even their slaves and "book carriers" (*tamquam casparii nostri sunt*).[47] The Qur'an will adopt this notion when it calls Jews, or, more precisely, those who do not keep the commandments of the Torah, "donkeys carrying books."[48]

Augustine's relationship with books, however, is not simply that of a writer. It is also, as Brian Stock has noted, that of an unusually gifted reader, and of course also that of a teacher. In the ancient world, teaching was an oral activity based upon books. Augustine determined to act in accordance with what he had gleaned from incessant study. Of all early Christian writers, it is Augustine who could consider most expertly questions on the nature of reading.[49]

For Augustine, the world was shaped by one book, and one book only: the Bible. In Stock's apt phrase, for Augustine, the Bible was "the only true book."[50] However, the ultimate end of human existence, the ineffable experience of the *visio Dei*, of the revelation of God's glory, remained for him always beyond the text. The saint reports this in his vision: "I have understood that no voice could reach God's ears, except for the expression of the soul."[51] Like other intellectual mystics, Augustine is in the paradoxical position of one whose world is constructed of books, and who is convinced simultaneously that what truly matters is irremediably situated beyond the written letter.[52]

As aforementioned, Marrou dedicated much of his vast knowledge and admirable *esprit de finesse* to both Augustine and the literary culture of his age. Marrou also wrote of the significance of Augustine's theory and practice of reading for the transformation of ancient Greco-Roman intellectual culture as a whole. And yet, his analysis of Augustine seems to miss a dimension. In *Saint Augustin et la fin de la culture antique* (first published in 1938, at a time when its author saw himself as living in a period of decadence and twilight), Marrou explicitly locates Augustine at the *end* of a long Greco-Roman tradition: both there and in his *History of Education in Antiquity*, he has little to say about the transformation of *paideia* under the impact of Christianity.[53]

In the past several decades, however, scholarship has begun to better appreciate the riches of late antiquity and the civilization of the Christianized Roman Empire. What was perceived as a period of decadence has now gained, thanks to its peculiar spiritual creativity (and partly thanks to Marrou himself) a dignity of its own.[54]

If Augustine ushered out Antiquity, he at the same time ushered in a new civilization, founded upon the relationship between two double cultures, that of Greece reinterpreted by its Roman conqueror, and that of Israel reread by Christianity, the new Israel. While the first was a culture of many books, the second was one of a single book (or rather established upon a single corpus of scriptures), revealed by God. Augustine, who had studied rhetoric in his youth, held that *belles lettres* were of little value, worthless as they were in achieving salvation. His *De doctrina christiana* (the first three books were written in 397, while the fourth dates from 426) reveals his ambivalence toward pagan literature. *De doctrina christiana* (and *doctrina christiana*, for Augustine, is equivalent to *doctrina pietatis* and to *scientia*)[55] reflects for Augustine the uncertain value of the *artes liberales*, which were the basis of ancient schooling and which became, to some extent thanks to Augustine himself, that of medieval Christian education.

Augustine's attitude has much in common with that expressed by John Chrysostom in his *Address on vainglory and the right way for parents to bring up their children* (probably written in the late 380s or in the 390s). There, Chrysostom argued that the ultimate goal of a good Christian education was "to raise an athlete for Christ" (*threpson athlētēn tōi Christōi*), that is, a monk.

Augustine, then, was a particularly valued witness to one of the most dramatic chapters in the history of Western culture, but he was also an active agent in this passage. This transformation meant, first of all, that much above the books of old were now placed the *hagia biblia*, or *hagiai graphai*, the divine, revealed books (the Latin singular, *sacra biblia*, would appear only in the thirteenth century). Augustine expected believers to come to church with their own books, although he tolerated women, instead of reading, singing hymns.[56] For Augustine, even a literate woman (*litterata*), does not read as a matter of course.[57]

In his *Confessions*, Augustine tells of his fascination at his discovery of Ambrosius reading silently.[58] Later in the same work, he describes how he himself read in silence.[59] Much has been written on Augustine's important testimony about the beginning of silent reading. Various metaphors used by Augustine (such as letters "shouting," "speaking," singing") would seem to imply that his practice remained one of reading out loud. In fact, on the contrary, these metaphors indicate that the letters were actually read silently. The emergence of silent reading, of course, would be a very long process indeed. It would take centuries before reading became, first of all, *lectio tacita,* a private and silent activity. Ancient monastic Rules clue us in to the link between silent reading and early Christian monasticism. The passage to such reading, actually, entailed a profound change in perception. Traditionally, in Rome, even prayer was said aloud.[60] Augustine's *Confessions* attest a double shift, both in reading habits and in the conception of prayer.[61]

As we have seen, scriptural authority had passed in the Christianized Roman Empire into the hands of the community of believers, or more precisely to its elites, who knew (thanks to the rules of interpretation) how to transform the holy text into a "sounding box." Scriptural authority allowed these *religious* elites, a class to which the monks certainly belonged and which was highly distinct from the old *cultural* elites, to effect the deep transformation of traditional education through a reading of the great Greek and Latin texts alongside the scriptural corpus. What soon became the holy Book of the Christians was a book of a new kind, which could be translated into any language without any loss of power. It could thus circulate throughout the ever-growing Christian *oikoumenē,* be read, commented upon, and listened to. Its stories were soon reproduced visually in what would become Christian art.

Religious creativity is by no means limited to the field of theological ideas. On the contrary, it seems that each successful new religious movement, at least among the "religions of the book," owes its success to novel literary publicity and propaganda. This is obviously true in the case of the Hebrew Torah scrolls and in early Christianity, as we have seen, but also in the case of Mani, who invented a new way of writing Middle Persian, one more efficient than the traditional Pahlavi alphabet. The same will also be true for the Muslims, who learned from the Buddhists to make use of paper on a large scale for religious propaganda. Such technical creativity is directly linked to the novelty of religious movements that are not tied to traditional ways of expression. It is precisely because the early Christians were, so to speak, beyond the pale, that they felt freed from cultural traditions.

Ancient Christianity, as we have seen, transformed the traditional framework of education, by establishing a system in which the single great book of God and the whole library of human books again and again recalled one another.[62] This system, along with the notion that while in theory the text belonged to God, in practice it belonged to the community, would flourish up to the end of the Middle Ages.

The scriptural side of the early Christian revolution was, then, one of its constitutive parts. Early Christianity was indeed a religion of the Book, but of a kind previously unknown. While the Jews had learned to launch, through the major enterprises of both the Septuagint and the Targumim, translations of their sacred scriptures, the Christians soon learned to offer dramatic developments to the translation movement, and made their scriptures (or at least their central parts) available to all languages spoken by people willing to listen to the new kerygma, within and without the Roman and Sasanian Empire. Hence, sections of the Bible were soon made available in Syriac, Coptic, Armenian, and Gothic, this demanding in some cases the invention of an alphabet for a language that had hitherto remained oral. Indeed, the success of Christianity in the ancient world can be attributed largely to the central importance of the book in general, and of scripture in particular. If Christ won over Mithras, to use a famous late nineteenth century metaphor, this may well be, to a great extent, because of the codex.[63]

In the scriptural universe of late ancient Christianity, however, the reinterpretation of Greco-Roman *paideia* in Christian education is not solely a matter of texts and commentaries. The new reading practices, in particular those developed by the early monks, also contributed much to relationships with books. It is to these aspects that we turn in Chapter 5.

5

THE NEW SELF AND READING PRACTICES

In Chapters 3 and 4, we sought to better understand the religious revolution of late antiquity and the cultural changes that it caused. We saw how the new Christian elites struggled to redefine the parameters of culture, between the scriptural corpus (*ta biblia*) on the one hand, and Greco-Roman *paideia* on the other hand. Chapter 4 confirmed the idea of early Christianity as a religion of the Book. Christian culture in the making, as we learned in that chapter, promoted a fresh approach to books, endowing them with a new status. This was particularly true in the monastic movement of late antiquity, where new reading practices eventually overturned the reading system altogether, as we shall presently argue. We shall understand now, moreover, how the Christian use of the codex reconstructed, on multiple levels, the way in which books would be approached from then on.

Interestingly, the topic of monasteries and their influence on early Christianity remains current news. In 2008, Pope Benedict XVI spoke at the Collège des Bernardins in Paris. The subject of the speech was medieval Christian monasteries and their function as treasuries of ancient culture as well as the locations of the emergence of a new, Christian culture.[1] Benedict clarified that the monks had not set out to achieve these goals. Rather, stated the Pope, they had intended to seek God, *quaerere Deum*. For Benedict, it was in the monasteries of the medieval

West that this great cultural transfer (of classical culture) and creation (of Christian culture) took place. While I agree with him on the central role played by the monastic movement, I propose a somewhat different frame for the phenomenon. Specifically, I shall argue here that it is precisely in the monastic movement of *late antiquity* that the roots of the cultural transformation of Western society should be sought, and that the new reading practices were directly linked to the new perceptions of the self that developed in early Christianity, in particular among the monks. The emerging attitude to books had much to do with the development, in late antiquity, of new conceptions of the person. More than anything else, Christianization processes reflect and incorporate the religious revolution of the Roman world.

As we have seen, the end of public sacrifices—until then the most concrete expression of public religion—emblemized this revolution. The Christian ascetic movement, culminating in the birth and burgeoning of monasticism in the Mediterranean and the Near East, and from there its move to other parts of the Empire, represents one of its most striking aspects.[2] In an instance of historical irony, the early monks, those radical opponents of traditional *paideia,* functioned as cultural brokers in a world where civil society—and the cultural *koinē* of pagans and Christians represented by *paideia*—was fast disappearing. To a great extent it was the monks of Christian antiquity, East and West, who laid the passage from Greco-Roman to Christian culture.

From the Pythagoreans to the Essenes, the Mediterranean had long hosted marginal communities of ascetics and religious "virtuosi" (again, a Weberian term). The early Christian monks were indeed following an old tradition of liminal, elitist communities of wisdom. But nothing on this scale had ever been seen before: right and left, young Christian men and women were rejecting the fundamental social imperative of procreation and joining the ranks of the cloistered.[3] A further change was brewing as well. The term *monachos* (Syriac *iḥidaya*) denotes a monk living *alone,* but the anchorites in the Egyptian and Syrian deserts were soon outnumbered by monks living together in *coenobia,* ascetic communities The monks themselves seem to have been aware of the linguistic paradox, and monastic literature, both in Greek and in Syriac, has the *monachos* having learned, through his ascetic practices, to *unify* his own self, to have become a new, fully integrated individual.[4] And this brings us to the final, crucial change in monastical behavior: in a world from which martyrdom had for all practical purposes disappeared, the demand for *imitatio Christi* was fast turning into the art of transforming the self.

During his last years, Michel Foucault became fascinated by Patristic literature and by the phenomenon of early Christian monasticism, whose revolutionary character he sought to interpret. Following in the footsteps of Pierre Hadot, Foucault was concerned with problems in Greek (or Greco-Roman) philosophy.[5] More precisely, the two philosophers were intrigued by the spiritual exercises, a Greek philosophical tradition involving the "care of the self" (*epimeleia heautou*), a care the nature of which the monks had transformed. Foucault argued that this transformation led to the suppression of the self.[6] Neither Foucault nor Hadot, however, were able to identify clearly the fundamental differences between the "care of the self" as understood by the Hellenic philosophers on the one hand and by the early Christian theologians on the other. A fuller understanding of the role of books in introspection might put us on the right track.[7]

A New Self

For the Greek philosophers, the individual sought to define himself both within the cosmos at large, and in counterpoint to it. For the Christians, the cosmic drama is epitomized by the life, death, and resurrection of Jesus Christ, both human and divine. This was a new form of the "care of the self," which I propose to call "sapiential activism."[8] Yet, it is through reflection upon the Holy Books of divine revelation that the Christian could find his own self: text and self would now be entwined, one deciphered through the other. The self-presentation of early Christianity as a "school" of wisdom was certainly useful for apologetic purposes. But it also reflected the deep conviction of a self-perception.[9]

From the first to the fifth centuries, a new perception of the individual formed in Christian literature, one that Hellenic thought was not likely to have conceived.[10] This perception eventually produced a newly reflexive self. The terms "reflexive self" and "person" both convey a late antique sensitivity to the individual. The Augustinian synthesis generated a radical reflexivity of the self—a reflexivity that was related to the awareness of sin, and that was quite absent in the ancient world until then. Bequeathed to the West, the Augustinian idea would dominate anthropological perceptions until at least the end of the Middle Ages. This idea was grounded in several points of Christian theology, and it concerned the reflection upon both God's nature and particular conceptions of man.

The first theological conception informing Christian (as well as Jewish) anthropology is of course the biblical idea of man having been created in God's image, *homo imago Dei* (*Gen* 1.26). This idea endowed the human body with dignity, and offered unity to the human person as a whole, body and soul. Both ran against the grain of Greek thought, or more precisely against Platonism, a leading philosophical trend in the Roman Empire. This new anthropology entailed a broadening of the self, no longer restricted to the intellect or the soul, and a new status of the body, supported by the idea of divine incarnation. Hence Tertullian could coin his famous lapidary expression: *caro salutis cardo,* the flesh is the axis of redemption, a sentence that would have been quite incomprehensible to a pagan.[11] The broadening of the concept of person coincided with another development: the fast-growing importance of the idea of sin—and in particular of original sin—with its ineluctable consequences. Together, these two developments would form the backbone of Augustinian anthropology, thus opening a major chapter in the history of Western consciousness.[12] Indeed, although Augustine's views cannot be said to have been representative of contemporary perceptions, their impact on medieval views in the Latin West were unequaled. Original sin, however, would be mitigated by the concept of *metanoia*, repentance, and the cleansing the individual of the blemish of his or her past sins. *Metanoia* presupposes the possibility of moral progress, which drives the dynamism of Christian anthropology.[13]

The new parameters of personal identity incorporated within the definition of the person a soul-body unity. Notwithstanding this integration, however, the new person was not quite a harmonious entity. Replacing the soul-body divide of Platonism, original sin offered a new schism, this time located within the soul. The break was effected by guilt, itself generated by inherited and thus unavoidable sin. This state of affairs demanded a salvation that went far beyond the individual. Indeed, it entailed ridding oneself of the consequences of the original sin. Greek philosophers hardly knew of such a tension within the soul. In this framework, faith became not only the condition *sine qua non* for salvation, but also the equivalent of it. Faith in Christ and His redemptive sacrifice, in itself, saved.

IDENTITY, however, is collective as much as it is personal. Social identity too underwent a radical reinterpretation in ancient Christianity. For the first time in the ancient world, identity was defined in religious terms, rather than in ethnic or cultural and linguistic ones, as had been the case in the Hellenistic and Roman contexts. Texts such as the second-century anonymous *Epistle to Diognetus* indicate this: the Christians were not associated with a single language, culture, or territory; they had no objective criteria of identification. This identity absence is perhaps best reflected in the corpus of laws established from Constantine to Theodosius II, and collected in the Theodosian Codex. These laws show the importance of defining the Church and the centers of authority within it.[14] This effort, in turn, meant defining the boundaries of the Christian community, as the traditional Jewish criteria, such as ethnicity, language and religious law, *halakha*, were no longer available. Dogma could provide the parameters of the new social identity; that is, the proper way to understand Jesus Christ, His nature, and His mission. Hence, collective identity would now be rooted in interiority and expressed in terms of belief. True belief, or orthodoxy, was itself defined by its negation, and showed up in the many faces of error: schism and heresy from within, Judaism and paganism from without. With the Christianization of the Roman Empire, the division of the heavenly world into the kingdom of God and the kingdom of Satan was mirrored in social identity: those who belonged, and would be saved, and those who did not belong, and would be lost.

The social definition of Church boundaries, however, did not only imply opposition to error, but also the desire, found in Christianity from its very beginnings, to broaden its appeal. In other words, these boundaries reveal Christianity's catholicity, its strong and successful urge to convert others to its way. Of course, conversion also betrays the essentially dogmatic stance of the new religion: it draws a firm line between truth and error.

Both individual and collective identities were defined in early Christianity in direct relation to the internalization process. And, as noted above, both attest the limitations of this process. The battle between faith and sin at the individual level and that between truth and error at the collective level seem to follow parallel lines. As truth comes from God and Christ, error comes from Satan and from the Antichrist. Choosing between true and false beliefs constitutes the core of both individual and collective identity, and it infused early Christian identity with a strong element of intolerance. Borrowing from Irenaeus, we might say that while truth is univalent, the hydra of heresy has multiple heads, all of which required severance.[15]

A New Status of Books

We recall that what has been dubbed the "scriptural movement" stands as one of the most striking facets of the religious and cultural revolutions of late antiquity. From early Christianity to early Islam, through the various Gnostic trends, Mandaeism, Manichaeism, and even the Neoplatonists, multiple religious movements granted prominence to holy books—prophetic or otherwise revelatory—as well as to their hermeneutics and to their ritual roles.[16] It is doubtless thanks to its Jewish roots that Christianity placed at center stage the collection of revealed books that became the *Biblia*. Of course, early Christianity shares many features with other religious movements of the ancient world. Judaism excepted, none of these maintained the priority of the revealed book as resolutely as Christianity.

The early Christian elites, both the religious hierarchy (i.e., the bishops) and the ascetic virtuosi (i.e., the monks), took reading and writing very seriously. In the entire Roman world, only the Jews had evidenced anything like this sort of book-centeredness.[17] The Logos, one might say, not only was incarnated in *Corpus Christi*, but also in the corpus of the *Biblia*.

Hence we move to the book as artifact, over and above being the material support of the text. This artifact was to be used for ritual purposes, but was also considered to possess magical powers. The study of books as objects, the roles played by their physical form in early Christian (and Jewish) rituals, public and private, as well as their apotropaic and magical uses, have only recently started to attract serious attention.[18] Perceptions percolate slowly, however, and we must deal with the *longue durée*.[19]

The status and role of books in the religious world of late antiquity is closely tied to the transformations in the production and form of books in the Roman Empire. As discussed in Chapter 1, from the second century on, more and more books were written as codices rather than in the traditional form of rolls; by the end of the fourth century, the codex had emerged as the clear winner.[20] Compared to its adoption in general society, the Christian adoption of the codex was immediate and universal. Very few of our extant biblical papyri do not come from codices. By the late second century, Christian writing was generally done on codices. In fact, the codex itself might even be understood as a Christian innovation. As we have seen, this revolution in the physical aspect of books is paralleled in the early centuries of the Common Era by the new development of silent reading—a development that would not become a widespread practice for centuries.[21]

Christians and Books

We know precious little about the Christian book culture in the Roman world. In *Books and Readers in the Early Church*, Harry Gamble Jr. adopted a broad perspective, integrating the Christian attitude toward the canonical books with the more general question of the status of literacy among Christians in the early centuries.[22] Gamble analyzed the various uses of books among Christians during the first centuries, both in public cults and in private. He found that up to the fourth century there was a clear distinction between public reading and private reading of canonical books. Considering contemporaries, Cyril of Jerusalem, for one, offers a strong warning against too much free access to the scriptures, writing that "what is read in church should not be read privately." This adjuration may not necessarily indicate an insatiable interest in scripture on the part of the masses. Gamble contended that the use and status of books and reading among Christians was similar to what obtained in society at large. This presumption seems somewhat dubious. There is little evidence that Christian attitudes to texts in general, and to their holy books in particular, reflected those of the surrounding society.

Rather, here as in other domains, the early Christians were likely both independent and original. Not bound by cultural and religious traditions, they were free to be innovative. Early Christian communities were "enclave societies," established upon a divinely revealed book (or upon a corpus of writings).[23] In such societies, the holy book was accorded great honor, but also was a fundament of ritual, as well of religious education. This status of the Bible had a significant impact upon ritualized reading and upon the relationship between reading and ritual.

In Chapter 1 we noted a paradox of early Christianity. Despite the major changes effected by Christians in the status and role of books, it seems that the literacy rate among Christians was not higher than that in Roman society at large. In antiquity (and far beyond it), cultures remained to a great extent oral, and literacy was, even in the best of times, a privilege of very few.[24] In such cultures, books were used as instruments for the authentication of texts, rather than as the means for their communication. This helps to explain why in the conversion movement launched by Christianity, books initially played a modest part. According to Keith Hopkins, "many or most Christian communities . . . simply did not have among them a single sophisticated reader or writer."[25] As such, Christians heard the holy texts, or rather parts of them, the most evocative stories, figures and words, through "preaching, catechesis, apologetic debates, intramural theological disputes, and personal edification." Robin Lane Fox, for his part, notes that "scriptural study must have ranked almost as low as sexual fidelity" among late antique Christians and that Christianity offered "a less reverential attitude to the written word" than that found in both Judaism and traditional culture in the Roman Empire.[26]

And yet, even if literacy rates were rather low within Christian communities, early Christian groups may still be defined as "communities of the book," whose cultural and religious capital was, to a large extent, constituted by their books. As Gillian Clark reminds us, "Christianity uniquely offered increased access to book-based education."[27] Furthermore, the early Christians soon learned to enjoy writing.[28] The horizons revealed by the existence of scripture and its almost infinite hermeneutical resonances and reverberations counts more than sociological facts. The latter can in no way account for the dialectical power of written and spoken words in the forging of a new scriptural universe, a universe unknown to pagans in the Roman world.

Christians and the Codex

The papyrologist Roger Bagnall has argued that the place of books in ancient society and the role of the Christians in the history of the codex have been misrepresented, mainly because much of the scholarship is lacking in cultural breadth.[29] To Bagnall's insight one might add a dimension rooted in the very logic of religious history. It is a remarkable fact that from the second century on the early Christians pioneered the use of the codex. While the passage from roll to codex was overall a gradual one, papyrologists have noted that almost all Christian papyri were originally part of codices, while very few were written on rolls. In this regard, a veritable "Christian *obsession* with the codex"[30] has been put forward. This preoccupation, as it were, with the codex seems to be quite related to early Christianity being a demotic form of a religion of the Book. For a religion that was at once outlawed and strongly missionary, the easy circulation of books of small dimensions was particularly significant.[31]

The clear Christian preference for the codex has been considered from multiple angles.[32] Practicality was surely one factor. The codex was cheaper to produce than the scroll—as it could be written on both sides of the page—and easier to manipulate, as there was no need to unroll it. And, unlike the scrolls of the Torah in the synagogue cult, Christian books were meant for practical use rather than cultic activity. As such, they were not overly elegant. A similar kind of functionalism can be found in the so-called Cologne Mani Codex, an official biography of the Prophet of light.[33] This codex, the smallest extant one from the ancient world, may share a further feature with the early Christian codex. Its tiny dimensions permitted, it seems, apotropaic use, and also might have helped to avoid police scrutiny in fourth-century Egypt. Books, including the scriptures, had become, quite literally, handy.

Yet, practicality alone does not account fully for the religious use of the new techniques. Lack of commitment to a certain textual format, such as the Jews might have had regarding the use of scrolls for the Torah and the other biblical books, is likely to have played a part in the Christian use of the codex. Further, this use may well be related to self-identification. The codex did not possess the hieratic character of the roll. Thus the codex suited the way that the early Christians perceived themselves: free from the sacerdotal habits of past traditions. Relatedly, the rise of the Christian codex may be considered in light of the marginal cultural position of Christians in late antiquity, a position that permitted disengagement from hallowed patterns.

Christian literacy, then, was a literacy of a new, revolutionary kind, an oral form of literacy, as it were. It does seem as though a marked ambivalence toward the written word existed among Christians in the Roman Empire. That the oral dimensions of their religion were paramount for early Christians does not imply, however, that its literary character was in the least negligible. Once again, we are witnessing a gap between ethos and praxis. The scriptural origin of Christianity prevented it from developing into a "textless" or oral religion. Early Christian literature privileges the "low," demotic language used by in the Gospels, a "language of fishermen" very different from the literary language of Greek *paideia*. Popular, spoken language was a central trait of earliest Christianity. Thus, the quarrel of the Church with the Empire can be encapsulated as that between two antithetical attitudes toward language. Consequently, Christianized Roman civilization developed conflicting systems of literacy.

The popular literary level of early Christian theology jibed poorly with contemporary Greco-Roman literature. Moreover, while early Christian literature sometimes follows known patterns (such as the Clementine "novel," both in the Greek *Homilies* and in the Latin *Recognitions*), its genres, such as Gospels, apocalypses, and theological treatises and commentaries, are often highly original, quite different from anything in Latin *belles lettres* or philosophical literature.[34] This literary creativity reflects a major transformation of the attitudes to reading in early Christianity. Reading, which had been in Rome an essentially recreational activity, became for the Christians a mainly normative one.

Anthony Grafton and Megan Williams have argued that early Christian intellectuals left a clear mark on the transformation of the book in the Roman Empire. Grafton and Williams used as a case study Caesarea Maritima and the figures of Origen and Eusebius.[35] In a book focusing on third- and fourth-century Caesarea, there is surprisingly little discussion of the interface between Christian and Jewish sages, which we know took place, precisely on biblical hermeneutics. True, while we know that Origen, whose scriptorium was unique, maintained close contacts with Rabbis in Caesarea, we know very little about Jewish books in late antiquity.[36] The Rabbis (probably under the impact of Christianity), who sought to obliterate these texts, would later identify most of them as marginal, dangerous, or simply heretical. As mentioned above, Rabbinic Judaism, just like Sasanian Zoroastrianism, functioned almost entirely within the oral realm. Texts such as the Mishna could be redacted, collected, fixed, and even canonized orally. Yet, as Jewish and Christian intellectuals could meet and discuss biblical hermeneutics, some of the Rabbis, at least, must have expressed intellectual curiosity about Christian books such as biblical commentaries and homiletics—just as some of the Church Fathers expressed interest in Jewish ways of interpreting scripture. It remains a matter of frustration, however, that we do not know more about this aspect of the Jewish–Christian intellectual interface. Grafton and Williams might have been able to say more, had they broadened their inquiry, their *Fragestellung*, from physical aspects of the book to the dynamics between written and oral texts in the life of Scriptures in late antiquity.

For Christian intellectuals, reading scripture and interpreting it meant becoming the successors of the ancient sages. It is through scripture that they learned to become wise men and spiritual guides. The ultimate codex, which contained the Word of God, fast became the new symbol of power in the ecclesiastical hierarchy. By extension, it seems, the codex itself was invested with a new dignity, also in secular civil society, and even (although only among the most affluent) in the family.

In the ancient world, texts were usually read aloud. Medical texts even recommended this as a physical exercise. Once the monastic copyists relinquished *scriptio continua*, the pace of reading could markedly improve. As noted in Chapter 4, from being mainly an *extensive* activity, reading was transformed into an *intensive* activity.[37] Moreover, the development of both silent and meditative reading granted the overall act new status. Reading was a kind of soul therapy, the reader now a *meditative* reader.[38] This is true, in particular, of the reading of scripture. Reading (or reciting) the scriptures constituted an opportunity to plumb the depths of one's psyche. In the early Christian world of late antiquity, reading had become a spiritual exercise.

The Reading System Redux

The reading system was thus irrevocably altered, together with writing methods. The way in which Christian intellectuals, after the Rabbis, read the text of the scriptures (of which they knew significant parts by heart) generated distinctly new attitudes to reading. Through reading (or reciting) the scriptures, one learned to search the depths of one's psyche: perception, knowledge, memory, emotions. Reading scripture and commenting upon it enabled Christian intellectuals—like the

Rabbis—to assume the mantle of the ancient sages. It is through scripture that they learned to become wise men and spiritual guides. All in all, the codex became the new symbol of power in the ecclesiastical hierarchy, secular civil society, and family. At the same time, the public reading of scripture had become a major aspect of Christian ritual. The monks' recitative reading (*Sprechgesang*) of the Bible constituted an act of intimacy with the texts.[39] Among the Christians, silent reading seems to be directly linked to the private reading of the Bible in the monastic milieus (in particular of the Psalms, a corpus also central to public worship), in meditation and oration.[40] Reading scripture in silence promoted its internalization. The book became an interior one, inscribed not on parchment, but on the heart of the believer. Indeed, the "Book of the Heart"—whose roots reach back to the ancient Near East—will have a long and rich future in the history of Christian spirituality. In other words, the development of silent reading among early Christian elites reflected the transformed status of the individual in the new religious system. Just like the use of the codex, silent reading must have been as closely related to that status of the individual.

We have dealt in this chapter with the religious roots of the cultural revolution that was effected, not quite purposefully, by the early monks. I started with a brief description of the emergence of a new, reflexive self, a self that is at once a sinner and a striver. Under such conditions, the individual, or at least the ascetic virtuoso, is no longer interested, as was the Greek philosopher, in *cultivating* the self. Rather, it is *transforming* this self that moves him. This inner work culminates in the *imitatio Christi* or, in the mystical Eastern tradition, in divinization (*theosis*) through the beatific vision. In his path toward transformation, the monk follows, as it were, the traces left by God's incarnation. It is through the reading of the scriptures and their meditation that such traces can be made visible.[41] By calling attention to the new Christian reflexive anthropology and to the new ways of reading, and by arguing that these two phenomena were evidenced most obviously in monasticism, I hope to have highlighted the tight ties between self and text among the early monks.

The momentous implications for the early monastic communities of these profound shifts in reading practices are the subject of Chapter 6.

6

COMMUNITIES OF KNOWLEDGE

The New Cultura Dei

In the late ancient world, new attitudes toward books were not only generated by the Christian culture in the making (Chapter 4) and by the new reading practices that developed, mainly, in the monasteries (Chapter 5). These attitudes were also the product of the establishment of ecclesiastical, and then monastic libraries.[1] The present chapter will analyze the relationship between knowledge, both soteriological and epistemological, and varieties of religious experience. As we have seen, early Christian intellectuals saw themselves as members of a "school" (modeled on the philosophical schools, but drawing from a truer wisdom).[2] While churches did not play an educational role similar to that of synagogues, we know of a number of important Christian schools in late antiquity.[3] These typically functioned around the community's library. This was true not only of Cassiodorus's Vivarium in the West and of the Nisibis Academy in the East, but also of Augustine's own library, in the vicinity of which his disciples lived, prayed, and studied.[4]

Chapter 5 presented early monastic communities as "communities of the book."[5] It was in the monasteries, I contended, that the book developed its contours, physical and otherwise, and that a new culture of the book was born. Indeed, it was in that setting that reading became a normative activity.

On first sight, it seems a strange idea that the late ancient Christian monks, alongside the urban theologians, drove the Christianization of Greek *paideia*.[6] Until recently, the commonplace was that, a handful of exceptions aside such as Evagrius Ponticus and the Origenist monks of fifth-century Palestine, whom we know to have been immersed in Neoplatonism,[7] the early Egyptian, Syrian, and Palestinian monks were not associated with the intellectual elites in the Eastern Roman Empire. Nonetheless, recent work on Greek culture among some of the first Egyptian monks has begun to cast doubt on this view. Samuel Rubenson, in particular, asserts vigorously that early monasticism was much more instrumental than previously thought in the transmission of the classical heritage.[8] Papyrological evidence, for instance, indicates that Antony was far from illiterate.[9] And we know that the Pachomian Rule did not tolerate illiterate monks.[10] According to Rubenson, the monks made short work of combining the Bible with classical (Greco-Roman) education; a figure like Evagrius Ponticus seems to have been less isolated than previously thought, and it is now clear that a location like Gaza, in Palestine, was active intellectually in late antiquity.[11] In this regard, the monastic canons of Shenoute published by Bentley Layton, by shedding new light on the history of Egyptian cenobitic monasticism, should tell us more about the activity of reading among the monks in late antiquity.[12]

While not dictating difference absolutely, then, location certainly enhanced variation. The desert monks, on the one hand, and the Christian urban elites, on the other, both in the East and in the West, had different reading practices.[13] In the East, the monks introduced an alternative cultural model, mostly oral, which expressed itself in the vernacular (i.e., Coptic, Syriac, or Armenian) rather than in Greek. This new *cultura Dei* was far from alien to books, however. The dialogical relationship between spiritual master and disciple was preserved in the monastic *Questions and Answers* literature, but the monastic milieu placed great weight on *listening to the book*.[14] Although much less has been written on oral than on written aspects of early Christian texts, Carol Harrison's elegantly written work, *The Art of Listening in the Early Church*, represents a major step forward in our understanding of the primacy of the verbal over the written, and of the intertwined nature of the relationship between the two in early Christian culture.[15]

In this vein, the monastery and the Rabbinic house of study (*beit ha-midrash*) shared a salient feature. In both venues, the Bible was read, recited—often by heart—translated, and interpreted. The monks, following in the footsteps of their counterparts in the Jewish religion of the Book, thrived in a like-minded community of religious *virtuosi* that situated the Book at its center.

The monks and the philosophers shared a system of education based on oral (or even silent) contact between master and disciple. The monks diverged, however, in their attitude toward reading. For them, reading was at the core of life.[16] The same cannot be said, at least not in the same way, of the philosophers.[17] Neither Epictetus nor Marcus Aurelius has much to say about reading and writing.[18] Plotinus, who taught orally, related to the texts of Plato and Aristotle in a different way than the monks approached the Bible. Although the later Neoplatonists sought to promote to a hallowed status the writings of Plato, this effort fell far short of the status accorded the scriptures by the Christians and the Jews.

Monks read in order to receive knowledge. The Pachomian Rule, for instance, stipulated that at least the Psalms and the New Testament were to be memorized. This activity was in fact soteriological. Here was a method to enhance concentration of the mind, a way of praying by the scriptures and with the scriptures, such that the Word of God entered the mind and the heart and repulsed Satanic thoughts. Thus, Abba Hilarion, father of the monastic movement in Palestine:

> He also said: "The acquisition of Christian books is necessary for those who can use them. For the mere sight of these books renders us less inclined to sin, and incites us to believe more firmly in righteousness."
>
> He also said: "Reading the Scriptures is a great safeguard against sin."
>
> He also said: "It is a great treachery to salvation to know nothing of the divine law."
>
> He also said: "Ignorance of the Scriptures is a precipice and a deep abyss."[19]

Cassian in the second century already demanded continuous prayer, and among the late-fourth-century Euchytes, or Messalians (literally, "those who pray," in Greek and Syriac), continuous prayer became the core of an important heresy. Silent reading of the Scriptures was essentially meditative (*meletē, meditatio, ruminatio*). This reading-meditation, developed in the early phases of Egyptian monasticism, had consequences of tidal-wave proportions. The *lectio divina* (or *sacra pagina*) would swamp the Middle Ages, both in Byzantine and in Western monasticism, as well as in later forms of Christian spirituality, for instance in the *devotio moderna* or among the first Jesuits.[20] Thus, even taking into account the variation in monastic form found across different divides such as urban and nonurban and East and West, one can say that altogether, the late ancient monks spearheaded a novel system: one in which reading morphed into meditation and meditation led back to reading.

Religion and Knowledge

Religion and knowledge form an odd yet inseparable couple. It seems a sort of universal truth that the two demand to be considered in light of one another.[21] This bond is underscored by the cognitive approach to religion, which has gained ground in the past decade or so, subsuming ritual studies and, in part, anthropology.[22] The emergence and growth of the history and anthropology of religions as well as of other forms of cultural knowledge can be conceived only through their intimate relationship with religion. Like any other couple, however, the relationship between religion and knowledge can show signs of strain. Under certain circumstances, this strain can result in rupture: knowledge (or science) breaking free from the close embrace of religion, or religion rejecting knowledge, which comes to be perceived as a threat.

Religion is notoriously undefinable. Yet, one can perhaps *describe* religion: an attempt to provide answers precisely where knowledge fails us. A primary paradox emerges, then, as religion, which engages with the unknown and the unknowable, offers irrefutable answers, in words and deeds, in the two apodictic modes of myth and ritual. By telling stories about the gods, by performing "speech acts," men and women, since the dawn of civilization, have claimed to know what they could not know, hence taking the sting out of the unknown.[23]

The long late antiquity evinces a new status of religion in society, much more central than ever before. Identity, which since Hellenistic times across the Mediterranean and the Near East had been viewed through cultural and linguistic lenses, became more and more defined in religious terms (i.e., in terms of belonging to a specific religious community). Alongside this overblown importance of religion, a dramatic weakening or shrinking of independent scientific curiosity took place. Intellectual creativity became directly linked to religion: on the one hand, the last Hellenic philosophers behaved like theologians, that is, like intellectual servants of religion, while on the other hand Christian theologians succeeded in assimilating Greek philosophy into their own system of thought. The "imperialistic" character, as it were, of the great religions of late antiquity, is not reflected only in the ecumenical ambitions of Christianity, Manichaeism, and Islam. More insidiously, it is present in the embrace by religion of all fields of knowledge—or at least of licit knowledge (illicit knowledge is usually stored in the apocryphal works cherished by various heretical movements—and as such, can be found in Rabbinic Judaism as much as in other religions of late antiquity). The late antique proliferation of religious communities, often groups of religious "overachievers," is observable throughout the Eastern Mediterranean and the Near East. Many of these communities were involved intensively in the creation, reproduction, and transmission of knowledge, mainly, but not exclusively, in the field of religion. One can mention here, alongside the Christian monasteries, the Jewish *yeshivot* (religious schools, mainly in Babylonia) and philosophical schools, as well as, later, the Islamic *madāris* ([sing. *madrasa*] religious schools).

From the canonization of the texts of the Old and the New Testaments, through the redaction of the Mishna and the Talmud (both the Palestinian and the Babylonian Talmuds), the early Manichaean writings, the "canonization" of some of Plato's texts by the late Neoplatonists, and the great legal codices, up to the sealing of the Qur'anic text, a series of revealed texts and "holy Scriptures" were redacted. These texts, which demanded highly complex hermeneutics, permitted the development of sophisticated educational systems. They did much to implant discursive knowledge at the very core of religion. Religions of the book thus also became religions of knowledge.[24]

The major transformation of religion in late antiquity has traditionally (though not perhaps most accurately) been considered the passage from polytheism to monotheism. This transformation certainly led to a striking simplification of the divine world. No more the baroque flourish of hosts of gods and goddesses vying for power and fighting for sex. Now we find the one God (surrounded by legions of angels and archangels) placing rigorous demands upon men and women such that they would not become prey to Satan and his demons. The simplification of the heavenly hosts, however, did not simplify, in a parallel manner, knowledge about religion. In fact, precisely the opposite outcome seems to have occurred. The idea of a single God brought with it a ceaselessly growing body of texts striving to explain the emergence of the many from the one (e.g., *creatio ex nihilo,* the haunting problem of evil [*unde malum?*], for the Jews, the conundrum of a universal God choosing his own people, and, for the Christians, the puzzle of the one and triune God and of the divine and human natures of Jesus Christ). This phenomenon is identified well in Flavius Josephus, who uses a neologism, *theokrateia,* to describe the political system of ancient Israel.[25] In *Against Apion,* Josephus explains that while in other societies religion was just one among various, fairly commensurate aspects of life, the Law of Moses accorded religion an all-encompassing status. Ethics, for instance, became part and parcel of religion. The idea of the one God does indeed require the development of a full-fledged theology. In lieu of a proliferation of myths, the monotheist ponders the nature of God and His relationship with the world and humanity, both of which He created single-handedly.

For archaic societies and those of the classical world, knowledge of religion had mainly meant knowledge of rituals. Such knowledge generally concerned the ability to deal with the precision these rituals required as well as with their associated symbolism. While Greek philosophers thought a great deal about religion, they did so as religious outsiders - even when, as citizens, they participated in the religion of the *polis*. Now, for the first time, at least on a grand scale, theology had been subsumed to religion: the consideration of God, his nature and his acts was now part of religion itself. This new status of theology is well illustrated in the writings of Philo. Indeed, it is within the context of the Jewish encounter with Greek philosophy that the concept of religion underwent major changes in late antiquity.

Philo, like the Hellenistic Jewish writers who preceded him, applied to the Hebrew Bible the hermeneutical rules developed by early Greek grammarians for the Homeric writings. And, as we have seen, the Jews borrowed another major element of Greek culture: the concept of *paideia. Talmud Torah,* the learning of the Torah (i.e., studying religious law and Biblical hermeneutics), perhaps the major aspect of Rabbinic Judaism, is essentially a cultural borrowing from the Greeks.[26] Yet the

Jews modified the loan concept by making study the cornerstone of their religion. This radical reshaping of the relation between religion and knowledge would be passed on to the Christians, and later to the Muslims. The teaching of a progressively growing body of knowledge, conceived as a religious duty, has informed monotheistic systems ever since. One may note the historical irony (Hegel would have spoken of "the cunning of reason") through which the early Christian appropriation of classical educational devices—thanks to its Jewish heritage—has engendered a mindset in which religion would remain entwined with knowledge, up to our own day. This mindset is as central to the Abrahamic religions as are more obvious categories such as "faith" or "prophecy."

Esoteric traditions and patterns of thought represented a further locus of change in the relationship between religion and knowledge in late antiquity. Across religions in the ancient Mediterranean and Near East, the deepest dimensions of truth were held close, transmitted solely to the select.[27] Esoteric trends protect these truths from outsiders, but from many insiders as well. True knowledge is imparted only to those who are deemed worthy of it, or are perceived as religious specialists. Esotericism can be found in Greek religion—in rituals, in particular in mystery cults, as well as in the most profound meaning of myths (the Neoplatonists were the major carriers of such esoteric hermeneutics of myths). Elitist communities such as the Pythagoreans were marked by esoterism; this community was divided between *akousmatikoi* and *mathematikoi* and only the latter were considered suitable recipients of the true meaning of beliefs and practices. The core ambivalence toward writing in the ancient world, so well exemplified in Plato's *Letter VII*, reinforced esoteric trends, by insisting that secret knowledge should not be put to writing, lest it be unwillingly divulged to outsiders. These trends are found across theistic systems, evident among Zoroastrians and Jews as well as Neoplatonists and early Christian Gnostics. Indeed, some of the earliest strata of Christian literature, such as the synoptic Gospels or the Gospel of Thomas, show vestiges of esoteric doctrines or tendencies. Such doctrines, then, which were intrinsic to the beliefs of the original Jewish-Christian communities, can be traced to first-century Palestinian Judaism.[28]

The second century witnessed major polemical debates about the legitimacy of these esoteric trends within the emerging theology of the new religion. For those Christian thinkers, such as Irenaeus of Lyon, who built the theological orthodox consensus, Christianity was a religion of a different kind, offering salvation equally to all and sundry. In such a religion, esotericism was less than welcome. The Church Fathers would thus in the second and third centuries free Christian theology in the making from Gnostic and dualistic trends. The latter sought to perpetuate in the new religion patterns of thought inherited from the ancient world, emphasizing esotericism, both in myths and in rituals.[29] It is only after the fourth century, with the disappearance, for all practical purposes, of the mystery cults, that Christian theologians would adopt and make systematic use of the langue of these groups. But this would be done with a twist. In this Christianized lexicon, the vocabulary of secrecy would be used in a metaphorical way, referring to that trend of personal religion that we call mysticism.

Gnosis

Thus far, I have dealt with religion and knowledge in highly general terms. Mention has been made above of knowledge *about* religion, the access to which remained limited in antiquity: some things (often, indeed, the core of religious life) were not considered fit to be revealed to all, and remained protected by the seal of esotericism. Moreover, some categories of religious knowledge—often core ones—remain consistently implicit. Indeed, certain concepts and behavioral patterns are so obvious to insiders that they need not be spelled out. Considering the other side of the coin, is the knowledge of a religion held by outsiders. Such knowledge is often of an ethnological character. There is a long tradition of the ethnological approach to religion in the ancient world, from Herodotus to Varro, Tacitus, and Lucian. The late-second-century Christian Clement of Alexandria offered a new slant on this tradition by proposing a serious comparative history of religion. For Clement, philosophy, in its function as a preparation for death, is an organ of religion. Hence, the history of philosophy is a branch of the history of religion. Both Greeks and barbarians retained, then, in their paganism, sparks of truth and wisdom.[30]

As we have seen, knowledge in late antiquity was entangled fully with religion. The very word *gnōsis* makes this clear; in the early Christian context, the Greek word refers to a *soteriological* knowledge: a knowledge that permits the individual possessing it to be saved from purgatory. Here, true religion *becomes* knowledge. Indeed, such a *gnōsis* became almost identified with the very core of religion—the concept of *gnōsis* is even reflected in the name of late ancient religious groups: both Epiphanius's *gnōstikoi* and the Mandeans (who draw their name from the Semitic root for knowledge, *d.'.t.*) are, quite simply, those who know: those to whom the secret myths and rituals of salvation have been revealed.

A further function of knowledge has little to do with the soteriological one just considered. This is its epistemic function, for which another Greek word, *epistemē*, is commonly used. This radical power of knowledge in religion is found in early Christian literature. For Clement of Alexandria, for instance, *gnōsis* was set in opposition to "faith," or *pistis*, and endowed with a new power, as the ideal state of the Christian virtuoso. In that sense solely, *gnōsis* had lost almost all epistemic qualities. It represented holiness rather than knowledge. Even the residual elements of epistemic value that remained in "heretical" Gnosticism, which the Church Fathers referred to as "the so-called *gnōsis*," had now been purged, in favor of a mind emptied of all knowledge that is not the knowledge of God. Hence, knowledge of God among late antique holy men had a negative bent: it entailed emptying the mind of everything coming from "the [non-divine]world." In the apophatic language of Gregory of Nyssa in the fourth century and the mystical theology of Pseudo-Dionysius a century later, knowledge would mean purging the mind of useless or noxious knowledge. God, for these mystics, is found not in light, but in darkness.[31] Some of those "holy mystics" will eventually claim to be madmen, "fools in Christ," seeking to remain innocent of worldly, corrupting knowledge in order to get closer to God—and stay away from men.[32] In parallel to this "negative mysticism" stands "negative theology": nothing positive can be predicated upon God, who cannot even be called "just" or "merciful." And so we have come full circle, back to religion as a bridge to the unknowable, the ineffable.

Knowledge coming from *curiositas*, an intellectual curiosity whose roots lie in *hybris*, must be rejected if one is to make spiritual progress. In Augustinian terms, knowledge stemming from the *civitas terrena* is harmful in the *civitas dei*.[33] In such a milieu, sciences are unwelcome: at best useless, at worst a serious obstacle to purity, sanctity, and salvation. Tertullian's fideist *cri du coeur*[34] concerning Athens versus Jerusalem represents only the first step in a long tradition of Christian antirationalism, for which knowledge, and in particular scientific knowledge, is an impediment to religion. This antirationalist tradition, in which religion and knowledge are fully and unalterably counterposed, will retain its place of honor for centuries, alongside the leading rationalist tradition, which insists on the integration of religion and knowledge. The latter trend will find its fullest expression in medieval scholasticism.

Epistemē

We have seen how knowledge became, in different ways, central to late ancient religious elites. The new status of knowledge is manifested particularly in educational practices. *Paideia* was the leading educational tradition in the Roman Empire, and the philosophical schools (and in particular the Neoplatonic school) had refashioned themselves into something very close to religious communities, largely under the influence of Christianity.[35] In a dialectical relationship with the ambient religious climate, then, the philosophical schools provided a model according to which religious education was approached among both Jews and Christians. We know how these last Hellenic schools functioned. Like those of the Christians and Jews (and also the Zoroastrians, in the Sasanian Empire), the learning communities of philosophers were under constant pressure to create, strengthen, and defend an orthodoxy based upon the correct interpretation of the foundational texts against competing approaches (*haireseis*).[36]

In such philosophical schools, the fundamental rule of hermeneutics was that of *symphonia:* Pythagoras, Orpheus, and Plato were always found to be in agreement with the *Chaldean Oracles*, a text the later Neoplatonists considered to be sacred, almost revealed.[37] Jews and Christians interpreted their Holy Scriptures using very similar rules, in which there could be no disagreement between any two scriptural passages. In the Neoplatonic school, there were two daily public prayers to the sun, morning, and evening, and pedagogy meant essentially psychagogy: through a canonical, or at least rigid list of texts, to be read and commented upon in a strict order, teaching meant not only progress of the mind, but also of the soul.[38]

While the Rabbinic ideal of a life of learning betrayed its early encounter with Greek *paideia,* the conditions of teaching, developed mainly in the Babylonian centers, and in Aramaic rather than in Greek, reflected a very different cultural world.[39] As we have seen, the early Christians in the Greco-Roman world did not formulate an autonomous educational system, but preferred to adapt traditional *paideia* to their own needs. Hence, in the Syriac speaking East, it is mainly in the monastic communities, rather than in the Christianized urban elites, that we can observe what constitutes the core of Christian *paideia*. In Byzantium, however, monastic education was usually reserved for the poor, rather than the urban elites. These did not give up Hellenic *paideia* without a fight, which may partly explain why the most important Christian academies in late antiquity were those that functioned in Syriac rather than in Greek.

Successively in Edessa and in Nisibis—on both sides of the frontier between the Roman and the Sasanian Empires—Miaphysite and Nestorian teachers developed a curriculum that included Syriac translations of Greek philosophy, alongside scriptural and Patristic texts. Syriac monastic education in general, and the school of Nisibis in particular, have been the topic of a number of important studies.[40] As Adam Becker points out, "the study of the East-Syrian school movement promises to shed light on the development of Christian *paideia* in Late Antiquity, the rise of the Babylonian Jewish academies, and the background of the burgeoning Muslim intellectual culture of the early "Abbasid period."[41]

The curriculum of these schools reflected their conception of Christian education: for them, Christianity was to be learned step by step, as it were, in successive stages. Indeed, the Syriac schools transformed study into ritual.[42] While the intellectual structures of these schools parallel to some extent those of the philosophers, their study cycle is strikingly similar to that of the Babylonian *yeshivot:* namely, two terms of intensive study, separated by long vacations in which the students were sent back to their families, in order to engage in agricultural duties, in particular sowing and harvesting. The school of Nisibis, with which Cassiodorus's Vivarium retained some historical links, was highly dynamic until the first half of the seventh century, when it entered its decline.[43] Its canons, which have been preserved, give us a rather concrete idea of how the school worked. It was run by a *rabban,* and various categories of teachers catered to the needs of the students (*eskolaye*) at all levels: above the *mhagyane* (in charge of orthographic precision), the *maqryane* (readers), the *mphashqane* (exegetes), there was the *kursia da-mphashqanuta* (chair of scriptural interpretation) and the *badoqe* (interpreters). The school followed a regular schedule: reading, writing, exegesis, and singing. Students were requested to dress simply, to treat with care the contents of the library, and to refrain from engagement in business. Teachers who neglected their duties were denied their salaries. The school of Nisibis thought of itself as the final heir of the "great and perfect philosophical school" (*eskula ravta d-philosophuta gamirta*) of Moses, later imitated by Solomon, the prophets, Plato, Aristotle, Pythagoras, Zoroaster, as well as in Babylonia and Alexandria.[44]

Like the schools of the Platonists, those of the Nestorians and of the Jews strove to both transmit knowledge and educate toward a specific way of life. They were communities of learning, where the great texts were studied, commented upon, and read or sung during liturgy. They offered at once the first elements of discursive knowledge to be transmitted and the best models for behavior. Knowledge and salvation were of a piece here. In these communities, books lay at the very heart of identity.

When Christian monks translated the classical Greek texts into Syriac, their intention was cultural rather than religious.[45] In the Greek tradition, *scholē* referred first of all to leisure time away from daily demands. The school functioned at one and the same time as the institutional and physical context in which *epistēmē* was to be acquired. It was clearly demarcated from the rest of the city's public space. Only those who could escape duties related to economic activity and the care of infants could attend school—hence married women usually remained outsiders to the educational system. Schools, however, were not only a place to exert the mind: the body was exerted as well. This exercise, *askēsis*, represented as much as *scholē* an essential element of the school's daily activities. In late antiquity, as we have seen, *gnōsis* took the lead, replacing *epistēmē* as the main educational thrust. But *gnōsis* never entirely supplanted *epistēmē*, and even monasteries, where salvation was privileged over knowledge, eventually engaged with *epistēmē* as well as with *gnōsis*.[46]

How did *gnōsis* become *epistēmē*, and vice versa? Religious *paideia* (we are dealing here with Christian *paideia*, but the same is true, *mutatis mu-*

tandis, of philosophical, Jewish, Islamic, or Buddhist education) intends, first of all, to educate. It does so by way of example: alongside the book, the teacher offers oral teaching and a living model. The institution (school, monastery, *yeshiva, madrasa,* etc.) is a hierarchical one, in which the relationship between master and disciple is paramount. The master's lesson is less important than the discussion that comes in its wake. The holy books are learned and the sacred teachings are committed to memory as the student moves from one stage to another. These stages, either fixed or flexible, are punctuated by various "rites of passage" culminating in the taking of vows or confirmation.

All communities of ascetics engaged in the ritualized reading and writing of sacred books, but in some locales such ritualized activities were more sharply accentuated than in others. In late antiquity, the highly demotic nature of Christianity promoted the legitimacy of scriptures' translations, hence depriving those scriptures of much of the hieratic character conferred by a holy tongue.[47] In different cultural contexts, religious communities approached knowledge in different ways. Some communities spotlighted the cognitive content of books, whereas others centered on ritualistic functions. In some, manual work was at the heart of life (and knowledge was peripheral); in others, it was the creation and transmission of knowledge that constituted the core of the community.

The ascetic communities were hothouses of intellectual and spiritual elitism, both carrying and transforming cultural traditions. They were communities of learning, "enclave societies" of sorts, slightly de-centered in their own society, a fact that permitted the organization of magnetic fields at the confluence of the particular and the universal, of cenobitic organization and individual ideal, of oral and written teachings and of discursive and mystical intellectual practices. As well, the communities were to some extent porous. While isolating themselves to some degree from the surrounding society, they survived by maintaining links with this society. To some extent, the porousness of these elite communities reflects the broader porous nature of the Christian scriptural universe, into which traditions stemming from various cultural worlds crept in before being transformed.

Thus far, we have dealt with the impact of Christianity on identity development and reading practices within the Roman Empire. Foreign traditions of wisdom were making themselves felt as well, however. This is especially true in the Eastern provinces, which were in continuous contact with patterns of thought and behavior from beyond the borders of the Empire. Chapter 7 will deal with these conceptions of Eastern wisdom in late antiquity.

7

EASTERN WISDOMS

East-West Contacts

At the core of the scriptural universe of early Christianity stood the two biblical Testaments. Thus far, we have seen how the books of the Bible, and the almost infinite interpretations of every verse in these books to be found in the hermeneutical tradition, became connected in the early centuries to many of the major textual monuments of Greco-Roman culture. Yet other stars shone, perhaps more distantly, in the firmament of early Christian culture. It is to some of those stars, pointing to cultural traditions alien to the Roman Empire, that the present chapter will be devoted.

In Chapter 6, I noted the view of Clement of Alexandria that elements of divine wisdom could be found also among barbarian peoples, who were ignorant of revelation. Moreover, we have seen how identities have been defined more as ways of life than as sets of beliefs, and how *paideia* provided a cultural common ground to those with different ethnic or religious identities. In Chapter 3, we referred to the important insights of Pierre Hadot on philosophy constituting a way of life, as well as to the seminal study of Henri-Irénée Marrou on education. These inquiries consider exclusively the Greco-Roman tradition. The Iranian and Jewish conceptions of wisdom, for instance, were not discussed. Here, we fill in some of those gaps, examining the representation among Greek writers, both pagan and Christians, of the traditions of soteriological knowledge from Iran, India, Israel, and Egypt. Indian traditions, or at least the perceptions of these traditions that were formed in the Greco-Roman world, were highly instrumental in granting the concept of wisdom a universal dimension in our period. The story of *Barlaam and Joasaph*, a Christian reworking of Buddhist traditions, attributed to John of Damascus, is a striking example of this.[1]

Tensions between "Eastern" conceptions of wisdom (including Christianity) and "Western" (i.e., Greco-Roman) schools of wisdom eventually realized a complete transformation of the concept of wisdom itself. The emergence of the medieval (theological) conception of wisdom among Christians and Muslims alike, in Greek, Latin, and Arabic, is typically taken to demonstrate the interface between Greek philosophy and Christianity or Islam. This grand historical narrative, however, may miscalculate the dynamics of religions and cultures in the late ancient Near East. Perhaps these would be better understood as the final products of a dialectical process that involved Eastern wisdom traditions and their reinterpretation in the late antique Roman Empire. The philological study of concepts and textual genres involving wisdom inevitably lead us to the domains of social, intellectual, and religious history. In societies in which religion had become the prominent factor of identity, both the carriers of wisdom and the social infrastructures granted to the schools of wisdom strongly shaped identities.

Wisdom in late antiquity, from the growth of the Gnostic Sophia myth to Christianized wisdom traditions and the attraction of "Eastern Wisdoms" for authors writing in Greek (and Syriac), must be tracked through the *longue durée*. The new formulations of wisdom can be considered a late avatar of the wisdom traditions in ancient Near Eastern religious and literary traditions, as well as the "abstraction" of wisdom in Greek philosophy and the growth of both theology and the intellectual critique of religion. The late ancient phase of the wisdom–religion dialectic reveals a synthesis of the religious roles played by wisdom in both Near Eastern and Greco-Roman cultures.

Geography follows perceptions. While Egypt may not properly belong to the "East" in the ancient world, it must be considered together with "Eastern nations" as it was perceived in late antiquity as a key link for the transmission of Eastern wisdom to Greece, be this wisdom of Iranian, or even originally Indian, origin. According to the fourth-century

Roman historian Ammianus Marcellinus, Zoroaster received knowledge of the systems of the universe and the pure rituals of religion from the Indian Brahmins, and had in his turn passed this knowledge to Pythagoras (according to Porphyry).[2] Egypt had held pride of place as the land of origins in Hellenic consciousness since the Classical period, and retained this honor in late antiquity, thanks in particular to Hermeticism.[3] But India was a strong contender for the title.

A GENERATION ago, the ancient historian Arnaldo Momigliano provided in his *Alien Wisdom* a seminal study of the meeting between Greek and foreign conceptions of wisdom in antiquity. We still await a late ancient sequel to what he did for the Hellenistic period.[4] A full-fledged study of the perception of foreign traditions of wisdom in the Roman Empire would do well to investigate the seduction exerted by the old *Kulturvölker* of Iran, India, Israel, and Egypt, "among the oldest and the wisest peoples," as Origen calls them, on late ancient intellectuals (both pagan and Christian) in the Eastern Roman Empire.[5]

Herodotus analyzed well the exceptionally convoluted saga of East-West contact in antiquity. A clash of civilizations and fruitful cultural exchange both, the saga entailed extensive military, commercial and religious activities. Here we shall hone in on the cultural dimensions of these contacts (what is called in German *Transkulturalität*), or more precisely on the perceptions of the great cultures of the East by intellectuals writing in the Roman Empire, both before and after its official Christianization.

Wisdom traditions in the ancient world could be expressed in both religion and "philosophy"; that is, in myths and their interpretation. Such traditions, which had circulated since early antiquity and through the Hellenistic period, kept their vigor in late antiquity. This attraction was expressed, over the centuries, in multiple ways. It is of major importance for a number of Greek- and Syriac-writing authors and for the formation of their own cultural and religious identities. Moreover, these traditions of Eastern wisdom had a major impact on the Arabization of Greek philosophy in the Islamic Caliphate. The powerful fascination they exerted surely is related to their resemblance to what we now call the "Oriental religions." This expression, coined by Franz Cumont more than a hundred years ago, oddly excluded both Judaism and Christianity, for reasons that have more to do with religious and cultural atavism than with scholarly rigor.[6] While Cumont assessed the results of this attraction somewhat positively (he credited it with the success of Christianity), other Classical scholars, such as André-Jean Festugière, saw in the seductive power of Eastern cultures and religions a clear sign of cultural decline in the early Empire.[7] Indeed, the Oriental fad has been understood as a "failure of nerve" (Gilbert Murray) and "the sleep of reason" (Festugière).[8]

Limes *Intellectuals and Barbarian Philosophers*

We shall at this point consider the patterns of transmission of knowledge between late ancient societies, and identify the carriers through which knowledge, both explicit and implicit, was transmitted. Among these carriers, some of the most prominent were those whom I call "*limes* intellectuals." By this term, I refer to those *literati,* usually living in the border areas of the empire, or coming from them, who were pulled between two cultures, their own ethnic one and the Greco-Roman cultural *koinē*. Such intellectuals were often bilingual, and, much more importantly, bicultural as well.[9] In cases of biculturalism, only *explicit* knowledge can be observed, while *implicit* knowledge, most revealing about core identity, may remain unnoticed. Bicultural persons, moreover, may not keep their two cultures snugly compartmentalized. More than a dual identity, theirs is a fluid one. While Hellenization surely colored the ethnic identity of its bicultural residents, the reverse was also patently true.

The Roman Empire saw among its thinkers an active quest, a pursuit of the unity of the ecumene beyond the plurality of cultures. Bicultural intellectuals advanced at once ethnographic curiosity and the search for underlying coherence beyond disparate patterns of behavior and of thought.[10] Cultural and religious transfer occurs continually between adjacent societies. Sometimes, such transfer is slow, or "cold." Late antiquity was an age of collision between the Roman and the Sasanian Empires, both cemented by a powerful religious ideology, in an area—the Near East—where a major *lingua franca,* Aramaic, crossed political borders.¹¹ Thus, late antiquity can be described indeed as an age of fast, "hot" transfer.

SINCE at least Herodotus and Plato, Greek culture showed a sustained curiosity for the wisdom traditions of Eastern peoples, as well as a strong attraction to them. For the Hellenistic ethnographer Megasthenes (ca. 300 B.C.E.), both the Brahmins (in India) and the Jews (in Syria) had anticipated basic concepts of Greek philosophy. In this view, which would remain current throughout antiquity, the Jews were a nation of philosophers, or the philosophers among the Syrians, parallel to the Brahmins among the Indians. This interest eventually was transmitted to European culture and ultimately adopted and transformed by modern Orientalist philology. How this curiosity played out in late antiquity might shed some light on the dynamics of this passage.

Both before and after the fourth-century religious revolution initiated by Constantine, several intellectuals, particularly in the Eastern provinces of the Roman Empire, expressed a lively interest in the wisdom traditions of several Eastern peoples endowed with a long cultural tradition. For these thinkers, these traditions expressed a truth deeper than the one found in Greek philosophy. These traditions lie at the core of the cultural and religious syncretism of late antiquity, in particular in the Near East, where Hellenism was in direct contact with a number of ancient and sophisticated literary cultures. Among the most important taxonomies is that of Themistius, one of the last pagan intellectuals of the fourth century. Themistius theorized a partition of culture and religion according to different regions: in his view, Greece was the original locus of paganism, while Syria, the country of the Jews, was that of monotheism, and Egypt that of the mystery religions.¹² Themistius's taxonomy came to be fundamental to Byzantine representations of religions and cultures, and of their identification with geographical areas.

Many of the *literati* interested in the dialogue between Greco-Roman thought and "barbarian philosophies" belonged to one or another of the Near Eastern ethnic groups. Hellenic thinkers of Syrian origin, in particular, seem to have been fascinated by non-Greek traditions of wisdom. One might mention here Hellenic (or "pagan") intellectuals such as Numenius of Apamea in the latter half of the second century,¹³ or Iamblichus of Chalcis in the late third and early fourth centuries, as well as Christian thinkers such as Tatian in the second half of the second century and Bardaisan in the late second and early third century. In a sense, the "seductive power of the East" reflects the resilience of ethnic identities in late antiquity and their refusal to surrender to the sway of Greco-Roman cultural traditions.[14] The phenomenon echoes in some respects the Hellenic "spiritual resistance" against Rome investigated by Harald Fuchs.[15] One can also find a powerful interest in "barbarian" religions and wisdom traditions among thinkers such as Clement of Alexandria (who in no way considered himself to be an Egyptian) or Philostratus of Athens. Some Hellenic thinkers of Syrian background, however, such as Porphyry, saw in Eastern traditions of wisdom no particular appeal—although Porphyry's ventriloquy, as it were, of his debate with Iamblichus, his own powerful disciple, through an Egyptian holy man, is singularly odd, and awaits explanation.[16]

A general interpretive framework for the enticement of "barbarian" wisdom traditions in late antiquity is in order. The attraction of Oriental wisdom traditions was a principal pattern through which Hellenized intellectuals in the Roman Empire coped with the presence of foreign cultures (often those of their own ethnic background) that lay beyond the boundaries of the empire or continued to resist Hellenization.[17] This interest demonstrates, on the one hand, ethnological and intellectual curiosity, and is a sign of respect expressed in architecture, administration, science, medicine, or magic. On the other hand, the interest, sincere as it may have been, almost never translated into an ability to fathom the secret of their cultural achievements, namely their languages, and even their systems of writing. In the absence of serious efforts to learn foreign languages—an absence underscored by Momigliano—few translations of major representative works from foreign literatures appeared in Greek. The Septuagint was here more an exception than a model. Under such conditions, foreign cultures became known mainly through oral reports, often of a mythical nature. It was only natural for Hellenic intellectuals to approach these reports in the manner they had learned to approach Greek myths. They developed a hermeneutics that put forward that myths, open to all at a superficial level, contained covert meanings only attainable by philosophers through sustained intellectual effort. In this view, beyond the exoteric level of myths lay esoteric wisdom. As well, the Hellenic thinkers assumed that a similar dual structure of myth and wisdom existed in foreign cultures. Finally, they assumed that wise men (philosophers) from all cultures had reached a similar understanding of the secrets of the universe. Such a conclusion, reflected, for instance, in Celsus's *Alethes Logos,* produced a twofold approach toward the highest among foreign cultures: although their exoteric level remained sealed, the kernel of their esoteric teaching, paradoxically, could be guessed, as it was presumed to correspond to Greek philosophical hermeneutics.

Late Antique Orientalism

As noted, a review of Oriental wisdoms in late antiquity requires the long view, starting with the emergence of Christianity and ending with the birth of Islam. The story reaches its conclusion with the Arabization of Greek philosophy and the establishment of the *dār al-ḥikma* (the "House of Wisdom") in ninth-century Baghdad.[18] Without question, the Arabization of Greek philosophy was smoothed by centuries of reflection on the potency of native traditions in their contact with Greco-Roman culture. This appropriation was prepared by a hermeneutical pattern for foreign cultures that had already developed in the late antique Near East, a pattern transmitted to the new rulers by Christian (as well as Sasanian) elites. It is this hermeneutical pattern that we now turn to decipher.

The military clashes between the Roman Empire (and later Byzantium) on the one hand and the Zoroastrian Sasanians (and later the Muslim Arabs) on the other hardly staunched the rich and bidirectional flow of ideas across the fluid boundaries. Travelers of all kinds—soldiers, merchants, pilgrims, slaves, and prisoners—criss-crossed cultural and linguistic as well as political borders.[19] They brought with them stories about foreign cultures, often of a mythical nature. These tales became the fundaments of the syncretistic religious systems of the late ancient Near East. It seems, indeed, that barbarian wisdom appealed especially to religiously minded Greek intellectuals. These were passionately engaged in the search for wisdom, and they sought it outside the Greek tradition. For them, the wise men of older peoples, such as the Egyptian priests, the Indian *brachmanoi,* the Persian Magi and the Jews were, like them, philosophers (or theologians) among their own peoples. As such, they were perceived as heirs to an esoteric and philosophical interpretation of their various myths. Serious intellectual effort was sure to yield a single tradition of wisdom common to the philosophers of the different ancient peoples.

Our topic has been considered extensively in the literature, but nearly always on a piecemeal basis. While this method has the advantage of providing detailed analyses of singular cases, only a comparative analysis can reveal the mechanisms through which late antique intellectuals dealt with the complex "globalization" of culture and the tensions between the ruling culture and the indigenous traditions of the conquered peoples. The diffusion of ideas among cultures in late antiquity is best approached by considering the various traditions related to the leading peoples from the East: Indians, Persians, Jews (and Assyrians, or Babylonians) and Egyptians. Inquiry concerning various "communities of wisdom" we have discussed, such as philosophical schools, Christian monastic communities, the Nisibis academy, Rabbinic *yeshivot* is called for. This study must go beyond the individual authors from the different philosophical schools and learning institutions, as well as the different translation efforts.[20]

A thread of Orientalism runs through late ancient intellectuals' writing in Greek, from Philostratus's description of Apollonius of Tyana's trip to India, the Hermetic writings and their Egyptian roots, Numenius and his conception of Plato as an "Atticizing Moses," the *Chaldean Oracles* and the construction of a hypostatized Assyrian tradition of religious wisdom, or else Plotinus' and Iamblichus' interest in Eastern (or Egyptian) wisdom traditions, up to the Neoplatonic philosophers' move to the court of the Sasanian king after Justinian's closure of the Academy in 529. A similar appeal of the East is of course present in Christianity from its inception, with the legend of the Magi and the Thomas traditions, which bring the Apostle to Mesopotamia and India. Clement of Alexandria was but one major Christian author who showed a strong interest in Indian and Egyptian wisdom traditions. Clement, for instance, is the first Greek author to mention the Buddha and Buddhism.[21] The formation and development of the Gnostic myth of Sophia, as well as the formation of Manichaean mythology, owe a great deal to Mesopotamian and Iranian mythical traditions. Gnostic and Manichaean myths, hence, belong to a superordinate intellectual framework, and are so many expressions of a *single* grand phenomenon: the deep attraction exerted by the (hidden) wisdom of the great *Kulturvölker* of the East. Their synthetic study can shed new light on the evolution of the interface between East and West in late antiquity.

Plotinus and Philostratus

An instance from the life of Plotinus will be illustrative here. In approximately 243, Plotinus, who was then thirty-eight years old and had already been Ammonius Saccas's student for eleven years, joined the Persian campaign of Gordian III, desiring to "investigate the Persian method [of philosophy] and the [philosophical] system adopted by the Indians." Thus, Porphyry, in the third chapter of his *Life of Plotinus* tells that Gordian's death, soon after a Roman defeat in Fallujah, in 244, cut short Plotinus's hopes to discover for himself Eastern patterns of wisdom.

Precisely what Plotinus—a contemporary of Mani, who might have heard of him—was seeking is lost to us.[22] Perhaps he had a taste for exotic traditions; perhaps he sought *sophia perennis*, the common ground among different intellectual (and spiritual) traditions of a world in the process of globalization. Plutarch might put us on the right track: he records that a friend of his, Cleombrotus of Sparta, traveled beyond the borders of Egypt into the Indian Ocean in order to collect materials for a work of theology he was writing.[23] Referring to Hermeticism, Festugière has spoken of "the end of an age of reason."[24] Was it the new, religious coloration of *sophia* in late antiquity that explains the growing attraction of India among intellectuals in search of the roots of the sacred?

Another Hellenic author, Philostratus of Athens, penned an important document on the contemporary perception of Indian wisdom. The *Life of Apollonius of Tyana* (written between 217 and 238 C.E.) tells us more about its author and his times than about its first-century hero. We do not know who the real Apollonius was, but thanks to this text we do know of a new kind of person, a holy man, for whom prophecy, or direct contact with the divine, counted more than received doctrine, and for whom religious observance and self-denial were the prerequisites of wisdom.[25] "My abstention from animal foods comes from [Pythagoras's] wisdom," he says (I.32.2).[26] Apollonius visits India with a specific purpose: to visit the Wise Men (*sophoi*) who live there. On his way, he meets the Magi in Babylon and Susa, a coincidence that he considers to be "an extra dividend." When asked about them, he answers that they are wise, "but not in every respect" (I.26). On his way to the Wise Men, Apollonius crosses the cultural *limes* of the Hellenic *oikoumenē*, signaled by a bronze tablet with the legend: "Alexander stopped there (*Alexandros entautha estē*)—a stele established by the Indians, presumably to boast that Alexander had advanced no further (II.43, at the end of Book II).

The limits of Alexander's empire, however, do not quite overlap with those of Hellenic impact, since one finds in India various idols of Greek gods (as well as of Egyptian ones), which the Indians "set up and worship with Greek rites" (II.14.3). Moreover, Apollonius's conversations with Iarchas, the leader of the Wise Men, take place in Greek, a language mastered by Iarchas, as well as by many others (III.16.2). Damis, Apollonius's companion, "never would have thought that an Indian could master Greek so completely" (II.36). Philostratus stresses the surprising character of this fact. Asked by Apollonius about the Wise Men's concept of the soul, Iarchas answers that it is identical to that taught by Pythagoras to the Greeks, which he himself had received from the Egyptians, to whom the Wise Men had originally transmitted it.

The Wise Men permit Apollonius to attend their rites, and during his four months among them, he absorbs their doctrines, both avowed and secret (*phanerous te kai aporrhētous pantas;* III.50). Their wisdom is summarized by Iarchas: "Those who love prophecy, my virtuous Apollonius, become divine under its influence, and act for the salvation of mankind" (III.42). Apollonius, on his side, in the letter he sends to Iarchas on his way back, thanks him for having shared his special wisdom with him, "showing him a path through heaven."

Before we end, we will glance at what Philostratus calls "the most famous story about Apollonius" (IV.6), purported to have occurred immediately upon his return to Greece from his trip to India (IV.25). The young Menippus had fallen in love with a foreign woman, at once beautiful, refined, and rich. He planned to marry her. It was Apollonius who revealed the harsh truth to him: alas, the object of his love was not a real woman, but a phantom (*phasma;* or a vampire, which had only the *appearance* of matter). The whole thing had been a delusion (*alla edokei panta;* IV. 25.2). A striking parallel to this docetic pattern appears in the Sanskrit *Vigraha-Vyavartani* ("Averting the Arguments"), a book of logic written by Nagarjuna, a great Buddhist philosopher of the third century C.E., to refute arguments of the Brahminical School of logic (Nyaya). In this work, we read (II.23.27): "A magically formed phantom destroys the erroneous apprehension concerning a phantom woman, teaching us that all phenomena are empty (*sunyata*)."²⁷ Should we then see the beautiful but threatening phantom, Apollonius's *femme fatale*, as the elusive guardian of wisdom at the confines of the Hellenic *oikoumenē*? If what we take to be the material cosmos is an illusion, then wisdom must, indeed, teach us the way to heaven.

The impact of Eastern traditions of wisdom on Greco-Roman late antiquity is a single chapter in the lengthy story of the interface between East and West. By late antiquity this interface already had a long history, and some patterns of thought from Eastern cultural traditions had already been internalized in the Greco-Roman world. One specific aspect of this phenomenon, the ontological status given to the letters of the alphabet as building blocks of the cosmos, is our next discussion.

8

A WORLD FULL OF LETTERS

Chapter 7 dealt with the imbrication of Greek and Oriental cultural traditions. As we saw, the balance between Greek and "barbarian" cultures remained heavily tipped toward the former, as thinkers in the Greco-Roman world were almost never able to function intellectually in a language other than Greek or Latin. If one adds to those linguistic limitations the interface between orality and writing, the intricacy of the matter becomes apparent. The present chapter will further investigate this cluster of problems, seeking to unveil levels of cultural contact between different social contexts. Using as a prism a highly original text that deals with the demiurgic power and religious significance of the letters of the alphabet, we shall see how Hebrew and Greek traditions on the letters, those fundamental elements of any literate culture, fused in the formative stages of Christian culture.

While as we have seen, full-fledged literacy was in the Roman world limited to a relatively small elite, the symbolic status of letters, words, and books was dramatically heightened for all. In this sense, one can speak not only of a "world full of gods," but also of "a world full of letters."[1] More than ever before, and perhaps also after, the late ancient world was one in which the letters of certain alphabets (i.e., the Greek, the Hebrew and the Syriac) were, like the Egyptian hieroglyphs, powerful symbols, even (or especially) when they were not understood. For late ancient people, these were, indeed, more than symbols: they were the building blocks of the universe. Hence, letters were the bread and butter of cosmogonical and cosmological speculations, and the *Urmensch* himself (or his consort) was conceived as being a *macranthropos* whose body was made up entirely of letters (*charactēres*).

Franz Dornseiff's seminal work of nearly a century ago taught us about the prominence of letters in late ancient magical theory and praxis, in cultures across the Mediterranean and Near East. Among Greeks, Iranians, Jews, Christians, Gnostics and Manichaeans one can follow the traces of letters' role and status.[2] The late ancient world, in which scriptures could be revealed, was also a world in which the individual characters composing the words of these scriptures were invested with divine power. The female cosmic Body of Truth (*sōma tēs alētheias*) in the teachings of the Valentinian theologian Mark the Gnostic echoes dramatically the *Shiʿur Qoma* (the cosmic body of God) in late ancient Hebrew texts and traditions, as well as some Manichaean mythological figures.[3] The *Infancy Gospel of Thomas* provides a well-known representation of this theme: As Zachaeus, the teacher, tries to teach the letters of the alphabet to the child Jesus, the latter objects, arguing that the teacher ignores "the true nature of the *alpha*." Only after grasping this cardinal point will the teacher be able to move on to the *beta*.[4]

Since Dornseiff's pioneering work on the mystical and magical dimensions of the alphabet in ancient Mediterranean cultures, much work has been done on different aspects of letters in late ancient religious traditions. In particular, remarkable isomorphisms have been discovered between some of the earliest strata of Jewish mysticism and gnostic mythological elements; these point clearly to contacts. We now begin to tackle patterns of impact between religious movements.

On the Mystery of the Greek Letters

On the Mystery of the Greek Letters is a valuable Greek text. Cordula Bandt's exemplary *editio princeps* includes a translation, a very thorough introduction that considers the place of the text in late ancient Christian literature, and copious notes.[5] Until Bandt's edition, this text was known only in a Coptic version preserved in a Coptic-Arabic manuscript from the fourteenth century published in 1900–1901 by A. Hebbelinck, under the title *Les mystères des lettres grecques*.[6] Both the Coptic-Arabic manuscript and the Greek one include various drawings, meant to explain the significance of the letters, as developed in the text. The text claims to have been redacted by Saint Sabas, the fifth-century founder of the Mar Saba monastery in the Judean wilderness. The Coptic version reads: "In the name of the Father and the Son and the Holy Spirit, one single God. Speech pronounced by Apa Seba, the priest, the hermit, about the divine mystery contained in the letters of the alphabet, a mystery which none among the ancient philosophers has been able to explain." Cordula Bandt has concluded that the text is pseudepigraphic, and likely was written by a follower of Sabas, a Melkite (and anti-Origenist) monk in sixth-century Palestine.[7]

The *mysterion* hidden in the letters (*stoicheia*) was revealed to Sabas by a Power *(kratos)* "as in ecstasy" (Chapter 1). It is with the Greek letters (or characters) that our text deals. These letters were given (by God) "before idolatry" in order to bring humankind to the true cult of God. For our text, however, there are only twenty-two, rather than twenty-four letters, in the original Greek alphabet. The text argues that both X and Ψ were not in the original alphabet, but were added later, by the "philosophers," that is, by the Hellenic pagan thinkers. The mystery of these letters, we are told, has been "hidden since the beginning of the world" (Chapter 2). There are twenty-two letters, like the twenty-two letters of the Hebrew (and the Aramaic, or Syriac) alphabet, just as there are twenty-two books of the Bible "according to the Jews," twenty-two works of God in the creation of the world, and twenty-two "marvelous works in the economy of Christ." Among these letters, there are seven vocal (Chapter 4) and fifteen "nonvocal" letters (Chapter 5). The seven vocal letters represent the seven *hypostaseis* of creation: heaven, water, firmament, air, earth, water between the two earths, and inferior earth. Elsewhere in the text, they also represent the seven creatures endowed with a voice. I have dealt elsewhere with the seven essential elements, or *hypostaseis* of creation, arguing that they are linked to the seven Iranian *Amesha Spenta,* later described in the first seven Kabbalistic *Sefirot*.[8] Here, I shall examine the meanings of the shapes of the letters themselves.

The Δ, as a triangle, is the figure of creation. It is also the figure of the holy Trinity, as its form alludes to the three hypostases. It is not only in metaphysical fashion that the Trinity is present in the whole universe, but also in its very physical structure. The cosmology of our text is neither rigorous nor presented in a systematic fashion. The four elements, air, fire, earth, and water are seen in parallel to the four cardinal points of the universe, the four directions of the wind, the four seasons and the four great rivers of the Garden of Eden: the Pishon, the Gehon, the Tigris and the Euphrates. The "T" is presented as a divine ray shining upon the earth. It also announces the cross of Christ "by its Hebrew name" as this name is "saddi." This obviously refers to the Hebrew letter *tsadi,* which is the first letter of the Hebrew *tslav* (cross) and also alludes to the *tsaddik,* the Just One. It interesting to note that the same interpretation attached to the letter *tav* (ת) is found in a rather late midrash, *Ottiyot de-Rabbi Akiva* (i.e., *"The Letters of Rabbi Akiva"*).[9] Π means arch (obviously because of its shape) or temple, and refers to "eight," while Σ is a figure of the world and of light.

Various elements of our text point to Jewish traditions. The most important of these elements is of course the number of letters, which points to the Hebrew—or to the Syriac—alphabet. According to our text, Syriac was Adam's language. The Syriac letters God Himself engraved on a stone tablet, like the Law, with His hand and finger. This tablet, upon which the theosophy was inscribed, was found after the flood by Cadmus, "the Greek philosopher," and was at the source of science in Palestine and Phoenicia, before the letters reached Greece (Chapter 19). For a late ancient Christian author from the Near East, Syriac was by far the most immediate reference as a Semitic language. This accounts for the confusion between Aramaic and Hebrew in ancient Christian Greek literature.

The number seven alludes to the Sabbath, and to "the observation of the Law." The text mentions that the Syriac word *or* means light. It is in Hebrew, rather than in Syriac, however, that *or* means "light." The reference to Hebrew *or* as "light" clearly points to a Hebrew context of the *Urtext,* or at least the Jewish origin of the exegetical traditions on the letters as they are conserved in our text. The text as we have it now, of course, presents an outspoken anti-Jewish polemic. According to it, the Jews have from the beginning of history belonged to Satan and are called "God-killers." *The Mystery of the Greek Letters* appears then, to be a potpourri of early Christian speculation, both on the letters and on cosmology.[10] While it shows some familiarity with some great names of Greek classical culture, such as Plato, Homer, Aristotle, Demosthenes, Pythagoras, Socrates, Hesiod, Democritus, Chrysippus, and Menander, it purports to proclaim the victory of "the Church of the illiterates" over the pagan philosophers, whom that Church instructs. The text presents, then, the victory of the Christianized Greek letters over Greek idolatry. The letters are not only the elements of Greek paganism, but also of a culture that permitted the development of true religion. For our text, the elements (*stoicheia*) of creation are the alphabet letters (*stoicheia;* Chapter 22). The (Greek) letters, thanks to their cosmogonical and cosmological status, can accomplish, as it were, a deconstruction of pagan (i.e., Greek) culture. *The Mystery of the Greek Letters* perceives Christianity as a cultural revolution: pagan books, which reflect mistaken and/or perverse structures have been destroyed, and new ones, faithful to the divine message, have now been built with different permutations of the same elemental letters.

On the Mystery of the Greek Letters preserves many Jewish or Jewish-Christian traditions. The *hexahemeron* (the six days of creation), together with the Sabbath and the Trinity, makes up "the mystery of the decade"). Number ten represents perfection (42). The text ends with this highlighting of ten. Notably, taken together, the twenty-two letters and the "mystery of the decade" are equivalent in number to the "thirty-two wondrous ways of wisdom" mentioned in the *Sefer Yezira* (the "Book of Creation"). The *Sefer Yezira* is an important late ancient Hebrew composition that deals with cosmogony and cosmology through speculation on the twenty-two letters of the Hebrew alphabet (*otiot yesod*) and the ten *sefirot belimah*.[11] These "ways of wisdom," composed of the ten *sefirot* together with the twenty-two letters, are mentioned already in the first paragraphs of the *Sefer Yezira*.[12] Thus, it seems that both the Greek and the Hebrew texts reflect an earlier tradition, probably stemming from Jewish-Christian milieus. Similar close parallelisms have been identified between the *Sefer Yezira* and the *Pseudo-Clementine Homilies*.[13]

On the Mystery of the Greek Letters clarifies that the shape of the letters represents, or figures, the form of the elements of the created world (Chapter 22). We shall return to this later, but at this point we shall simply note that *stoikheia*, "letters," since Plato at least, also denotes "elements," that is, the four elements of all cosmology: water, earth, fire, and air. Plato, as we shall see, introduced the notion that the components of both language and of the world somehow were bound together.

Mystical Alphabets

We turn now to the immediate context of the theosophy preserved in *The Mystery of the Greek Letters*. While our text reflects rather uncommon patterns of thought in Patristic literature, it is not totally *sui generis*. Yet, in order to grasp its central message, namely, the affinity between the letters of the alphabet and cosmology, we shall first look to related discussions in Patristic literature.

The classicist and historian of religion Albrecht Dieterich spearheaded an investigation of *On the Mystery of the Greek Letters* in his *ABC Denkmäler*.[14] Dieterich referred to Jerome's *Preface* to his translation of the *Rules of Pachomius*, where he mentions the "mystical alphabet" that permits the monks to converse with the angels. They spoke, then, a secret language, which simple human beings could not understand. The *Letters* of Pachomius and Theodore, which Jerome also translated, attest as well an esoteric language used by at least some Egyptian monks. The interlocutor in Pachomius's *Letter VI* grasps the importance of understanding the spiritual elements of the spiritual alphabet.[15] Similarly, in the *De viris illustribus* attributed to Gennadius of Marseille, abbots are said to use ciphers made from the letters of the alphabet.[16] Elsewhere in these letters, reference is made to the language that was revealed to both Pachomius and Cornelius by an angel. While others can hear the sounds, they are unable to understand their meaning. Jerome also tells us that Pachomius organized the monks of his monastery into twenty-four groups, to represent the twenty-four letters of the Greek alphabet. In his first letter to Cornelius, Pachomius offers a list of the meanings of the letters: I stands for Jesus,[17] Y for God, P (the numerical value of which is 100) for Christos, O for God the Judge, H for the ogdoad, that is, *Christos*, or Jesus,[18] T for the cross (*stauros*), Σ for Sabaoth (i.e., Jesus), Δ for the Trinity (as it includes the first three letters), and A for *archē*, that is, Jesus.[19]

We thus have before us an Egyptian tradition that may have reached Palestine around (or before) the turn of the fifth century. Jerome may provide a link with the monastic milieu of the Judean wilderness. But Jerome's own preoccupation with the individual letters is presented in his famous *Letter 30* to Paula, in which he reveals to Paula, at her insistent demand, the meaning of the Hebrew letters. Like the multilayered significance of the biblical text, the meaning attached to each letter of the Hebrew alphabet is also multiform, at both the literal and the spiritual levels. The literal level concerns the name of each letter: "*Aleph* means 'doctrine,' *beth* 'house,' *gimel* 'fullness,' *daleth* 'door.' (Aleph interpretatur 'doctrina,' beth 'domus,' gimel 'plenitudo,' deleth 'tabularum' . . .)."

In approaching the spiritual meaning of the alphabet, Jerome notes that there are seven groups of letters (and points to the mystical nature of the number seven). He then asks Paula: "What is more sacred, I ask you, than this mystery? (Oro te, quid hoc sacratius sacramento?)" Here again, we find the mystery of the twenty-two letters.

Jerome was not the first Christian intellectual to reflect on the Hebrew language. Eusebius, in his *Praeparatio Evangelica,* had offered a sustained review of language in general and of Hebrew in particular.[20] As the first philosopher, long before the Greeks, Moses had taught a realist, antinominalist theory of language: "names are given to things by nature and not conventionally." According to Eusebius, Plato, in his *Cratylus,* only follows his predecessor Moses. Hence names, such as *adam* and *ish* have a signification of their own, linked to the meaning of their sound: "earth" (*adama*) and "red" (*adom*) for the former, "fire" (*esh*) for the second. "Isaac," similarly, means laughter (this etymology is already biblical: Gen 17: 17). Hebrew, adds Eusebius, reflects etymologies much more clearly than Greek. Hence, A (*aleph* in Hebrew) means "learning" (the root a.l.p. means "learn" in Aramaic), *beth*, a house, etc. . . . Eusebius then quotes a few verses from the *Greek Anthology,* which reveal that the name of "the everlasting Father of mankind" is composed of seven vowels.

In *Praeparatio Evangelica* X,5, Eusebius offered a consideration of the Phoenician origins of the Greek alphabet: likely it was the Phoenician Cadmus who introduced the letters to the Greeks. According to him, the letters were first devised, it seems, by the Syrians, that is, the Hebrews living in Syria, the country neighboring Phoenicia. Eusebius adds that, unlike the Greek letters, each Hebrew letter has a meaning. This comment is repeated toward the end of this chapter.

A similar perception of Greek (and Latin) letters as stemming from the Hebrew letters is given by Isidore of Seville, an encyclopedic writer summarizing the world of knowledge of late ancient Christianity in the early seventh century.[21] The origin of the Hebrew letters is the Law of Moses—a fact reflecting their relative belatedness. Indeed, Syriac and

Chaldaean letters are older, as they can be traced to Abraham. Queen Isis discovered the Egyptian letters when she came from Greece to Egypt and brought them to her country. Cadmus brought to Greece the first seventeen letters of the alphabet, while the other letters were added during the Trojan War and also by the poet Simonides. Isidore adds that there are five "mystical" letters in the Greek alphabet[22]: Y represents human life, Θ represents death (*thanatos*), T figures the cross of the Lord. Α and Ω signify the beginning and end of things, i.e., cosmology, the very topic of our text.[23] The Greeks, like the Hebrews—and unlike the Romans—also used letters to represent numbers.

Another work of interest is the *Gospel of the Egyptians*. This is a puzzling text found in two slightly different Coptic versions at Nag Hammadi after the Second World War. The *Gospel of the Egyptians*, dubbed by scholars as "Gnostic," presents various traditions that seem to echo Jewish or Jewish-Christian ones. The Father of all comes from Silence, and His name is an invisible symbol, a hidden mystery.[24] Then come the vowels O, I, H, O, Y, E, A, Ω each repeated twenty-two times. This series of vowels seems, then, to represent the esoteric divine name.

Jewish Traditions

Jewish traditions about the secret or unpronounceable name of God, the Tetragrammaton, have a long history. I have argued elsewhere that these were retained, and developed, among the first Jewish Christians, and then passed into the Gnostic world.[25] Esoteric conceptions of language, and speculations about the divine names, were common in many ancient cultures. What was peculiar to the Jews was the utter inexpressibility of the name of their god. The Nag Hammadi codices have been called "a Gnostic library." In all likelihood, the codices were used in Pachomian monasteries. It seems that these texts were copied to serve as edifying reading material, as postulated by Frederik Wisse.[26] Hence, we have here a possible link between *The Mystery of the Greek Letters*, probably stemming from Palestinian monasteries, and the traditions on esoteric language from early Egyptian monasticism, where the secret alphabet seems to have focused on the esoteric name of God.

The Jewish traditions on the Hidden Name of God made their presence felt in early Jewish-Christian and Gnostic traditions. This Jewish origin explains both the number of the letters and the various traits in our text.

At the core of these traditions lies the esoteric name of God. Probably the most striking among these traditions is that of Marcus Gnosticus, the Valentinian teacher whose conceptions were preserved by Irenaeus[27]: the Divine feminine emanation, Truth (*Aletheia*) is a cosmic figure whose body is uniquely made of the letters of the alphabet. Her head is Α and Ω, her neck Β and Ψ, her hands Γ and Χ, her breasts Δ and Φ and so on. This is, according to Mark, "the body of Truth, this is the scheme of the Element, this is the character of the Letter!" This element he calls *Anthropos:* he is, says Mark, "the source of all Logos, the principle of all Voice, the expression of everything inexpressible, the mouth of silent Silence."[28]

This last text has received a great deal of attention—especially by scholars of early Jewish mysticism—who have made much of the striking similarities between the figure of *Aletheia* and the idea of *Shiʿur Qomah*, the measurements of the cosmic Divine body. How such conceptions can be traced directly to early monastic practice, both in Egypt and in Palestine, is now clear.

Rabbinic literature is replete with discussions of the importance of the letters in general and of those in the Divine name (*ha-shem ha-mephorash*) in particular. In this context, a long passage in tractate *Shabbat* of the Babylonian Talmud (103b–104a) stands out. Another passage, from tractate *Berachot* of the Babylonian Talmud (56a), refers to the letters from which the world was created. By far the most important text for our current investigation, however, is the *Book of Creation*, the *Sefer Yezira*. This text (which the Jewish tradition considers to have been redacted by Abraham) would become one of the foundational texts of medieval mystical and theosophical Jewish speculation, at least from the tenth century on.[29] One of the vexing questions about *Sefer Yezira* is the date of its composition. In a monograph on this text, Yehuda Liebes made a strong case for a very early dating.[30] Liebes argues that the text was known in the Rabbinic period and that it must stem from the Second Temple period. Other scholars date it to late antiquity or even to the early Islamic period. Without entering into this particular scholarly fray, I shall note simply that our consideration of probable Jewish (or Jewish-Christian) origins of the Christian speculation on the letters of the alphabet supports Liebes's view, if not regarding the redaction of the book itself, then at least about the early date of its main underlying conceptions. Such a provisional conclusion is also supported by the close similarities between the *Sefer Yezira* and the *Pseudo-Clementine Homilies* demonstrated by Shlomo Pines.[31]

Greek Origins

We are left with a crucial question: What are the origins of Jewish thinking on the alphabet's letters? The rather original pattern of thought shown in Jewish texts typically is taken by modern scholars to be endogenous to the Jewish tradition. This presumption is unlikely to have much validity, and is certainly not very useful from a heuristic point of view.

In the late antique Near East, the letters of the alphabet exerted a pull that was by no means limited to Jewish and Christian milieus. In Iran, for instance, the heretic Mazdak is supposed to have said that:

> the King of the upper world rules by means of the letters of the alphabet, whose sum yields the highest name. Whoever can form a conception of these letters, to him is revealed the greatest mystery. But whoever is excluded remains in the blindness of ignorance, forgetfulness, dullness and sorrow with respect to the four spiritual powers.

Werner Müller, who has called attention to this tradition, links it to the monastic speculations on the letters that we have surveyed.[32] He makes no attempt, however, to account for the corresponding Jewish conceptions.[33]

As mentioned above, antiquity already knew of a long tradition of discussion on the letters of the alphabet. In the Semitic world, the *Book of Aḥiqar* offers the commonly accepted view on the significance of the letters. The longest and most detailed of these traditions, however, is found in the Greek world. Herodotus says in his *Histories* (II.36), that the Egyptians, who are "the most religious nation in the world," write from right to left, unlike the Greeks, and have two sorts of writing, "the sacred and the common." Diodorus Siculus (*Bibl.* I.74) develops Herodotus's brief note:

> And the priests teach the boys two kinds of letters, those called sacred by the Egyptians and those containing the more common sort of learning.... Of the two kinds of Egyptians letters, the demotic are taught to all, but those called sacred by the Egyptians are known to the priests alone.

Egyptian hieroglyphs were a point of intellectual curiosity in Greek society, up to Horapollo's *Hieroglyphica*. This was the sole surviving work (from fifth-century C.E. Alexandria) to deal at length with hieroglyphs.[34]

Democritus of Abdera, who was born thirty-three years before Plato, in 460, compared the atoms from which the world was made to the letters of the alphabet. Before Democritus, Pythagoras had compared the numbers to the letters and to the world at large. Plato, who was so impressed by Egypt, also devoted much effort, in various dialogues, such as the *Cratylus*, the *Theetetus*, and the *Timeaus*, to reach a proper understanding of language. In *Theetetus*, 202c ff. and in *Timeaus* 48b, Plato extends metaphorically the word for "letter" (*stoicheion*) to cover the elements of the universe. In this text, the letters are not conceived as writing signs, but rather as sounds elemental to the syllables. More precisely it seems that *stoicheion* referred mainly to the sound of the letter, while *gramma* referred to the written sign.[35] In *Cratylus* 393c, Plato reflects on the names of the letters. Most relevant for us, however, is *Timeaus* 47e–48b. There, Plato discusses the creation of the world, and compares the elements of the universe to the letters of the alphabet. This text, then, which was awarded a long life and was to become one of the topical texts in Christian references to Plato's writings, states in so many words the relationship between *stoicheia* and cosmogony.

The doctrine of the four elements of the universe was first put forward not by Plato, but by Empedocles, as we are told by Aristotle: "Empedocles was the first to speak of the four material elements."[36] Although this doctrine was soon rejected by Anaxagoras and the atomists, Aristotle proposed a revised version of the theory, which maintained its authority throughout antiquity and the Middle Ages.[37] Aristotle followed Plato in substituting *stoicheia* for *archai* in referring to the elements.

The semantic evolution of the word *stoicheion* is well charted, as is that of its Latin counterpart, *elementum*. In the Byzantine period, *stoicheion* came to mean, in a dramatic semantic transformation, "heavenly body" (star, constellation) and "spirit" or "demon." In Christian literature, repeated reference is made to the *stoicheia tou kosmou* in Colossians 2, 8. Little discussed, however, is the polysemic character of the word itself. As we have seen, since Plato *stoicheion* denoted both element and letter. Without question, *The Mystery of the Greek Letters* betrays this line of thought.

It is also, however, clearly colored by a strong Jewish background. Hellenistic Judaism is the obvious locus wherein Greek traditions about the letters of the alphabet could have been reinterpreted to fit Jewish conceptions. Philo, in particular, has a striking remark on the education of the young Moses, when he states: "The Egyptian men of learning taught Moses the philosophy which is expressed in symbol which is exemplified in the so-called sacred letters (*en tois legomenos hierois grammasin*)."[38] The learned Egyptians "further instructed him in the philosophy conveyed in symbols, as displayed in the so-called holy inscriptions. . . ." What seems to be going on in this fragment is the following. Hellenistic Jews were aware of Greek traditions about the sacred letters of the Egyptian priests, and their esoteric character. For them, however, Hebrew was the sacred language. For Philo, who might well reflect an earlier Hellenistic Jewish tradition, Moses, who had as a child been initiated into the esoteric tradition of the Egyptian hieroglyphs, could later apply to the Hebrew letters the traditional Greek understanding of the Egyptian "letters."[39]

Hellenistic Jewish traditions about Moses and the esoteric character of Egyptian priestly language was not, however, the only source of Jewish and Christian (including Jewish-Christian and Gnostic) speculation about the letters of the alphabet, their esoteric (or "mystical") meaning, and their cosmogonic connection. Other traditions about the letters of the alphabet that might well have influenced Jewish speculation were circulating in the Western Semitic world. Nonetheless, Hellenistic Jewish speculation, branching out from Greek traditions, was likely a major proximate channel through which this speculation reached Palestine.

The *Mystery of the Greek Letters* has not revealed all its mysteries to us. But we have gained some insight into how "the Church of the Illiterate" came to instruct "the pagan wise men." Essentially, our strange text demonstrates the deconstruction of Hellenic literary culture through its own alphabet. What counts is not anymore what is written, but rather the constituent elements of this culture, decontextualized and stripped of their original semantical meaning. The books of Hellenic culture, ineluctably linked to idolatry, can disappear. The letters alone will remain, imbued with the esoteric power of God's creation. *The Mystery of the Greek Letters* stands precisely at the intersection of Judaism and Christianity, of the Hebrew and the Greek cultures, of the exoteric and the esoteric hermeneutical traditions, of the East and the West, and finally, of the oral and written traditions.

Thus Christian *paideia,* or at least the monastic *paideia* considered in this book, is Greek in form and Hebrew in content. Its hybrid nature demonstrates definitively the Christian innovation, reinventing traditional education to accord with what was for them the only true text. The creation of the world with the letters of the (Hellenized and Christianized Hebrew) alphabet represents the true mystery and power of the letters, from A to Ω, from creation to salvation, from revelation through Scripture. The world and the script are to be deciphered through one another. We have here, in a nutshell, the idea of the two revelations, one by the revealed Book of God, the other by the Great Book of nature. This double revelation would continue to appear up to Newton, and even beyond.[40] Traces of God can be found both in nature and in the letters of the alphabet. The cultural revolution of early Christianity would be the fruit of a new religious outlook established upon a book. Puzzlingly, it almost seems as if the very idea of a revealed book would eventually sap the legitimacy of a literary culture.

In this chapter, we have seen how Jewish and Greek traditions were imbricated in the developing scriptural counterculture promoted by early Christian monks. Cultures (and countercultures) are meant, at least in a certain sense, to serve individuals, and it is by individuals that they are advanced. In this vein, then, the next and last chapter will attempt to delineate the dialectical relationship between textual and personal authority in the transmission of scripture in ancient Christianity.

9

SCRIPTURAL AND PERSONAL AUTHORITY

Oral and Written Transmission of Scriptures

The new and striking primacy of the written word, which we saw manifested in letter speculation in Chapter 8, was the engine that powered the cultural transformation of late antiquity. In the wake of this change came the creation of a Christian culture. As we have seen as well, the ascendance of the written word irrevocably tipped the balance between orality and literacy. The new confluence of the written and the spoken word birthed religious leaders and spiritual virtuosi. These were charismatic, prophetic personalities who, in accordance with their outlook, heralded or battled the emerging scripture-based orthodoxies.

The present chapter takes up our final concern, the dialectical relationship between scriptural and personal authority. I wish to develop here at least the bare bones of a model that will help us to grasp the transformation of religious authority in the late ancient Eastern Mediterranean and Near East. While the problems dealt with in this chapter pertain to different religious groups in late antiquity, I shall draw most heavily on Patristic Christianity, with some reference to Rabbinic Judaism.

Jesus, Mani, Muhammad: prophecy was alive and well all during this period. The hermeneutical "orthodox" elites within the different communities most certainly did not represent the sole type of personal authority in late ancient religion. Alongside them lay the charismatic authority of the prophets and the heretics (not infrequently one and the same). Jesus, Mani, and Muhammad, charismatic leaders all, were possessed by the prophetic spirit. At the same time, each took a distinct approach to the idea of the religious book. Jesus teaches, but does not write down those instructions; Mani makes sure to record his teachings, in a deliberate departure from his predecessors, such as Jesus, Buddha, and Zarathustra; and Muhammad is portrayed as illiterate, but the recipient of divine revelations that must be written down in a book. The strong impression is that of a late ancient religious scene in which religious authority must be viewed through the lens of a dialectical relationship between scriptures and individuals.

As discussed in Chapter 1, a central aspect of the transformation of religion in the long late antiquity was the "scriptural movement."[1] This movement refers not only to the new (scriptural) texts, but also to their canonization, their translations as well as hermeneutical literature. A number of religious movements grew that were established upon the biblical scriptures.[2] The first two centuries saw a literary war over the proper Biblical hermeneutics, through the elaboration of interpretive texts, which resulted in a "parting of the ways" between Judaism and Christianity. From the first texts of the New Testament (Paul's letters), through the redaction of the Mishna, toward the end of the second century, and, at the same time (around 180), the first reference to a "new testament" (*kainē diathēkē*) by Irenaeus of Lyon, we can follow the competition between Jewish and Christian communities about the proper interpretation of the Scriptures, which were then still, for Christians and Jews alike, the texts of the Hebrew Bible or of its Greek translation, the Septuagint. As I have argued elsewhere, it is no coincidence that the idea of a "New Testament" and the Mishna (that is, as its Greek name indicates, *deuterosis*, repetition [of the Law]) appear at approximately the same time: both offer more or less the same key to the correct interpretation of the biblical text: through the oral law or through the new prophecy.[3] To this, one should add the fact, which to the best of my knowledge has not yet been noted, that the end of the second century is also when one started to make an academic choice among the many Greek tragedies, at the peak of the Stoic influence in the Greco-Roman world, up to the Emperor Marcus Aurelius.[4] The appearance of Mani's texts and the canonization of the texts of the New Testament in the third century, as well as the finalization of the list of the thirty seven books of the New Testament in Athanasius's *Easter Letter* of 367, would be paralleled by the identification of a great number of texts as apocryphal, to be rejected as heretical. Most such texts thus were fated to disappear, either through destruction or benign neglect. In the main, serendipity determined which would survive. While it is almost impossible to date with any precision the first appearance of the Mandaean texts, there seems to be little doubt that the Qur'an was originally, at least for some decades, an *oral book*.[5]

Oral Books

What, though, would an oral book be? In the ancient world, some texts were held in such regard that they were memorized without being committed to writing, or before (in some cases much before) they became written texts. The ancient world offers a fine example of such a work: the Avesta, which remained oral for a millennium, and was preserved in remarkably precise fashion in a language no longer understood by its reciters. In the fifth and sixth centuries, the redaction of the two versions of the Talmud, both in Palestine and in Babylonia, is best considered alongside the redaction of the great legal codices in the Roman Empire, the Theodosian Codex, the great compilation of laws since 312 published by Theodosius II in 429, and the Justinian Codex published a century later. Similar scriptural attitudes can be discerned among pagans; for instance, among Platonist philosophers or trends influenced by Platonic philosophy. In these circles, the texts of Plato functioned more or less like religious scriptures, to which were appended a hermeneutical apparatus and reverence that rivaled those associated with Christian scripture, for example.[6] In this respect, the classical scholar E. R. Dodds could write: "Christians and pagans were alike schoolmen: they could not challenge the authority of the ancient texts."[7]

The "scriptural movement" of our period is concerned mainly with the systematic building up of new interpretive layers over existing scriptures. This is patently so with regard to the Mishna and the Talmud, as well as to the great Roman legal codices. It is also the case for the huge and diverse Patristic literature, a veritable cathedral of glosses on both the Old and New Testaments. Shaul Shaked's characterization of "uneasy ambivalence," coined with respect to the Talmud, covers some ground here too, in the context of the relationship between oral and written modes of transmission in late antiquity.[8]

These monuments of words became the backbone of emerging orthodoxies: Christian, but also Jewish and Zoroastrian, in both the Roman and the Sasanian Empires. As there is no orthodoxy without its corresponding heterodoxy, soon decried as heresy, the fixation of scriptural canons as well as the creation of hermeneutical corpora also means the censorship of apocryphal and heretical writings. As orthodoxies emerged, then, other texts, authors, and ideas disappeared from view.

Religious writings are multiplex, and so are religious specialists. Each community has its scriptural interpreters, who develop and enforce hermeneutical rules through which the scriptural text is meant to be understood. For instance, the Greek tradition has such rules (the Homeric writings were interpreted in metaphoric terms by the philosophers since at least the fourth century B.C.E.) and so does the Jewish one, both in Palestine and in the Hellenistic world (where the influence of the Greek allegorical philosophical tradition was dominant).

Types of Authority

Max Weber identified three main types of authority in human societies: (1) what he called "rational-legal authority," (2) establishing legitimacy upon a complex system of written rules, traditional authority, including customs, habits, and social structures, and (3) charismatic authority, mainly that of the individual leader, either political or religious in nature. Charismatic authority is central in the context of religion, and in particular of religious traditions stemming from the inspiration of a prophet. Weber perceived the evolution, with time, of the original charismatic element of prophecy into more structured social patterns, which he called the "routinization" of religion. This routinization replaces the charismatic element of the first generation (or generations) with hierarchical structures and fixed patterns of decision making, in particular for the formulation of rules of interpretation of scriptures. The Weberian paradigm thus posits two main kinds of religious authority: one that stems from charismatic prophecy, and another that is embedded in the routine of ecclesiastical hierarchy. Hence, tensions between prophets and bishops soon give way to conflict among heretical leaders and orthodox rulers.

A similar dichotomy can be discerned with respect to the authority of scriptures. Even before the canonization process has run its course completely, an elaborate hermeneutical system is established, methods of interpretation are developed, and alternative scriptures are discarded as apocryphal or heretical. The remaining texts, those accepted into the canon, along with the accepted rules for their interpretation, become the core of the educational system of the religious elites.

Alongside this routinized scriptural authority, however, scriptures exert a further, much more immediate impact. I propose to call this phenomenon "charismatic scriptural authority." Instances of this direct reference to scripture include prayer, recitation or chanting, incantation, and *sortes biblicae*. Thus, we find the immediacy of the biblical calling in such behavior as Augustine's famous *"Tolle, lege!"* Like personal authority, scriptural authority can thus be charismatic or routinized.

In line with Weber, the social anthropologist Harvey Whitehouse has developed a theory of religion that differentiates between two fundamental modes of religiosity. He calls these modes doctrinal and imagistic, and claims that they are found in all societies.[9] The doctrinal mode of religiosity, which is highly routinized (in the Weberian sense of the word), is characterized by high frequency and low arousal. The opposite is true of the imagistic mode. Whitehouse contends that all patterns of religious life offer different admixtures of these two modes. His theory has been well received, although perhaps more by historians of religions than by social anthropologists. Whitehouse acknowledges the nonradical nature of the dichotomy between the two modes of religiosity in his theory, of its inability to reflect fully the complexities of historical reality.

Building on Weber and Whitehouse, we can say that doctrinal religiosity is mediated by routinized authority, both personal and scriptural.[10] Similarly, imagistic religiosity is mediated by charismatic authority, both personal and scriptural. In other words, scriptural authority, in its charismatic mode, informs imagistic religiosity, in much the same way that in its routinized mode it informs doctrinal religiosity. In a parallel manner, the mode of personal authority, as charismatic, informs imagistic religiosity, while as routinized, it informs doctrinal religiosity. It might be useful, for our purposes, to replace the terms "imagistic" and "doctrinal" with "charismatic" and "structural." This is summarized in the following schema:

Person: *charisma:* prophet, holy man, heretic
structure: bishop, rabbi, priest

Text: *charisma:* oral, prophetic, eschatological
structure: commentary, legal text

Like all schemas, this one offers a drastically simplified representation of archetype interplay between charisma and structure, people and texts. According to it, a charismatic person may link up with either a charismatic or a structural text, and a structural person may do the same; in each case, a different case figure obtains. Now charisma is notoriously unstable, and easily rigidifies. *Mutatis mutandis,* the reverse holds true for structures, which tend to break into supple, charismatic frames. Of course, reality never quite conforms to the neat delineations provided in such schemas, but they remain useful for understanding the vectors that undergird historical realities.

Authority in the Early Church

Research on personal authority in the early Church vastly exceeds work on scriptural authority in the same context. The early textual evidence references several different categories of people invested with authority in the early church: ministers, prophets and teachers. Very early mention is made as well of the authority of scripture. Tertullian, before the end of the second century, is one of our first witnesses for this usage.[11] He also mentions the Apostles.[12] Cyprian deals with episcopal succession and the relationship between bishops and priests.[13] In Patristic Latin texts, "authority" and "power" imply different things. Thus, Pope Gelasius distinguishes *auctoritas sacra pontificum* from *regalis potestas*. The Roman pontiff has *plenitudo potestatis*. The functions of authority are, first, the ordination and the laying on of hands. For Cyprian, "All must recognize that the bishop is in the church and the church is in the bishop."[14] Authority permits the formulation of laws, the exercise of justice, the suppression of errors, and conciliar legislation, which is the richest and most elaborate source of authority. From the start of the third century, the papacy intervenes in disciplinary matters.

Thus, scriptural and personal authority in late ancient religion could be charismatic or structural. We now turn to the relationship between scriptural and personal authority and the different combinations between them. What has been called "the scriptural movement" of late antiquity was actually only one aspect, albeit a central one, of what in actuality was a much broader phenomenon. Such a phenomenon is to be considered in light of societies in which the status of reading and writing was ambiguous.[15] Although their knowledge was by no means limited to technicians such as scribes, as it was in archaic societies, it was not shared by large segments of the population.[16] Among Christian rank and file, however, analphabetism was far from rare, although the traditional image of Christian monks as often being illiterate now appears to have been more a cliché than a faithful representation of reality.

As antiquity moves to a close, from the fifth century on, the holy man becomes the umpire of the holy and the moral and spiritual arbiter of his community, almost its "pole"—a term which will be used to describe the Sufi master (*qutb*) in Islam.[17] What is of relevance here is that the holy man embodies not only the Savior but also the scriptures. That the holy text is also represented by a man should not surprise or puzzle us, as the letters of the alphabet had for a long time acted in figurative images of the body's members. We might speak here of a sort of symbiosis between book and body, the second literally incorporating the first. Hence, Greek philosophers already were asked to represent their books in their body. Some philosophers, and then some Rabbinic sages, were thus considered to be living libraries.[18] The holy man was the new embodiment of the wise man, of the philosopher, of the Jewish sage, of the Gnostic. Presence had replaced knowledge. This presence, in itself, had become a source of power, one that could perform miracles. But such miracles were accomplished in the name of the divine scriptures embodied by the holy man (or, more rarely, holy woman).[19] Hence, as Claudia Rapp has noted, "the holy book and the holy man are the most powerful icons for our interpretation of the culture and mentality of late antiquity," adding that

> a double movement connects the two: the pious scribe acquires holiness from copying a sacred text, but at the same time the holy man—whether as a scribe or as the subject of a hagiographical work—is also able to impart holiness to the written text.[20]

Derek Krueger has convincingly argued a similarly bold thesis.[21] According to him, various late ancient Christian authors granted writing a new meaning, turning it into a religious activity. Probing various aspects of writing habits in Christian literature from the Eastern side of the Mediterranean, from the fourth to the seventh century, Krueger focuses his attention on early Byzantine hagiography, including texts such as Athanasius' *Life of Antony,* Gregory of Nyssa's *Life of Macrina,* Theodoret of Cyrrhus' *Religious History,* The *Hymns* of Romanos the Melodist, and the *Teaching of Addai*. These works show how, together with fasting or prayer, writing became a major instrument of early Christian authors in their ascetic ambitions. This development, according to Krueger, reflects the double meaning of the word *mimēsis,* both representation and imitation. Hence, for instance, the virtues exemplified by the saints are to be imitated, or the audience is asked to become like holy images. The images function as do words: they are, like biblical characters, types to be imitated by the believer.

Here the text of the Bible plays a central role: for early Byzantine hagiographers, for instance, the biblical authors are perceived "as typological precedents for their activity of narrating the lives of holy people." These hagiographers, who belonged to the monastic movement, described their heroes, the holy men, as patterned along the lines of leading biblical figures, in particular Moses.

One wonders whether this phenomenon of the spiritual transformation of writing and reading, of the religious authority given to the text (which is no longer the text of scripture, but that of the saint, the holy man who has become the embodiment of scripture) is limited to Christianity, or whether similar phenomena can be detected in other late ancient religious cultures. It would be illuminating to ask, for instance, what happens in Hellenic or in Jewish literature in the same period, or whether biographies of philosophers reflect related trends. The nature of Midrash, for instance, might be clarified by reading late ancient Midrashic texts in light of the insights provided by Christian hagiography. Moreover, the new attitude to writing ought to be studied in direct relation to the new approach to reading, including intensive and silent reading, emerging in late antiquity, mainly among Christian authors.[22] Further research might also probe Western Christian literature, in order to clarify how East and West differed in this matter.

The One and the Many: Revelation and Education

As we saw in Chapter 4, late ancient Christianity experienced a serious tension between the one Book (or literary corpus) of revelation and the many books of education. The monks and the theologians make a good case study of this never-quite-resolved tension: while the former held the sole authority of the books of divine revelation, the latter combined the authority of the scriptures with the rules of interpretation received from a long cultural tradition of hermeneutics first applied to the Homeric texts. There were, indeed, two "programs of truth," the first making as its cynosure the One Book, the other the whole cultural tradition.[23] Each of these choices demonstrates a different attitude to personal authority. *"Sola scriptura"* entails a certain type of personal authority, while the larger Hellenic tradition, for its part, demands a different approach to the same.

For the Rabbis, the destruction of the Temple marked the cessation of revelation; for them, "the gates of prophecy" had closed. The sages were now identified as the correct interpreters of God's will.[24] *Inter alia*, new texts claiming to be prophecies were perforce spurious, coming from false prophets. The Jewish writings from Palestine during the Second Temple period, in both Hebrew and Aramaic, were largely pseudepigraphical in nature. Texts were not signed by their authors, but rather were attributed to a hero of the Urzeit, such as Adam, Seth, Noah, and Abraham. Similarly, commentaries and targums were typically left unattributed. Hellenistic Jewish literature, which functioned according to the rules of Greek literature, found among its authors proud signatories. Tellingly, we do not have a single authored Jewish work after Philo and Josephus. Works written by Jews during the Second Temple period were censored, and hence effectively destroyed, by the late ancient rabbis. It is thanks mostly to the Christians that certain texts (for example, the apocrypha and pseudepigrapha of the Old Testament, together with Philo and Josephus) were preserved. In the sixteenth century, the great Julius Scaliger had already investigated this phenomenon, concluding that the early Christian preservation of this literature could be accounted for, at least to some extent, by the crucial role it played in the formation of Christian mythology.

Late ancient Jewish literature was written, for the most part, in Hebrew and Aramaic, and, like the Jewish literature of the Second Temple period, was usually anonymous. This is the case with the various Midrashic compilations and Talmudic treatises, which are tantamount to stenographic notes from the discussions in the Academies. One might say that one finds in Rabbinic literature a distinct absence of authorship.

For the Rabbis, then, the Bible was in a bibliographic category all its own. No other book could equal it. Consequently, Rabbinic literature would be called "Oral Torah," in contradistinction to the "Written Torah." In the Oral Torah, scholars' statements are not produced by an author but are memorized and transmitted over centuries, each generation building on the cumulative body of tradition through interpretation and innovation. In such a system, the "relationship of scholar, text, and interpreter is a complex one, each member contributing at all times to the overall authority of the tradition in the academy."[25]

The absence of the notion of textual authorship in Rabbinic Judaism had enormous implications for textual authority in late ancient Judaism and Christianity. For the Rabbis, the "text" of the Oral Torah is not identified as that of one authoritative voice. It is the polyphony itself that constitutes the authority, and while it is the voice of tradition, it is also a voice that belongs to the "reader" who becomes part of this tradition.

The personal authority of a rabbi is directly related to his scriptural knowledge. More precisely, he is the embodiment of scripture. In this schema, scriptural and personal authority achieve some kind of *unio personalis*. The rabbi embodies scripture, and he becomes the revealer of scripture, through his exposition of "Oral Torah" (*torah she-be-al-peh*). Such a union is possible precisely because there is little concept of personal authorship of a text in the Rabbinic world.[26]

For the Patristic world, Christ is God's *Logos*, and the ecclesiastical authority is that of the bishop, or *episkopos*, a figure modeled on that of the *mevaqer* (or supervisor) at Qumran. The authority of the bishop can be said to be more *ex officio* than personal, as it is rooted in his function in the ecclesiastical hierarchy. Rabbinic Judaism, in many ways a more demotic religion than early Christianity (which retained the priestly element of Second Temple Judaism), knew of no similar hierarchy. Scriptural authority, for the Christians, is that of the text itself (in its recognized translation, inspired by the Holy Spirit). The biblical text spoke directly to the early Christian believer; Rabbinic Jews, in contrast, had this text relayed to and interpreted for them by the Rabbis.

As such, scriptural authority in early Christianity had a more direct impact on its communities than it did in Rabbinic Judaism.

Patristic Christianity held within it different kinds of personal authority. Alongside that of the bishop, the theologian and the spiritual writer, was that of the author of treatises on scriptural interpretation and *theosis*. Second only to mystical union with the divine, Christianity privileges *imitatio Christi*, following Jesus—up to martyrdom. Typically, it is the holy man who will show the way to this *imitatio*, thus becoming himself a model. Holy men developed a pattern of personal authority based upon their own charisma, which competed with the authority of the bishop and that of the theologian. Overall, then, personal authority appears to have been more conspicuous, elaborate, and direct in Patristic Christianity than in Talmudic Judaism. Scriptural authority stood its ground, however, mostly thanks to the power of Jesus as the ultimate model. Judaism, as against this, set up as a model for imitation—the teacher. The authority of scripture was mediated through the polyphonic voice of tradition, yet it was expressed by a single individual: a teacher and not a priest or holy man.

I SUBMIT that in the long late antiquity, the complex interface between literacy and orality caused an extraordinary imbrication of scriptural and personal modes of authority in religions of the book; that is, among Jews and Christians. This relationship was contextualized as well by varying levels, among Christians and Jews, of integration to, or rejection of, surrounding culture. Speaking in a general sense, both scriptural and personal authority seem to have been more clearly expressed among Christians than among Jews. Among the latter, authority of both types remained more mediated. This variance in networks of authority can be considered one of the major structural differences between the two emerging religions.[27] Without doubt, it had a major impact on attitudes toward religious education among Jews and Christians.

CONCLUSION

Alexandria, Jerusalem, Baghdad

We have reached the end of our short trip around the scriptural universe of ancient Christianity. Let us then take stock. While our stargazing has been limited by several considerations, I hope that we have succeeded in training our sights on a major constellation: the mechanisms through which Greco-Roman culture was Christianized and the centrality of this fact for the new relations between religion and knowledge in late antiquity. We have seen how the complex creation of Christian culture was not only an affair of educated Greek Fathers and elevated Greek texts but also of Jews, monks, and heretics. As in other contexts, individuals from the cultural *limes* acted as cultural brokers, as agents of change. Indeed, it is as much at the margins of late ancient society as at its core that the mechanism of its transformation was situated.

Knowledge transmittal drove the cultural transformation in antiquity, but this transmittal was heavily indebted to the restructuring of knowledge according to new values. Like poetic creativity, cultural transformation draws a map of misreading, and its grammar cannot be studied in isolation from the history of religions. In Western history, as elsewhere, cultural change and religious revolution were frequent bedfellows. Among the major transformations of the attitude to books in late antiquity is that reading, as well as writing and copying, became for Christians a normative activity, a religious duty, infused with spiritual meaning. As much as holy men, holy books may be considered the iconic symbol of late ancient religion.

This book has assumed the hermeneutical principle of *perpetuum mobile,* with interpretive communities holding on to traces of different hermeneutical accretions, like so many layers of rock formation. Breakthroughs occur when an overwhelming urge is felt to return to the roots, to obliterate the accretions. It is at the moment of such breakthroughs that the concept of an implicit cultural memory receives its full meaning. Ideas and traditions may well be expunged from public memory, but they don't disappear from cultural memory, and remain, as older layers of a palimpsest, underlying the newer story. The old French dictum, "la culture, c'est ce qui reste quand on a tout oublié," ("culture is what remains after one has forgotten everything") holds true here. This unconscious cultural memory also underlies new interpretive traditions of the old biblical stories.

We have made use of the palimpsest metaphor to show that any new story is only the latest revision of an older one and that the previous versions, although they are no longer read or told, continue to echo. Moreover, this metaphor showcases the existence of two systems of religious memory: implicit memory functioning alongside explicit memory. Averil Cameron has pointed out how "the familiar term 'religion of the book' encompassed a whole world of writing and dissemination of religious texts, and that outside the Qur'anic context it must be understood in much wider terms than simply in relation to a set of scriptures."[1] Yet, the end of this book, and that of late antiquity, is not the end of the story.[2] We have watched act one in the "Great Game" between East and West in the formation of European culture, which began when Greece and Iran clashed in early antiquity. In the next act, Christianized Greco-Roman *paideia,* reformulated in the Syriac Academies, would be translated into Arabic, become the foundation of *adab* in the world of medieval Islam, and be reinterpreted by the sages of Baghdad. As it had been baptized, it would now become circumcised, and it is this new avatar that would be translated from Arabic into Latin in medieval Toledo.

According to a story reported in Ibn al-Kiftī's *Ta'rīkh al-Ḥukamā'* (*Chronicle of the Physicians*), after the conquest of Alexandria in 640 the Caliph Omar ordered Emir 'Amr Ibn al-'Ās to destroy the contents of the great library. The rationale, so the story goes, was that the books were either in agreement with the Qur'an, or contradicted it. They were, then, either superfluous or false, and in both cases should be destroyed.[3] Only the works of Aristotle, the sources tell us, escaped destruction, while all other works fed the stoves of the public baths during six long months. This legend was meant to set forth two claims. The first of these is that the Islamic Empire was built on a single book, a divine one that contained all wisdom. The second claim was that Islam was culturally autarkic; that is, excepting Aristotle there had been no transfer of knowledge from antiquity to early Islam. Both claims, whether Muslims made them (*in bonam partem*), or Christians (*in malam partem*), are patently false.

Crucial here is the perception, fostered by both sides, that the coming of Islam as a new player on the scene meant not only a fresh start in religious history, but also a radical departure from a revered cultural attitude, the wholesale rejection of a whole literary tradition. There is of course a grain of truth to such a narrative. The coming of Islam meant not only a new religion, which was to sweep far beyond the Near East in a series of whirlwind conquests, but also the linguistic ascendance of Arabic, which, after the Abbasid revolution, would replace Greek as the main official language in the areas taken over from the Roman Empire.[4] In the dialectics of religious relationship and intellectual exchanges between East and West, the great religious transformation of the Roman Empire can be understood, then, only through the profound impact of the Near East on the Greek world. The intellectual synthesis achieved in tenth-century Baghdad would represent the next major station in the great dialogue between East and West across the ages. This time, it would reflect the Greek impact on Arab culture.

Yet the vision of a radically new Arabic culture, built solely upon the Qur'an, is a far cry from the truth. For more than a century, until the Abbasid revolution, Greek was retained, at least side by side with Arabic, as the administrative language of the Umayyad Caliphate.[5] Under the new concept of *adab*, the Arabized ideals of *paideia* often reappear.[6] The central reference to Aristotle in Arabic literature is a striking exception to the overall disappearance of Greek literature in the Arabized *paideia*. It is a truism that it was largely through the Arabs that Greek philosophy was transmitted to Western Europe in the Middle Ages. Yet Aristotle was not translated directly from Greek into Arabic. It is mainly through Syriac and Pahlavi translations prepared for the curriculum in the Syriac late antique academies that those texts eventually made their way into Arabic.⁷ The so-called translation movement in Baghdad, which reached its apogee in the tenth century, had its roots in the Syriac academies, as well as in the monasteries of the Judean wilderness near Jerusalem, the locus of the first Arabic translations of the Bible in the seventh and eighth centuries, as well as in the Sasanian Empire.⁸ John of Damascus, whose father was a high-ranking official at the Caliph's court, still wrote in Greek. His student Theodore Abu Qurra, however, wrote Christian theological tracts in Arabic. Jews, like Christians, were active coauthors of this major chapter in the transfer of knowledge and passage of cultural contents between societies. Dāwūd ibn Marwān al-Muqammas, a figure from early ninth-century North Mesopotamia, stands as a superb example. Muqammas, born a Jew, converted to Christianity and studied at the Christian Academy of Nisibis, eventually returning to the religion of his youth. The first systematic Jewish thinker since Philo, Muqammas penned in Arabic the first Jewish theological *Summa*, which owed a great deal to his Christian education.⁹ His Bible commentaries, moreover (also a first for medieval Judaism) were straightforward translations from Syriac. Similarly, in the early tenth century, the Jewish theologian Sa'adia Gaon echoes in his works (in Arabic) whole passages of Syriac (Christian) theological texts.¹⁰ Polemics had long been a major mode of contact between religious communities in the late antique Mediterranean and Near East. However, there was another side of the polemical coin: the formation of a new mode of religiosity, established upon the synoptic presentation of opposing theological arguments. The literary genre of *Religionsgespräche* and the long tradition of *Questions and Answers* literature in late antiquity, reflect that religiosity.¹¹ The theological *Questions and Answers* literature had a long history within Christianity, both in Greek and in Syriac literature. Particularly significant here is the impact it had on the formation of Kalam, Islamic dialectic theology, which also retains a strong dialogical element, certainly in its early layers.¹² Thus, the term "Abrahamic triangle," while far from perfect, reasonably describes reality.

IN THE Near East on the eve of Islam, a mosaic of "midrashic communities" were telling a number of different stories. These tales were constructed from the same narrative kernels, organized slightly differently each time, in kaleidoscope fashion. The Semitist John Wansbrough demonstrated definitively that the midrashic, oral mode of scriptural hermeneutics, which permitted scriptural authority to be "naturally" channeled through charismatic authority, was central to the communities that would come to constitute the cradle of the Qur'an.[13] With the early development of Islam, the late antique triangle formed by pagans, Jews, and Christians would be transformed into a new hermeneutical triangle formed by Jews, Christians, and Muslims. Throughout the long Middle Ages, important Jewish communities lived (and sometimes even thrived) in the two theologico-political realms of the Islamicate world and Christendom, East and West. Together, and including these Jewish communities, they formed what may be called the "Abrahamic ecosystem." It is mainly within this ecosystem that cultural transmittal and religious interchange would take place from then on.

Notes

Acknowledgments

Index

NOTES

Introduction

1. On late antiquity and recent polemics about its historiography, see for instance Polymnia Athanassiadi, "Antiquité tardive: construction et déconstruction d'un modèle historiographique," Chapter I in her *Mutations of Hellenism in Late Antiquity* (Farnham: Variorum Ashgate, 2015). Cf. my review in *Bryn Mawr Classical Review*, 2016.01.19.
2. The bibliography is huge, and constantly growing. It would be futile to even attempt to offer updated references. I opt, therefore, to refer to the classical article of Carten Colpe, "Heilige Schriften," *Reallexikon für Antike und Christentum* 14 (1987), 184–223. For a less technical study, in English, see for instance John F. A. Sawyer, *Sacred Languages and Sacred Texts* (New York: Routledge, 1999).
3. On modes of religiosity in late antiquity, see Guy G. Stroumsa, *The Making of the Abrahamic Religions in Late Antiquity* (Oxford Studies in the Abrahamic Religions) (Oxford: Oxford University Press, 2015), 50–55.
4. On Marcion, see now Judith M. Lieu, *Marcion and the Making of a Heretic: God and Scripture in the Second Century* (Cambridge: Cambridge University Press, 2015).
5. Guy G. Stroumsa, *The End of Sacrifice: Religious Transformations in Late Antiquity* (Chicago: Chicago University Press, 2009). The book was originally published as *La fin du sacrifice: mutations religieuses de l'antiquité tardive* (Paris: Odile Jacob, 2004).
6. The privatization of ritual and the transformation of sacred space are confirmed by the testimony of archaeology, as shown by Kim Bowes, for whom the Christianization of the aristocracy goes hand in hand with the development of private rituals. See K. Bowes, *Private Worship, Public Values, and*

Religious Change in Late Antiquity (Cambridge: Cambridge University Press, 2008).

7. Rémi Brague, *Modérément moderne* (Paris: Flammarion, 2014), 238–246. Cf. Harold Bloom, *A Map of Misreading* (Oxford: Oxford University Press, 1975).
8. On the idea of a religious revolution in late antiquity, see Guy G. Stroumsa, *Barbarian Philosophy: The Religious Revolution of Early Christianity* (Tübingen: Mohr Siebeck, 1999).
9. On Patristic ambivalence about Greek *paideia,* see the fine analysis of Monique Alexandre, "La culture grecque, servante de la foi: de Philon d'Alexandrie aux Pères grecs," in Arnaud Perrot, ed., *Les chrétiens et l'hellénisme: identités religieuses et culture grecque dans l'antiquité tardive* (Paris: Ecole Normale Supérieure, 2012); see also, in the same volume, Olivier Munnich, "La place de l'Hellénisme dans l'autodéfinition du christianisme," 61–122.
10. On religious mobility in the Roman Empire, see for instance Simon Price, "Religious Mobility in the Roman Empire," *Journal of Roman Studies* 102 (2012), 1–19.
11. See Stroumsa, *The Making of the Abrahamic Religions in Late Antiquity,* Introduction. On the complex problems related to monotheism in late antiquity, see for instance Athanassiadi, "The gods are God: polytheistic cult and monotheistic theology in the world of late antiquity," Chapter IV in her *Mutations of Hellenism in Late Antiquity.*
12. See Robert N. Bellah and Hans Joas, eds., *The Axial Age and Its Consequences* (Cambridge, MA: Harvard University Press, 2012), and Guy G. Stroumsa, "Robert Bellah on the Origins of Religion—A Critical Review," *Revue de l'Histoire des Religions* 229 (2012), 467–477.
13. See Peter Jackson and Anna-Pya Sjödin, eds., *Philosophy and the End of Sacrifice: Disengaging Ritual in Ancient India, Greece and Beyond* (The Study of Religion in a Global Context; Sheffield: Equinox, 2016).
14. See for instance Sanjay Subrahmanyam, *Explorations in Connected History: From the Tagus to the Ganges* (Delhi: Oxford University Press, 2004) *and Explorations in Connected History: Mughals and Franks* (Delhi: Oxford University Press, 2004).
15. See the caveat raised by Eric Rebillard, *Christians and Their Many Identities in Late Antiquity, North Africa, 200–450 C.E.* (Ithaca, NY: Cornell University Press, 2012), where, speaking of "beyond groupism," he proposes to deal with the interactions of religious groups rather than to study their activities in isolation. The intense turn toward the social sciences and social history in the study of early Christianity since the 1970s and 1980s has brought to a constant refining of our toolkit. Hence, networks of communities have become more and more commonly used in order to understand interaction between them. See, for instance, Stanley Stowers, "The Concept of 'Community' and the History of Early Christianity," *Method and Theory in the Study of Religion*

23 (2011), 238–356. In a sense, the present work is an attempt to apply the concept of network also to scriptures.
16. We owe the concept of a "theological triangle" to Philippe Borgeaud; see his *Aux origines de l'histoire des religions* (Paris: Seuil, 2004), 83–87.
17. Guy G. Stroumsa, *The Making of the Abrahamic Religions in Late Antiquity*, 189–198.
18. I use "whirlpool effect" as defined by Sarah Stroumsa, "Whirlpool Effects and Religious Studies: A Response to Guy G. Stroumsa," in V. Krech and M. Steinicke, eds., *Dynamics in the History of Religions between Asia and Europe: Encounters, Notions and Comparative Perspectives* (Boston: Brill, 2012), 159–162.
19. For a fresh application of the network approach to ancient religious history, see Anna Collar, *Religious Networks in the Roman Empire: The Spread of New Ideas* (Cambridge: Cambridge University Press, 2013).
20. Similarly, I have not endeavored to refer in the footnotes to all relevant primary texts and secondary literature, but only to those texts and scholarly works I have found more directly relevant for my present purpose.

1. A Scriptural Galaxy

1. Andreas Bendlin, "Wer braucht "heilige Schriften? Die Textbezogenheit der Religionsgeschichte und das 'Reden über die Götter' in der griechisch-römische Antike," in C. Bultmann et al., eds., *Heilige Schriften: Ursprung, Geltung und Gebrauch* (Münster: Aschendorff, 2005), 205–228. See also, Jörg Rüpke, "Heilige Schriften und Buchreligionen : Überlegungen zu Begriffen und Methoden," in Christoph Bultmann, Claus-Peter März, Vasilios N. Makrides, eds., *Heilige Schriften: Ursprung, Geltung und Gebrauch* (Münster: Aschendorff, 2005), 191–204. Another version of this chapter will appear in Josef Lössl and Nicholas Baker-Brian, eds., *A Companion to Late Antiquity* (Hoboken, NJ: Blackwell, 2016 [in press]).
2. See in particular Urs App, *The Birth of Orientalism* (Philadelphia: Pennsylvania University Press, 2010).
3. Jack Goody, *The Power of the Written Tradition* (Washington, D.C.: Smithsonian Institution Press, 2000).
4. See for instance Joachim Schaper, "Scriptural Turn" und Monotheismus: Überlegungen zu einer (nicht ganz) neuen These," in J. Schaper, ed., *Die Textualisierung der Religion* (Forschungen zum Alten Testament, 62; Tübingen: Mohr Siebeck, 2009), 276–291.
5. For a recent authoritative and comparative presentation of the status and role of scriptures in the religions of the Book, see F. E. Peters, *The Voice, The Word, The Books: The Sacred Scriptures of the Jews, Christians and Muslims* (Princeton, NJ: Princeton University Press, 2007).
6. Jan Bremmer, "From Holy Book to Holy Bible: An Itinerary from Ancient Greece to Modern Islam via Second Temple Judaism and Early Christianity,"

in Mladen Popovic, ed., *Authoritative Scriptures in Ancient Judaism* (Leiden: Brill, 2010), 327–360.
7. Mary Beard, "Writing and Religion," in Sarah Iles Johnson, ed., *Religions of the Ancient World.* (Cambridge, MA: Harvard University Press, 2004), 127–138.
8. Marshall McLuhan, *The Gutenberg Galaxy: The Making of Typographical Man* (Toronto: Toronto University Press, 1962).
9. See Larry W. Hurtado, *The Earliest Christian Artifacts: Manuscripts and Christian Origins* (Grand Rapids, MI: Eerdmans, 2006). On magical uses of scriptures, see Christoph Markschies, "Heilige Texte als magische Texte," in A. Kablitz and Ch. Markschies, eds., *Religion und Rationalität* (Berlin: de Gruyter, 2013), 105–120.
10. Guglielmo Cavallo, "Lire, écrire et mémoriser les Saintes Ecritures," in Luce Giard et Christian Jacob, ed., *Des Alexandries, II: Les métamorphoses du lecteur* (Paris: Bibliothèque Nationale de France, 2003), 87–101.
11. Judith Herrin, "Book Burning as Purification," in Philip Rousseau and Manolis Papoutsakis, eds., *Transformations of Late Antiquity* (Farnham: Ashgate, 2009), 205–222.
12. The literature here is huge. From the preeminent scholar in the field, Guglielmo Cavallo, see for instance, "Du volumen au codex: la lecture dans le monde romain," in G. Cavallo and Roger Chartier, eds., *Histoire de la lecture dans le monde occidental* (Paris: Seuil, 1997), 85–114. See also, G. Cavallo, "Libri, lettura e biblioteche nella tarda antichità: un panorama e qualche riflessione," *Antiquité Tardive* 18 (2010), 9–19. For a clear presentation of the issues, see Hurtado, *The Oldest Christian Articrafts,* 61–83.
13. E. J. Kenney, "Books and Readers in the Roman World," in E. J. Kenney, ed., *Cambridge History of Classical Literature,* vol. II (Cambridge: Cambridge University Press, 1982), 3–32, esp. 20.
14. On libraries in the ancient world, see, for instance, Jason König, Katerina Oikonomopoulou and Greg Woolf, eds., *Ancient Libraries* (Cambridge: Cambridge University Press, 2013). One should note that of the twenty-one chapters dealing with libraries in the Greek and Roman worlds, not a single one is devoted to the question of Christian libraries.
15. William Allen Johnson and Holt N. Parker, eds., *Ancient Literacies: the Culture of Reading in Greece and Rome* (Oxford: Oxford University Press, 2009).
16. The expression "textual communities" was coined by Brian Stock for medieval monasteries; see Stock, "Textual Communities: Judaism, Christianity, and the Definitional Problem," in B. Stock, *Listening for the Text: On the Uses of the Past* (Baltimore: Johns Hopkins University Press, 1990); cf. "interpretive communities," an expression famously coined by the specialist of English literature Stanley Fish.
17. William V. Harris, *Ancient Literacy* (Cambridge, MA: Harvard University Press, 1989).
18. See note 7.

19. See note 12.
20. There were, however, also some disadvantages to the new form of books. While scrolls offered a "panoramic" view of the text, having to turn pages meant getting a broken text. As codices became bigger and bigger with time, they were sometimes made to be consulted rather than to be read.
21. Martin Wallraff, *Kodex und Kanon: Das Buch im frühen Christentum* (Hans-Lietzmann Vorlesungen 12; Berlin: de Gruyter, 2013).
22. See, for instance, Jan Assmann, *The Price of Monotheism* (Stanford, CA: Stanford University Press, 2010) [originally published as: *Die Mosaische Unterscheidung, oder der Preis des Monotheismus* (Munich: Carl Hanser, 2003), 145–151.
23. Reading the Psalms would remain central through the centuries; see for instance Derek Krueger, *Liturgical Subjects: Christian Ritual, biblical Narrative, and the Formation of the Self in Byzantium* (Philadelphia: Pennsylvania University Press, 2014), 17–23, on the Psalms and the penitential self. See further Georgi R. Parpulov, "Psalters and Personal Piety in Byzantium," in Paul Magdalino and Robert Nelson, eds., *The Old Testament in Byzantium* (Washington, D.C.: Dumbarton Oaks, 2010), 77–105. Cf. David Brakke's Review of Brouria Bitton-Ashkelony and Lorenzo Perrone, eds., *Between Personal and Institutional Religion,: Self, Doctrine and Practice in Late Antiquity, Medieval Review* 15.6.40 (online). István Czachesz is doing important work on cognitive aspects of Early Christian writing. See for instance his "Rewriting and Textual Fluidity in Antiquity: Exploring the socio-cultural and psychological context of earliest Christian literacy," in J. H. F. Dijkstra, J. E. A. Kroesen and Y. B. Kuyper, eds., *Myths, Martyrs, and Modernity* (Leiden: Brill, 2010), 425–441.
24. On the exegetical nature of late ancient culture, see Hervé Inglebert, Introduction to Scott Fitzgerald Johnson, ed., *Oxford Handbook of Late Antiquity* (Oxford: Oxford University Press, 2012), and Garth Fowden, *Before and After Muhammad* (Princeton, NJ: Princeton University Press, 2014), Chapters 5 and 6.
25. Doron Mendels, *The Media Revolution of Early Christianity: An Essay on Eusebius'* Ecclesiastical History (Grand Rapids, MI: Eerdmans, 1999).
26. On Jewish literacy, see Catherine Heszer, *Jewish Literacy in Roman Palestine*, as well as her "Crossing Enemy Lines: Network Connections Between Palestinian and Babylonian Sages in Late Antiquity," *Journal for the Study of Judaism* 46 (2015), 224–250.
27. See AnneMarie Leuijendijk, *Greetings in the Lord: Early Christians and the Oxyrhynchus Papyri* (Harvard Theological Studies 60; Cambridge, MA: Harvard University Press, 2008), Chapter 5: "The Business of the Bishop: Fundraising, Travel, and Book Production."
28. Brian Stock, *Implications of Literacy, Written Language and Models of Interpretation in the Eleventh and Twelfth Centuries* (Princeton, NJ: Princeton University Press, 1983).

29. William A. Johnson, *Readers and Reading Culture in the High Roman Empire: A Study of Elite Communities* (Oxford: Oxford University Press, 2010).
30. Claudia Rapp, "Holy Texts, Holy Men, and Holy Scribes: Aspects of Scriptural Holiness in Late Antiquity," in William E. Klingshirn and Linda Safran, eds., *The Early Christian Book* (Washington, D.C.: Catholic University of America Press, 2007), 194–222.
31. Anne S. Kreps, *The Crucified Book, Textual Authority and the Gospel of Truth* (Doctoral Thesis, University of Michigan, Ann Arbor, 2013). Cf. Chagall's paintings of the crucified Jew with scrolls.
32. Jörg Rüpke, *Von Jupiter zu Christus: Religionsgeschichte in römischer Zeit* (Darmstadt: Wissenschaftliche Buchgesellschaft, 2011), Chapter 9: "Buchreligionen als Reichsreligionen? Lokale Grenzen überregionaler religiöser Kommunikation," 133–141.
33. See Chapter 8.
34. See Guy G. Stroumsa, *The End of Sacrifice*, 36–38.
35. Shaul Shaked, "Reflections on Modes of Transmission in Late Antiquity," in Julia Rubanovich, ed., *Orality and Textuality in the Iranian World: Patterns of Interaction across the Centuries* (Jerusalem Studies in Religion and Culture 19; Leiden: Brill, 2015), 43–62. Shaked adds that while most affairs of importance, in late antiquity, were concluded and sealed in writing, not everything was considered to be fit for writing, a fact that explains the interplay between teaching and esotericism, and also bears upon the concept of an "oral book."
36. See Guy G. Stroumsa, "Early Christianity: A Religion of the Book?" in Margalit Finkelberg and Guy G. Stroumsa, eds., *Homer, The Bible, and Beyond: Literary and Religious Canons in the Ancient World* (Jerusalem Studies in Religion and Culture, 2; Leiden: Brill, 2003), 153–173.
37. G. G. Stroumsa, "Mystère juif et mystère chrétien: le mot et la chose," in Laurent Pernot, Yves Lehmann, Marc Philonenko, eds., *Les mystères: nouvelles perspectives. Entretiens de Strasbourg* (Recherches sur les Rhétoriques Religieuses; Turnhout: Brepols, 2016 [in press]).
38. Sarah I. Johnson, "Sacred Texts and Canonicity," in S. I. Johnson, ed., *Religions of the Ancient World*. (Cambridge, MA: Harvard University Press, 2004), 622–639.
39. See for instance Lourdes Garcia Urena, "The Book of Revelation: A Written Text Towards the Oral Performance," in Ruth Scodel, ed., *Between Orality and Literacy: Communication and Adaptation in Antiquity: Orality and Literacy in the Ancient World*, volume 10 (Mnemosyne Supplements 367; Leiden: Brill, 2014), 308–330.
40. Wilfred Cantwell Smith, *What Is Scripture? A Comparative Approach*. (Minneapolis: Fortress Press, 1993).
41. The Talmudic texts, however, are a complicated instance, as they may well reflect a legal as well as a religious codification. Despite some older works, the comparative study of the redaction of the Talmudim and the Roman legal codices remains to a great extent a desideratum.

42. Robert Lamberton, *Homer the Theologian: Neoplatonist Allegorical Reading and the Growth of the Epic Tradition* (Berkeley: University of California Press, 1986).
43. See Polymnia Athanassiadi, "Apamea and the Chaldean Oracles," in her *Mutations of Hellenism in Late Antiquity* (Farnham: Variorum Ashgate, 2015), V, 117 ff. See also her *La lutte pour l'orthodoxie dans le platonisme tardif, de Numénius à Damascius* (Paris: Belles Lettres, 2006), 31–70. For Athanasiadi, the *Chaldean Oracles* were viewed as their sacred scriptures by the late Neoplatonists.
44. Since the days of Müller, historians of religions have noted striking similarities, in either content or structure, between various literary corpora in different religious traditions. They use the Islamic concept of "peoples of the Book" in a generic sense quite naturally, without reflecting upon its significance or applicability. Rightly or wrongly, the modern concept seems to be used as a more "neutral" and less loaded term than "monotheism" when referring to Judaism, Christianity, and Islam. On Müller, see Lourens van den Bosch, *Friedrich Max Müller: A Life Devoted to the Humanities* (Studies in the History of Religions 94; Leiden: Brill, 2002).
45. *Ahl al-kitāb* generally refers to Jews, to Christians, and at times to Jews and Christians together, in the Qur'an.
46. I am unaware of any study of the theme. Moshe Halbertal, *People of the Book: Canon, Meaning, and Authority* (Cambridge, MA: Harvard, 1997) does not discuss its origins.
47. On the possible contacts between Manichaeism and the earliest strata of Islam, see M. Gil, "The Medinan Opposition to the Prophet," *Jerusalem Studies in Arabic and Islam* 10 (1987), 65–97, and *idem*, "The Creed of Abu Amer," *Israel Oriental Studies* 12 (1992), 9–58.
48. See Chapter 4.
49. Guy G. Stroumsa, *Barbarian Philosophy: The Religious Revolution of Early Christianity* (Tübingen: Mohr Siebeck, 1999), "The Christian Hermeneutical Revolution and Its Double Helix," 27–43.
50. Maren Niehoff, *Jewish Exegesis and Homeric Scholarship in Alexandria* (Cambridge: Cambridge University Press, 2011).
51. On Nisibis and Vivarium, see Chapter 6.
52. For a comparative analysis of Rabbinic and Hellenic education, see Catherine Hezser, "The Torah versus Homer: Jewish and Greco-Roman Education in Late Roman Palestine," in Matthew Ryan Hauge and Andrew W. Pitts, eds., *Ancient Education and Early Christianity* (London: Bloomsbury, 2016), 5–24.

2. A Divine Palimpsest

1. "What is the human brain, if not an immense and natural palimpsest? My brain is a palimpsest, and so is yours, reader. . . . And the divine palimpsest created by God, which is our incommensurable memory. . . ."

2. Yadin Dudai and Micah Edelson, "Personal Memory: Is it personal, is it memory?" *Memory Studies* (2016), in press. The material of this chapter forms the bulk of "Religious Memory between Orality and Writing," *Memory Studies* (2016), in press.
3. See Maurice Halbwachs, *La mémoire collective*, éd. crit. G. Namer (Paris: Albin Michel, 1997) [1st. ed. 1950].
4. Jan Assmann, *Religion und kulturelles Gedächtnis* (Munich: Beck, 2000). Cf. Jan Assmann, "Gedächtnis," *Religion in Geschichte und Gegenwart* (=*RGG*) 3 (2000), 523–525. See also, Michael Welker, "Memory, Imagination, and the Human Spirit," *Memory Studies* (2016), in press.
5. M. Halbwachs, *La mémoire collective*, 96.
6. Larry Squire and Eric Kandel, *Memory: From Mind to Molecules* (Greenwoods, CO: Roberts, 2009 [2nd ed.]).
7. Maurice Halbwachs, *Les cadres sociaux de la mémoire* (Paris: Félix Alcan, 1925), 193 and 221.
8. Yadin Dudai, *Memory from A to Z: Keywords, Concepts, and Beyond* (Oxford: Oxford University Press, 2002).
9. M. Halbwachs, *Les cadres sociaux de la mémoire*, 193.
10. M. Halbwachs, *La mémoire collective*, 99.
11. Ibid., 52.
12. Ibid., 98.
13. See Danielle Hervieu-Léger in Maurice Halbwachs, *La topographie légendaire des Evangiles en Terre Sainte: étude de mémoire collective*, éd. M. Jaisson (Paris: Presses Universitaires de France/CNRS, 2008), 37 [Halbwachs's book was first published in 1941]. As evidenced in the first chapters of Marc Bloch's *La société féodale* (first published in 1939), the study of historical and social geography was particularly strong in France at the time. (I owe this remark to Brian Stock.)
14. Danielle Hervieu-Léger, *Religion as a Chain of Memory* (New Brunswick, NJ: Rutgers University Press, 2000).
15. M. Halbwachs, *La topographie légendaire des Evangiles en Terre Sainte*, 47.
16. Alan Kirk and Tom Thatcher, eds., *Memory, Tradition, and Text: Uses of the Past in Early Christianity* (Leiden: Brill, 2005).
17. Jan Assmann, "Gedächtnis." See also Carlo Severi, "La mémoire rituelle: expérience, tradition, historicité," in A. Becquelin and A. Molinié, éds., *Mémoire de la tradition* (Société d'ethnologie, Université de Paris X Nanterre, Nanterre, 1993), 347–363. See also, Scott Atran, *In Gods we Trust: The Evolutionary Landscape of Religion* (Oxford: Oxford University Press, 2002). Like other scholars, Assmann prefers to reserve "collective memory" for a more homogenized, often ideological type of memory.
18. The question of transgenerational religious memory begs to be broached. Can the impact of an event be transmitted to future generations? This question, a far from trivial one, has until very recently remained in the domain of science fiction. But researchers have shown how long-term memory can

modify brain structure, and epigenetics today refers to a "cellular memory" and to the transmission between generations of nonbiological characters. Nonetheless, the results of this inquiry remain highly speculative.
19. Harvey Whitehouse, "Modes of Religiosity: Towards a Cognitive Explanation of the Sociopolitical Dynamics of Religion," in *Method and Theory in the Study of Religion* 14 (2002), 293–315. See G. G. Stroumsa, *The Making of the Abrahamic Religions in Late Antiquity* (Oxford: Oxford University Press, 2015), 50–55.
20. See Luther H. Martin and Panayotis Pachis, eds., *Imagistic Traditions in the Graeco-Roman World: A Cognitive Modeling of History of Religious Research* (Thessaloniki: Equinox, 2009).
21. Harvey Whitehouse and James Laidlaw, eds., *Ritual and Memory: Towards a Comparative Anthropology of Religion* (Walnut Creek, CA: Alta Mira, 2004).
22. Jack Goody, *The Interface between the Written and the Oral* (Cambridge: Cambridge University Press, 1987), chapter 1.
23. Jack Goody, *The Power of the Written Tradition* (Washington, D.C.: Smithsonian Institution Press, 2000).
24. Ibid.; see also, Walter J. Ong, *Orality and Literacy: The Technologizing of the Word* (London: Routledge, 1988) [1st. ed. 1982].
25. Philippe Borgeaud, "Pour une approche anthropologique de la mémoire religieuse" in Borgeaud, éd., *La mémoire des religions* (Geneva: Labor et fides, 1988), 7–20. See also, Fritz Stolz, "Tradition orale et tradition écrite dans les religions de la Mésopotamie antique," in Borgeaud, éd., *La mémoire des religions*, 21–35.
26. W. Ong, *Orality and Literacy*.
27. Josef Lössl, "An Inextinguishable Memory: "Pagan" Past and Presence in Early Christian Writing," in Carol Harrison, Caroline Humfress, Isabella Sandwell, eds., *Being Christian in Late Antiquity* (Oxford: Oxford University Press, 2014), 74–89. See also, Guy G. Stroumsa, "Cultural Memory in Early Christianity: Clement of Alexandria and the History of Religions," in S. N. Eisenstadt, J. P. Arnason and B. Wittrock, eds., *Axial Civilizations and World History* (Jerusalem Studies in Religion and Culture 4; Leiden: Brill, 2005), 293–315.
28. On *figura*, see in particular Erich Auerbach, "Figura," originally published in his *Neue Dantestudien* (Istanbul, 1935), and in English in his *Scenes from the Drama of European Literature* (New York: Meridian Books, 1959), 11–78. Thanks to Brian Stock for suggesting the reference to this seminal text.
29. Michel Tardieu, "Théorie de la mémoire et fonction prophétique," in Philippe Borgeaud, ed., *La mémoire des religions*, 105–113.
30. See Chapter 5.
31. On the development of silent reading in the Middle Ages, see, for instance, Paul Saenger, *Space Between Words: The Origins of Silent Reading* (Stanford, CA: Stanford University Press, 1997).

32. Philippe Borgeaud, "Pour une approche anthropologique de la mémoire religieuse" in Borgeaud, ed., *La mémoire des religions*, 7–20.
33. Einar Thomassen, "Some Notes on the Development of Christian Ideas about the Canon," in E. Thomassen, ed., *Canon and Canonicity: The Formation and Use of Scripture* (Copenhagen: Museum Tusculanum Press, 2010), 3–29.
34. Doron Mendels, *Memory in Jewish, Pagan and Christian Societies of the Graeco-Roman World: Fragmented Memory, Comprehensive Memory, Collective Memory* (London: T. & T. Clark, 2004).
35. Yosef Hayim Yerushalmi, *Zakhor: Jewish History and Jewish Memory* (Seattle: University of Washington Press, 1996) [1st. ed. 1982].
36. Jean-Claude Basset, "L'anamnèse: aux sources de la tradition chrétienne." in Philippe Borgeaud, ed., *La mémoire des religions*, 91–104. See also, Andrew C. Itter, *Esoteric Teaching in the Stromateis of Clement of Alexandria* (Supplements to *Vigiliae Christianae* 97: Leiden: Brill, 2009).
37. Birger Gerhardsson, *Memory and Manuscript: Oral Tradition and Written Transmission in Rabbinic Judaism and Early Christianity*, ASNU 22 (Copenhagen: Ejnar Munksgaard, 1961).
38. In a recently published bestseller, the psychologist Daniel Kahneman demonstrated two distinct thought patterns; one more intuitive, or fast, the other more analytical, or slow. Kahneman argued that we make simultaneous and constant use of these systems (D. Kahneman, *Thinking Fast and Slow* [London: Penguin, 2011]). It would be interesting to investigate a similar kind of dual functioning in the modes of religious memory.
39. William V. Harris, *Ancient Literacy* (Cambridge, MA: Harvard University Press, 1991).
40. Eric R. Kandel, *In Search of Memory: The Emergence of a New Science of Mind* (New York: Norton, 2006).
41. Sigmund Freud, *Fragen der Gesellschaft; Ursprünge der Religion* (Frankfurt am Main: Fischer, 1974).
42. Guy G. Stroumsa, *The Making of the Abrahamic Religions in Late Antiquity* (Oxford: Oxford University Press, 2015).

3. Religious Revolution and Cultural Change

1. Jerome, *Letter* 22. 30; see J. N. D. Kelly, *Jerome: His Life, Writings and Controversies* (Peabody, MA: Hendrickson, 1998 [1975]), 42. The story is so powerfully told by Jerome that some scholars have thought the story to have rhetorical value only, but there is no reason to doubt its authenticity. A former version of this chapter was published in French as "Les sages sémitisés: nouvel *ethos* et mutation religieuse dans l'empire romain," in Corinne Bonnet and Laurent Bricault, eds., *Panthée: Religious Transformations in the Graeco-Roman Empire* (Leiden: Brill, 2013), 293–307.
2. See the Introduction, and Guy G. Stroumsa, *Barbarian Philosophy: The Religious Revolution of Early Christianity* (Tübingen: Mohr Siebeck, 1999).

3. Philippe Borgeaud, *Aux origines de l'histoire des religions* (Paris: Seuil, 2004), 83–87.
4. The relationship between either two of the sides of the triangle are best understood when one does not forget the third side. Was not Philo considered, after all, to have been the first among the Fathers of the Church?
5. H.-I. Marrou, *Histoire de l'éducation dans l'antiquité* (Paris: Seuil, 1948); Eng. transl.: *History of Education in Antiquity* (New York: Sheed and Ward, 1956). See also, P. Brown, *Power and Persuasion in Late Antiquity: Towards a Christian Empire* (Madison: University of Wisconsin Press, 1992), 36.
6. On which, see Christoph Markschies, *Does it Make Sense to Speak about a "Hellenization of Christianity" in Antiquity?* (Dutch Lectures in Patristics 1; Leiden: Brill, 2011).
7. Peter Brown, "Late Antiquity and Islam: Parallels and Contrast," in Barbara Daly Metcalf, ed., *Moral Conduct and Authority: The Place of Adab in South Asian Islam* (Berkeley: University of California Press, 1977), 23–27.
8. See Samuel Rubenson, "Christian Asceticism and the Emergence of the Monastic Tradition," in Vincent Wimbush and Richard Valantasis, eds., *Asceticism* (Oxford: Oxford University Press, 1998), 49–57; Samuel Rubenson, "Philosophy and Simplicity: The Problem of Classical Education in Early Christian Biography," in Tomas Hagg and Philip Rousseau, eds., *Greek Biography and Panegyric in Late Antiquity,* (Berkeley: University of California Press, 2000), 110–139. See also, Elizabeth A. Clark, *Reading Renunciation: Asceticism and Scripture in Early Christianity* (Princeton, NJ: Princeton University Press, 1999), where Clark studies, *inter alia,* aspects of reading in early Eastern monasticism.
9. As argued by Tim Whitmarsh, *Greek Literature and the Roman Empire: The Politics of Imitation* (Oxford: Oxford University Press, 2001), 91, referring to *Vit. Pyth.* 44.
10. See Christoph Markschies, *Kaiserzeitliche christliche Theologie und ihre Institutionen: Prolegomena zu einer Geschichte der antiken christlichen Theologie* (Tübingen: Mohr Siebeck, 2007), 43–109.
11. I am grateful to my colleague David Satran for having shared with me the manuscript of his *In the Image of Origen: Eros, Virtue and Constraint in the Early Christian Academy* (Berkeley: University of California Press, in press), which offers a close reading and in-depth analysis of Gregory Thaumaturgus's *Panegyric* of Origen.
12. See, for instance, Sara Rappe, "The New Math: How to Add and to Substract Pagan Elements in Christian Education," in Yun Lee Too, ed., *Education in Greek and Roman Antiquity* (Leiden: Brill, 2001), 405–432.
13. He had even less interest in other educational patterns, such as that of Talmudic Judaism. In this book, Marrou was still following the conception that had sustained his doctoral thesis, *Saint Augustin et la fin de la culture antique*. (Paris: de Boccard, 1938), informed by a sense of the ending of an era. The work offered tremendous insights, however, one of which was to

the recognition of the fact that pagans and Christians shared in the traditional forms of *paideia*. Indeed, Marrou was seeking to understand the *final stages* of ancient culture in the late Roman Empire, rather than its transformation under the impact of Christianity.

14. Hervé Inglebert, *Interpretatio Christiana: les mutations des savoirs (cosmographie, géographie, ethnographie, histoire) dans l'Antiquité chrétienne, 30–630 après J.C.* (Paris: Etudes Augustiniennes, 2001).
15. One way for the Christians to counter the charge that they were uneducated was to devalue formal education. This was often done, even when they themselves, like Origen for instance, were highly educated.
16. Peter Garnsey and Caroline Humfress, *The Evolution of the Late Antique World* (Cambridge: Cambridge University Press, 2001). See p. 151 in the French translation, *L'évolution du monde de l'antiquité tardive* (Paris: La Découverte, 2004).
17. See Leonardo Lugaresi, *Il Teatro di Dio: Il problema degli spettacoli nel cristianesimo antico (II–IV secolo)* (Brescia: Morcelliana, 2008).
18. Guy G. Stroumsa, *Barbarian Philosophy: The Religious Revolution of Early Christianity* (Tübingen: Mohr Siebeck, 1999), chapter 10, 168–190. The chapter had originally been published in 1990.
19. See in particular Ramsey MacMullen, *Christianizing the Roman Empire, (A.D. 100–400)* (New Haven, CT: Yale University Press, 1984).
20. H. Inglebert, "Introduction," in Hervé Inglebert, Sylvain Destephen et Bruno Dumézil, eds., *Le problème de la christianisation du monde antique* (Paris: Picard, 2010), 7–17.
21. Susanne K. Langer, *Philosophy in a New Key: A Study of Symbolism in Reason, Rite and Art* (Cambridge, MA: Harvard University Press, 1942).
22. Among his many books, see especially Pierre Hadot, *Qu'est-ce que la philosophie antique?* (Paris: Gallimard, 1995). On the relationship between Christianity and philosophy, see, for instance, Winrich Löhr, "Christianity as Philosophy: Problems and Perspectives of an Ancient Intellectual Project," *Vigiliae Christianae* 64 (2010), 160–188.
23. The first English edition dates of 1911; the French original was published in 1906 (the book's chapters were originally delivered as lectures at the Collège de France in 1905).
24. André-Jean Festugière, *La révélation d'Hermès Trismégiste, vol. I: L'astrologie et les sciences occultes* (Paris: Gabalda, 1943), 20.
25. It is perhaps symptomatic that the Belgian Cumont retained more common sense than the French Dominican Festugière. Indeed, the schism between classics and theology, which existed since the early nineteenth century, had been radicalized in France by the suppression of the Faculties of Theology and the separation between Church and state.
26. On the question of Christianity as model or exception as an "oriental religion," see Christoph Auffarth, "Les religions orientales dans le monde grec et romain," *Trivium* 4 (2009) (http://trivium.revues.org/3370, accessed Oc-

tober 2, 2009). German original in C. Bonnet, S. Ribichini, D. Steuernagel, eds., *Religioni in contatto nel Mediterraneo antico* (*Mediterranea* 4 [2007]; Pisa: Fabrizzio Serra, 2008), 333–356.

27. See Stephen Mitchell, *A History of the Later Roman Empire, A.D. 284–641: The Transformation of the Ancient World* (Malden, MA: Blackwell, 2007). In his seminal work, *Gnosis und spätantiker Geist*, Hans Jonas sought to identify the ethos of late antiquity. In the first volume, published in 1934, Jonas insisted upon the *Geworfenheit*, the subjective state of man being "thrown into the world." *Geworfenheit* was of course a concept fundamental for the existential philosophy of his teacher, Heidegger. For Jonas, Gnostic texts from the early centuries of the Common Era reflected a sense of *Geworfenheit*, which he considered to be typical of late antiquity, its *Zeitgeist*, partaken by different intellectual and religious system under the Empire. Claiming that the Gnostics and Plotinus shared the same basic attitude, however, was less than fully convincing, as this entailed ignoring the fact that Plotinus had spent many efforts fighting the Gnostics, whom he considered to be nothing less than intellectual perverts. For Jonas, this *Zeitgeist* was originally expressed by a small minority of intellectuals in the globalized *oikoumenē* of the Roman Empire. Similarly, E. R. Dodds could explain, in *Pagan and Christian in an Age of Anxiety*, a book published in 1965 (Cambridge: Cambridge University Press), at the time of the great fear, in the West, of a nuclear apocalypse, how the religious radicalism of the early monastic movement reflected the deep crisis of the third century.
28. Werner Jaeger, *Early Christianity and Greek Paideia* (Cambridge, MA: Harvard University Press, 1961).
29. Jaeger refers here to Josephus, *Contra Apionem*, II. 171.
30. David Dawson has criticized Jaeger's conception of the relationship between Greek *paideia* and early Christianity. For Dawson, it is a mistake to position Christians (even with their religion) outside "Greek culture." Dawson proposes, rather, to see the conflict between early Christian and late Hellenic thinkers as a contest between different participants of a common Greek culture, over competing constructions of their identity, as authorized by alternative religious texts. Although much is dated in Jaeger's approach, this particular criticism strikes me as unsatisfactory. The refusal to recognize a religious realm for Christianity that remained independent from Greco-Roman culture stems, I think, from mental schemes inherited from Richard Niehbur's *Christ and Culture*, and ignores the weight of its Jewish roots in the early developments of Christianity. See David Dawson, "Christian Teaching," in Frances Young, Lewis Ayres, Andrew Louth, eds., *The Cambridge History of Early Christian Literature* (Cambridge: Cambridge University Press, 2004), 222–238. It is interesting to recall that the twelfth-century Jewish thinker Maimonides already noted that early Christian theologians made good use of philosophical thought patterns when addressing pagan audiences.

31. On the "true doctrine" common to the philosophers of all nations, see, for instance, Michael Frede, "Celsus' Attack on the Christians," in Jonathan Barnes and Miriam Griffin, eds., *Philosophia Togata II: Plato and Aristotle at Rome* (Oxford: Oxford University Press, 1997), 218–240, as well as his "Origen's Treatise *Against Celsus*," in Mark Edwards, Martin Goodman and Simon Price, in association with Christopher Rowland, eds., *Apologetics in the Roman Empire: Pagans, Jews, and Christians* (Oxford: Oxford University Press, 1999), 131–155. See also Chapter 7.
32. On Porphyry, see in particular Aaron P. Johnson, *Religion and Identity in Porphyry of Tyre: The Limits of Hellenism in Late Antiquity* (Cambridge: Cambridge University Press, 2013). I am indebted to Aaron Johnson for having provided me with the text of his important study ahead of publication. See also, Jeremy M. Schott, *Christianity, Empire, and the Making of Religion in Late Antiquity* (Philadelphia: University of Pennsylvania Press, 2008), as well as Zlatko Pleše, "Platonist Orientalism." in A. Perez Jimenez and F. Titchener, eds., *Historical and Biographical Values of Plutarch's Works* (Malaga: International Plutarch Society, 2005), 355–381. For the Stoic background of the interest in Ancient Wisdom as reflected in some foreign cultures—and in particular among the Jews, see G. R. Boys-Stones, *Post-Hellenistic Philosophy: A Study of its Development from the Stoics to Origen* (Oxford: Oxford University Press, 2001).
33. Jaeger chose not to address the deep differences between the two systems.
34. See in particular Polymnia Athanassiadi and Michael Frede, eds., *Pagan Monotheism in Late Antiquity* (Oxford: Oxford University Press, 1999) as well as Stephen Mitchell and Peter van Nuffelen, eds., *One God: Pagan Monotheism in the Roman Empire* (Cambridge: Cambridge University Press, 2010) and S. Mitchell and P. van Nuffelen, eds., *Monotheism between Pagans and Christians in Late Antiquity* (Leuven: Peeters, 2010). It is noteworthy that some of these pagan conceptions seem to have Jewish or Jewish-Christian roots.
35. The Buddha, Zarathustra, and Jesus, but not Moses, whom the Manichaean theological anti-Semitism excludes from the list of the prophets of humanity, together with all other biblical prophets of Israel.
36. Paul Veyne, *Quand notre monde devint chrétien (312–394)* (Paris: Albin Michel, 2007), esp. For a less idiosyncratic study offering a more complete vision of the conversion of the Roman world, see Marie-Françoise Baslez, *Comment notre monde est devenu chrétien* (Paris: CLD, 2008).
37. I quote the English edition: Paul Veyne, ed., *A History of Private Life, I, From Pagan Rome to Byzantium* (Cambridge, MA: Harvard University Press, 1987), chapter I, 5–234; see 43, 69, 214.
38. "Culte, piété et morale dans le paganisme romain," in Paul Veyne, *L'empire gréco-romain* (Paris: Seuil, 2005), 419–543, esp. 440, 472, 490, 530.
39. "Païens et charité chrétienne devant les gladiateurs," in *L'Empire gréco-romain*, 545–631. See esp. 573. On gladiator games in the Roman world, see

in particular Georges Ville, *La gladiature en Occident des origines à la mort de Domitien* (Rome: Ecole Française de Rome, 1981).
40. See ibid., 530–531, 589, and 464.
41. On the origins of the concept of late antiquity, see J. H. W. G. Liebeschuetz, "The Birth of Late Antiquity," in his *Decline and Change in Late Antiquity: Religion, Barbarians and their Historiography* (Aldershot: Variorum/Ashgate, 2006), chapter XV.
42. See Robin Lane Fox's new, massive and impressive biography of Augustine, *Augustine: Conversions to Confessions* (New York: Basic Books, 2015).
43. Peter Brown, *Authority and the Sacred: Aspects of the Christianisation of the Roman World* (Cambridge: Cambridge University Press, 1995), 10–25.
44. *A History of Private Life*, 235–312; see esp. 251, 260, 292.
45. Peter Brown, *The Body and Society: Men, Women, and Sexual Renunciation in Early Christianity* (New York: Columbia University Press, 1988).
46. Garnsey and Humfress, *The Evolution of the Late Antique World*; I quote according to the French translation, *L'évolution du monde de l'antiquité tardive* (Paris: Maspéro, 2004), 151.
47. G. W. Bowersock, *Hellenism in Late Antiquity* (Ann Arbor: University of Michigan Press, 1990).
48. See in particular Basil of Caesarea, *Oratio ad adolescentes* (I quote according to Mario Naldini, Basilio di Cesarea, *Discorsi ai giovani* [Florence: Nardini, 1984]). Cf. Jean Chrysostom's *Address on Vainglory and the Right Way for Parents to Bring Up their Children*, in M. L. W. Laistner, *Christianity and Pagan Culture in the Later Roman Empire* (Ithaca, NY: Cornell University Press, 1951).
49. See Robert Browning's essay on Homer in Byzantium, in Robert Lamberton and John J. Keaney, eds., *Homer's Ancient Readers: The Hermeneutics of Greek Epics Earliest Exegetes* (Princeton, NJ: Princeton University Press, 1992). See also Kurt Treu, "Antike Literatur im byzantinischen Ägypten im Lichte der Papyri," in *Byzantino-Slavica: Revue internationale des études byzantines*, 1 (1986), 1–7.
50. See Chapter 1, p. 52 and note 52.
51. Elias J. Bickerman, "The Historical Foundations of Post-Biblical Judaism," in Louis Finkelstein, ed., *The Jews, their History* (New York: Schocken, 1970), 111.
52. This is, for instance, how the Platonic philosopher Alexander of Lycopolis perceives the Christians, in the fourth (?) century. See André Viley, *Alexandre de Lycolopis, Contre la doctrine de Mani* (Paris: Cerf, 1985).
53. On the Christian version of the philosophical spiritual exercises, so well studied by Pierre Hadot, see, for instance, Winrich Löhr, *Pelagius: Portrait of a Christian Teacher in Late Antiquity* (The Alexander Souter Memorial Lecture 1; Aberdeen: University of Aberdeen, 2007).
54. An expression from the *Aleinu* prayer, from late antiquity. On *tikkun 'olam*, see, for instance, Babylonian Talmud, *Gittin* 32a.

55. See G. B. Ladner, *The Idea of Reform: Its Impact on Christian Thought and Action in the Age of the Fathers* (Cambridge, MA: Harvard University Press, 1959).
56. *I Clement* 62.3. To be sure, this does not mean that there is no relationship between religion and ethics among the pagans. Such a relationship actually seems to have become stronger in the first two centuries of the Common Era. See, for instance, Liebeschuetz, "Religion A.D. 68–196," in his *Decline and Change in Late Antiquity,* VI, esp. 1002–1003.

4. Scripture and Culture

1. See Chapter 1, note 40. A former version of this chapter was published as "Scriptures and *paideia* in late antiquity," in Maren R. Niehoff, ed., *Homer and the Bible in the Eyes of Ancient Interpreters* (Jerusalem Studies in Religion and Culture 16; Leiden: Brill, 2012), 29–41.
2. J. E. Wansbrough, *The Sectarian Milieu: Content and Composition of Islamic Salvation History* (London Oriental Studies 34; Oxford: Oxford University Press, 1978).
3. Keith Hopkins, "Conquest by Book," in Alan K. Bowman and Greg Woolf, eds., *Literacy and Power in the Ancient World* (Cambridge: Cambridge University Press, 1994), 133–158.
4. *Pirke Avot,* 5.2.
5. See Catherine Hezser, *Jewish Literacy in Roman Palestine* (Texts and Studies in Ancient Judaism 81; Tübingen: Mohr Siebeck, 2002), 34–36, despite Hezser's methodological skepticism.
6. See C. F. Evans in *Cambridge History of the Bible,* I, 232; cf. A. C. Outler, "The "Logic" of Canon-making and the Tasks of Canon-criticism," in W. E. March, ed., *Texts and Documents: Critical Essays on the Bible and Early Church Fathers* (San Antonio: Trinity, 1980), 264–265, and H. Y. Gamble, Jr., "Christianity: Scripture and Canon," in F. M. Denny and R. L. Taylor, *The Holy Book in Comparative Perspective* (Columbia: University of South Carolina Press, 1985), 36–62, esp. 37. See also, C. F. Evans in the *Cambridge History of the Bible,* I, 232, and S. Morenz, "Entstehung und Wesen der Buchreligion," in his *Religion und Geschichte des alten Ägypten* (Vienna: Böhlau, 1975), 382–394. Elsewhere in the same volume, Morenz states: "Das Christentum ist eine Buchreligion" calling the idea of a Book religion "Israel's gift to the world" (8).
7. Eusebius, *Historia Ecclesiastica* 3.7. Cf. ibid., 6.23, for the development of commentaries since the time of Origen.
8. This is one of the main arguments of Celsus in his *Alethes Logos.* See Origen, *Contra Celsum,* I.
9. See for instance M. Tardieu, *Le manichéisme* (Que sais-je? 1940; Paris: Presses Universitaires de France, 1981).
10. A taxonomy quite similar to the one presented by Müller, although much more precisely developed, has been proposed by Carsten Colpe, who sug-

gested seeing two main and complex vectors (*Filiationen*) of religious canons, the one launched by the Buddhist texts and the other starting with the Hebrew Bible. This last vector, obviously, goes through the New Testament, the Mishnah, and Mani's works, up to the Qur'an and beyond. See C. Colpe, "Sakralisierung von Texten und Filiationen von Kanons," in J. Assmann and A. Assmann, eds., *Kanon und Zensur* (Munich: Fink, 1987), 80–92.

11. Bowman and Woolf, eds., *Literacy and Power in the Ancient World*, 12. R. Lane Fox, "Literacy and Power in Early Christianity," in ibid., 126–147 and notes; M. Halbertal, *People of the Book*, 1 et passim.

12. I have studied this phenomenon in *Hidden Wisdom: Esoteric Traditions and the Roots of Christian Mysticism* (Numen Book Series 70; Leiden: Brill, 2005 [1st ed. 1996]), esp. 92–108.

13. Lactantius, *Epitomé des Institutions Divines* (Sources Chrétiennes 335; Paris, 1987), 25.1; p. 111. On the question of the place of the *Epitome* in Lactantius's work, see Hervé Inglebert, "Lactance abbréviateur de lui-même: des *Institutions Divines* à l'*Epitomé des Institutions Divines*: l'exemple de l'histoire des religions," in Marietta Horster et Christiane Reitz, eds., *Condensing texts/condensed texts* (Palingenesia 98; Stuttgart: Franz Steiner, 2010), 491–515.

14. Ibid., 36.4–5: . . . Ubi autem utraque conjuncta sunt, ibi esse veritatem necesse est, ut si quaeratur ipsa ueritas quid sit, recte dici possit aut sapiens religio aut religiosa sapientia.

15. It had now become part of religion, permitting it to broaden its horizons dramatically. This new conception of religion, in which theology retains a central role, will permit the fast development of polemics on the nature of true faith, thus encouraging the reorganization of religious space between orthodoxy and heresies. At the same time, it will entail the multiplication of sects, each proposing a different hermeneutics of the same sacred scripture.

16. For a new reading of this important text, see Neil McLynn, "The Manna from Uncle: Basil of Caesarea's Address to Young Men," in Christophe Kelly, Richard Flower and Michael Stuart Williams, eds., *Unclassical Traditions: Alternatives to the Classical Past in Late Antiquity, Proceedings of the Cambridge Philological Society*, 2011, 106–151.

17. His aliquis forsitan quaerit utrum auctores nostri, quorum scripta divinitus inspirata canonem nobis saluberrima auctoritate fecerunt, sapientes tantummodo an eloquentes etiam nuncupandi sunt . . . Nam ubi eos intellego, non solum nihil eis sapientius, verum etiam nihil eloquentius mihi videre potest. *Doct. Christ.* IV. 6. 9. See the edition of R. P. H. Green, *Augustine: De Doctrina Christiana* (Oxford Early Christian Texts; Oxford: Oxford University Press, 1995).

18. It is strikingly similar to the Islamic concept of the "inimitability" of the Qur'anic language (*i'jaz al-Qur'an*); on the latter, see R. C. Martin, "Inimitability," in J. D. McAuliffe (ed.), *Encyclopaedia of the Qur'ān* (Leiden: Brill, 2002), 6 vols., 2.526–536.

19. *Doct Christ* IV. 6. 10. Cf. Michael Cameron, "Augustine on Scripture," in Mark Vessey, ed., *A Companion to Augustine* (New York: Wiley-Blackwell, 2012), 200–214.
20. See especially H.-I. Marrou, *Saint Augustin et la fin de la culture antique* (Paris: Etudes Augustiniennes, 1983 [first edition 1938]), 211–275, and C. M. Chin, "The Grammarian's Spoils: *De Doctrina Christiana* and the Contexts of Literary Education," in K. Pollmann and M. Vessey, eds., *Augustine and the Disciplines: from Cassiciacum to Confessions* (Oxford: Oxford University Press, 2005), 167–183, as well as H. Hagendahl, *Augustine and the Latin Classics,* two volumes (Göteborg: Acta Universitatis Gothoburgensis, 1967).
21. The complex question of Christianity and *paideia* has given birth to a vast literature. Let us only mention here, since Werner Jaeger's seminal *Early Christianity and Greek Paideia,* Robert A. Kaster, *Guardians of Language: The Grammarian and Society in Late Antiquity* (Berkeley: University of California Press, 1988); Christoph Markschies, *Kaiserzeitliche christliche Theologie und ihre Institutionen: Prolegomena zu einer Geschichte der antiken christlichen Theologie* (Tübingen: Mohr Siebeck, 2007), 43–109; Gillian Clark, *Christianity and Roman Society* (Cambridge: Cambridge University Press, 2004), 78–92, Frances Young, "Christian Teaching," in F. Young, C. Ayres and A. Louth, eds., *Cambridge History of Early Christian Literature* (Cambridge, New York: Cambridge University Press, 2004), 91–104, and J. David Dawson, "Christian Teaching," in ibid., 222–238. See in particular, Sara Rappe, "The New Math: How to Add and to Subtract Pagan Elements in Christian Education," in Yun Lee Too, ed., *Education in Greek and Roman Antiquity* (Leiden: Brill, 2001), 405–432. Cf. Chapter 3.
22. See Claudia Rapp, *Holy Bishops in Late Antiquity: The Nature of Christian Leadership in an Age of Transition* (Berkeley: University of California Press, 2005), who shows how these versions of *paideia* were often intertwined.
23. See Robert Browning, "The Byzantines and Homer," in Robert Lamberton and John J. Keaney, eds, *Homer's Ancient Readers: the Hermeneutics of Greek Epics' Earliest Exegetes* (Princeton, NJ: Princeton University Press, 1992), 134–148.
24. On Homer in early Christian literature, see Hugo Rahner, *Griechische Mythen in christlicher Deutung* (Basel: Herder, 1984), 241–328. Averil Cameron, "Education and Literary Culture," in A. Cameron and Peter Garnsey, eds., *The Cambridge Ancient History XIII; The Late Empire* A.D. *337–425* (Cambridge: Cambridge University Press, 1998), 665–707; and Robert Browning, "Education in the Roman Empire," in Averil Cameron, Brian Ward-Perkins, M. Whitby, eds., *The Cambridge Ancient History, XIV, Late Antiquity: Empires and Successors,* A.D. *425–600* (Cambridge: Cambridge University Press, 2000), 855–883. Education provided a set of values common to people of all religions, as mentioned by Edward J. Watts, *City and School in Late Antique Athens and Alexandria* (Berkeley: University of California Press, 2006), 21. On *paideia* and identities in the early Roman Empire, see Barbara E. Borg, ed., *Paideia: The*

World of the Second Sophistic (Berlin: W. de Gruyter, 2004). On the status of *paideia* in late ancient society, see Peter Brown, *Power and Persuasion in Late Antiquity: Towards a Christian Empire* (Madison: Wisconsin University Press, 1992).
25. Tertullian, *De Praescr. Haer.* 7.
26. On this literature, see for instance, William Harmless, S. J., *Desert Christians: An Introduction to the Literature of Early Monasticism* (Oxford: Oxford University Press, 2004). According to Samuel Rubenson, the opposition between Christian and pagan wisdom does not reflect the cultural status of fourth-century monasticism, but was projected by later writings. For him, the early Christian monks (and Antony among them) were no uneducated peasants, but rather were coming from a well-educated socioeconomic class. See Samuel Rubenson, "Christian Asceticism and the Emergence of the Monastic Tradition," in Vincent L. Wimbush and Richard Valantasis, eds., *Asceticism* (New York: Oxford University Press, 1995), 52.
27. Such ambivalence had already been present in Alexandrian Judaism, as Monique Alexandre notes in "La culture grecque, servante de la foi, de Philon d'Alexandrie aux Pères grecs," in Arnaud Perrot, ed., *Les chrétiens et l'Hellénisme: Identités religieuses* (Paris: Ecole Normale Supérieure, 2012. See also, Olivier Munnich, "La place de l'Hellénisme dans l'autodéfinition du christianisme," in Perrot, ed., ibid., 61–122.
28. See for instance, Robert L. Wilken, "Alexandria: A School for Training in Virtue," in P. Henry, ed., *Schools of Thought in the Christian Tradition* (Philadelphia, PA: Fortress Press, 1984), 15–30; Alain Le Boulluec, "La rencontre de l'Hellénisme et de la "philosophie barbare" selon Clément d'Alexandrie," in A. Le Boulluec, *Alexandrie antique et chrétienne: Clément et Origène* (Paris: Etudes Augustiniennes, 2006), 82–93; G. G. Stroumsa, "Philosophy of the Barbarians: on Early Christian Ethnological Representations," in *idem.*, *Barbarian Philosophy: the Religious Revolution of Early Christianity* (Tübingen: Mohr Siebeck, 1999), 57–84.
29. On this concept, see Winrich A. Löhr, "The Theft of the Greeks: Christian Self Definition in the Age of the Schools," in *Revue d'histoire écclésiastique* 95 (2000), 403–26; and Arthur J. Droge, *Homer or Moses? Early Christian Interpretations of the History of Culture* (Tübingen: Mohr Siebeck, 1989). See also, Daniel Ridings, *The Attic Moses: The Dependency Theme in Some Early Christian Writers* (Göteborg: Acta Universitatis Gothoburgensis, 1995).
30. This approach reappeared in the East toward the end of the fourth century, for instance in the epistle of John Chrysostom on the role of Greek literature in Christian education. It allowed the great patrician families to give their children an education that was "traditional" yet also thoroughly Christian. Thus, these families (such as that of the brothers Basil of Caesarea and Gregory of Nyssa, and that of their cousin Gregory Nazianzen, in Cappadocia) established the foundations of European culture, a culture based on both traditional *paideia* and on the divine books.

31. Pier Franco Beatrice, "The Treasures of the Egyptians: A Chapter in the History of Patristic Exegesis and Late Antique Culture," in *Studia Patristica* 39 (2006), 159–184.
32. See Tim Whitmarsh, *Greek Literature and the Roman Empire: the Politics of Imitation* (Oxford: Oxford University Press, 2002), 91.
33. See *Barbarian Philosophy*, 27–43 ("The Christian hermeneutical revolution and its double helix"). As is the case with all metaphors, the heuristic value of this metaphor disappears if we take it at face value.
34. On this, see the effort of Dennis MacDonald to present the New Testament as a corpus comparable to the Homeric writings. D. MacDonald, *The Homeric Epics and the Gospel of Mark* (New Haven, CT: Yale University Press, 2000), and *Does the New Testament Imitate Homer?* (New Haven, CT: Yale University Press, 2003).
35. Cf. Chapter 1, note 41.
36. Cf. Chapter 3.
37. The canonization of the New Testament will not be treated here. On this topic, scholarly literature is huge, and constantly growing. A classical study remains that of Bruce M. Metzger, *The Canon of the New Testament, Its Origin, Development, and Significance* (Oxford: Clarendon Press, 1987).
38. I have offered a tentative explanation for this puzzling synchronicity in "The Body of Truth and Its Measures: New Testament Canonization in Context," in my *Hidden Wisdom: Esoteric Traditions and the Roots of Christian Mysticism*, 79–91.
39. R. Travers Herford, *Some Ancient Safeguards of Civilization* (London: Lindsey, 1933).
40. For a striking, famous Talmudic parable that shows that such a hermeneutical situation was well known in late antiquity, see the story of "Akhnai's oven," Babylonian Talmud, *Baba Metzi'a* 59a, which concludes: "[The Torah] is not in heaven!"
41. The mechanism just described does not work only among Jewish and Christian communities. In publishing himself his own writings, Mani precisely intended to avoid the problems plaguing Christian, Zoroastrian, or Buddhist communities, as Jesus, Zarathustra, and the Buddha made the mistake of not having redacted their own writings themselves.
42. See for instance, Gillian Clark, "City of Books: Augustine and the World as Text," in W. Klingshirn and L. Safran, eds., *The Early Christian Book* (Washington, D.C.: Catholic University of America Press, 2007), 122–138. See further Matilde Caltabiano, "Lettura e lettori in Agostino," *Antiquité Tardive* 18 (2010), 151–161.
43. In the conversion scene, Augustine discovers truth to be beyond books.
44. See the chapters in Mark Vessey, ed., *A Companion to Augustine*, Part IV, Texts, 159–254, and in particular Michael Stuart Williams, "Augustine as a Reader of his Christian Contemporaries," 227–239.
45. In any case, he is the only ancient author whose *Retractationes* have survived.

46. Pierre Petitmengin, who has done extensive research on this topic, discusses the important role played by books in general, and by the Book par excellence (*scriptura sacra*), the Bible, in late antique intellectual and spiritual life.
47. See, respectively, *En. Ps.* 56.9 and *En. Ps.* 40.14.
48. Q. 62: 5; cf. already Babylonian Talmud, *Avoda Zara* 5b.
49. He also gives us the first technical description of reading, and of the role played by memory in this process.
50. B. Stock, *Ethics Through Literature: Ascetic and Aesthetic Reading in Western Culture* (The Menahem Stern Lectures; Hanover, NH: University Press of New England, 2007), 32.
51. *De Catech. Rudibus,* IX. 1.
52. In his new biography of Augustine, Robin Lane Fox offers detailed analyses of Augustine as an intellectual mystic. See R. Lane Fox, *Augustine: Conversions to Confessions* (New York: Basic Books, 2015), *passim*.
53. See H.-I. Marrou, *Histoire de l'éducation dans l'antiquité* (Paris: Seuil, 1965 [1948]). Many of Marrou's ideas have been overturned by patient research into Augustine's sources; see Goulven Madec, Saint *Augustin et la philosophie: notes critiques* (Paris: Etudes Augustiniennes, 1996). I owe this reference to Brian Stock. Similarly, Marrou's magisterial synthetic work on education in antiquity barely mentions the highly significant chapter of Rabbinic Judaism. For Jewish education and literacy, see Catherine Hezser, *Jewish Literacy in Roman Palestine.* Early Islam remained of course beyond the book's chronological span.
54. The catalogue for a 1977 exhibition on Christian and late antique art at the Metropolitan Museum, as well as the Proceedings of a symposium organized by Kurt Weitzmann on that occasion were both entitled: *An Age of Spirituality.*
55. As argued by Pier Franco Beatrice; see his "Canonical and Non-Canonical Books in Augustine's 'De Doctrina Christiana,'" in *Miscellanea Patristica reverendissimo Marco Starowieyski septuagenario professori illustrissimo viro amplissimo ac doctissimo oblata* (Warsaw: *Warszawskie Studia Teologiczne* 20/2, 2007), 23–35.
56. They often knew these hymns by rote. Thus Melania, who reads both the Old and the New Testament three or four times yearly, and knows the Psalms by heart.
57. *Soliloq.* I. 10. 17. A similar point is made by Cyril, Jerusalem's bishop in the fourth century, through whom we learn that prayer books were used in liturgy.
58. *Conf.* VI.3.
59. *et legi in silentio, Conf.* VIII.29. The text is unclear as to whether he trained himself to read silently. For references to silent reading, one has to turn to medieval writers such as the Victorines in the twelfth century. See further Jean Leclercq, *The Love of Learning and the Desire for God: A Study of Monastic*

Culture (New York: Fordham University Press, 1982 [3rd ed.]). I owe this reference to Brian Stock.
60. Valette-Cagnac, 42–47, referring to Martial, *Epigrams* I. 39, verse 56.
61. We still need an anthropological history of the book, of writing and of reading in Late Antiquity.
62. On the fact that the classical Greek authors remain part of *paideia* among the Christians, see for instance Peter Brown, *The World of Late Antiquity, A.D. 150–750* (London: Thames and Hudson, 1971), 115–125.
63. See D. Diringer, *The Book before Printing: Ancient, Medieval and Oriental* (New York: Dover, 1982), 275–335 (chapter 7, "The Book follows Religion"). In his *Creation of the Sacred: Tracks of Biology in Early Religions* (Cambridge, MA: Harvard University Press, 1996), the late historian of Greek religion Walter Burkert speculates that in the world of the future, established upon totally new communication patterns permitted by computers, religion, which permits contacts and connections between individuals, may not be needed, or even possible. Such a daring hypothesis may well not be proven true. Judging from the example of early Christianity, however, it is quite probable that the contemporary revolution in the means of communications will also bring us to a parallel religious revolution.

5. The New Self and Reading Practices

1. Benedict XVI's September 12, 2008, speech is available on Youtube. An earlier version of this chapter formed the bulk of "Reading Practices in Early Christianity and the Individualization Process," in Jörg Rüpke and Wolfgang Spickermann, eds., *Reflections on Religious Individuality: Greco-Roman and Judeo-Christian Texts and Practices* (Religionsgeschichtliche Versuche und Vorarbeiten 62; Berlin: De Gruyter, 2012), 175–192.
2. There is a vast and constantly growing literature on early monasticism. For a broad picture, see for instance, Susanna Elm, *Virgins of God: the Making of Asceticism in Late Antiquity* (Oxford: Clarendon Press, 1994). For a few more focused studies, see for instance, David Brakke, *Demons and the Making of the Monk: Spiritual Combat in Early Christianity* (Cambridge, MA: Harvard University Press, 2006); Mark Sheridan, *From the Nile to the Rhone and Beyond: Studies on Early Monastic Literature and Scriptural Interpretation* (Studia Anselmiana 156, Analecta Monastica 12; Rome: Pontificio Ateneo Sant' Anselmo, 2012).
3. Peter Brown, *The Body and Society: Men, Women, and Sexual Renunciation in Early Christianity* (New York: Columbia University Press, 1988).
4. See Antoine Guillaumont, "Monachisme et éthique judéo-chrétienne," in his *Aux origines du monachisme chrétien: pour une phénoménologie du monachisme* (Spiritualité orientale 20; Bégolles en Mauges: Abbaye de Bellefontaine, 1979).
5. For a discussion of Foucault and other contemporary thinkers, see Christopher Gill, *The Structured Self in Hellenistic and Roman Thought* (Oxford: Oxford

University Press, 2006), esp. Part III, "Issues of Selfhood." See also, A. A. Long, "Representations of the Self in Stoicism," in Steven Everson, ed., *Psychology* (Companions to Ancient Thought 2; Cambridge: Cambridge University Press, 1991), 102 ff., and for other studies, Richard Sorabji, *Self: Ancient and Modern Insights about Individuality, Life, and Death* (Chicago: Chicago University Press, 2006).

6. Michel Foucault, *L'herméneutique du sujet: Cours au Collège de France. 1981–1982* (Paris: Gallimard, Seuil, 2001). Cf. Pierrre Hadot, *Exercices spirituels et philosophie antique* (Paris: Albin Michel, 2002). As shown by Winrich Löhr, spiritual exercises in the philosophical vein can also be found among Christian teachers. See W. Löhr, *Pelagius: Portrait of a Christian Teacher in Late Antiquity: Souter Memorial Lectures on Late Antiquity, I* (Aberdeen: School of Divinity, University of Aberdeen, 2011), 16–17.

7. I wish to call special attention to Foucault's *Du gouvernement des vivants, cours au Collège de France, 1979–1980* (Paris: Gallimard, 2012), where the author analyzes the early Christian concept of *metanoia*, as it appears in Patristic texts, and in particular in Tertullian's *De poenitentia*. Foucault seeks to show that early Christianity established what he calls a "régime de vérité" different from the one that existed in Greco-Roman philosophy. More precisely, Christianity moved between two polar "régimes de vérité," that of faith and that of confession (*aveu*)—the former representative of the Greek East, the latter of the Latin West. Foucault then follows the historical implications of the early Christian conception of confession in Western Christianity in general, and in monastic practice in particular. I cannot elaborate here on Foucault's ideas, but this text should be read seriously by scholars of early Christianity, as it has a great deal to offer to Patristic studies.

8. See Chapter 3, pp. 53–54.

9. See Frances Young, "Christian Teaching," in Frances Young, Lewis Ayres, Andrew Louth, eds., *Cambridge History of Early Christian Literature* (Cambridge: Cambridge University Press, 2004), 464–484. One should further note that in Rabbinic Hebrew usage, the "house of study" (*beit ha-midrash*) is more prominent than the synagogue (*beit ha-knessset*).

10. For an analysis of this capital fact, see G. G. Stroumsa, *The End of Sacrifice*, chapter 1. Long ago, I offered a more detailed study of the early Christian transformation of the self, seeking to show that it was predicated upon some of the central tenets of Christian theology; see G. G. Stroumsa, *Barbarian Philosophy: The Religious Revolution of Early Christianity* (Tübingen: Mohr-Siebeck, 1999), 168–190 ("*Caro salutis cardo:* Shaping the Person in Early Christian Thought").

11. *De ressurectione mortuorum*, 2

12. See David Hunter, "Augustine on the Body," in Mark Vessey, ed., *A Companion to Augustine* (Malden, MA: Blackwell, 2012), 353–364.

13. Hebrew for *metanoia* is *teshuva*, in contradistinction to Greek *epistrophē*. For further developments, see G. G. Stroumsa, *Barbarian Philosophy: The Religious*

Revolution of Early Christianity (Tübingen: Mohr Siebeck, 1999), 158–167 ("From Repentance to Penance in Early Christianity: Tertullian's *De paenitentia* in Context").

14. See Caroline Humfress, "Judging by the Book: Christian Codices and Late Antique Legal Culture," in William E. Klingshirn and Linda Safran, eds., *The Early Christian Book* (Washington: Catholic University of America Press, 2007), 141–158.

15. See G. G. Stroumsa, "On the Roots of Christian Intolerance," in Francesca Prescendi and Youri Volokhine, eds., *Dans le laboratoire de l'historien des religions* [Religions en perspective 24]; (Geneva: Labor et Fides, 2011), 193–210.

16. See in particular Wilfred Cantwell Smith, *What Is Scripture? A Comparative Approach* (Minneapolis: Fortress Press, 1993). For this and the following paragraphs, cf. Chapter 1.

17. Books were of course also important in the Orphic tradition, but we simply do not know enough about possible Orphic communities in the Roman world.

18. See for instance, Larry W. Hurtado, *The Earliest Christian Artifacts: Manuscripts and Christian Origins* (Grand Rapids: Eerdmans, 2006). See also, the doctoral dissertation of Zeev Elizur, *The Book and the Holy: Chapters in the History of the Concept of Holy Book from the Second Temple Period to Late Antiquity* (Beer Sheva: Ben Gurion University, 2012 [in Hebrew]). Elizur deals primarily with books in Jewish context, but also offers interesting comparisons with early Christian aspects of the question. See also, Jean-Marie Carrié, "Le livre comme objet d'usage, le livre comme valeur symbolique, *Antiquité Tardive* 18 (2010), 181–190.

19. I do not deal here with the complex case of late antique Rabbinic Judaism, in which reverence for the Holy Book was so high that it seems to have prevented, or at least strongly impeded, for a long time the writing of books, with the consequence that much of the hermeneutical involvement of the elites with the Torah remained oral for many years.

20. Cavallo, "Du volumen au codex: la lecture dans le monde romain," in Guglielmo Cavallo and Roger Chartier, eds., *Histoire de la lecture dans le monde occidental* (Paris: Seuil, 1997).

21. See in particular Chapter 4.

22. Harry Y. Gamble, Jr., *Books and Readers in the Early Church: A History of Early Christian Texts* (New Haven: Yale University Press, 2000).

23. See Ian H. Henderson, "Early Christianity, Textual Representation and Ritual Extension," in Dorothea Elm von der Osten, Jörg Rüpke, and Katerina Waldner, eds., *Texte als Medium und Reflexion von Religion im römischen Reich* (Heidelberg: Franz Steiner, 2006), 81–100.

24. Jack Goody, who has done so much to help us understand the differences between oral and literate societies, offered too-rigid distinctions between oral and literate societies. See for instance, Goody, *The Interface between the*

Written and the Oral (Cambridge: Cambridge University Press, 1968). Cf. Chapter 1, note 3.
25. Keith Hopkins, "Conquest by Book," in Mary Beard et al., eds., *Literacy in the Roman World Journal of Roman Archaeology*, Supplementary Series, 3 (Ann Arbor: Department of Classical Studies, University of Michigan, 1991), 133–158.
26. Robin Lane Fox, "Literacy and Power in Early Christianity," in A. K. Bowman and G. Woolf, eds., *Literacy and Power in the Ancient World* (Cambridge: Cambridge University Press, 1994), 126–147.
27. Gillian Clark, *Christianity and Roman Society* (Cambridge: Cambridge University Press, 2004), chapter 5, 78–92.
28. See for instance, William V. Harris, *Ancient Literacy* (Cambridge, MA: Harvard University Press, 1989), who can refer to the "acute logorrhea of Christian authors."
29. Roger Bagnall, *Early Christian Books in Egypt* (Princeton, NJ: Princeton University Press: 2009).
30. See for instance, Graham Stanton, *Studies in Matthew and Early Christianity*, in Markus Backmuehl and David Lincicum, eds. (Wissenschaftliche Untersuchungen zum Neuen Testament 209; Tübingen: Mohr Siebeck, 2011), 153–176.
31. This is why I have described early Christianity, a bit irreverently, perhaps, as a religion of the paperback; see Chapter 4.
32. See Bagnall, *Early Christian Books*, 69–80.
33. See Eduard Iricinschi, *"Tam preciosi codices uestri:* Hebrew Scriptures versus Persian Books in Augustine's Anti-Manichaean Writings," in Philippa Townsend and Moulie Vidas, eds., *Revelation, Literature, and Community in Late Antiquity* (Tübingen: Mohr Siebeck, 2011), 153–176.
34. See for instance, Christoph Markschies' discussion In his *Haupteinleitung* to the new edition of the *Antike christliche Apokryphen in deutscher Übersetzung* (Tübingen: Mohr Siebeck, 2012), 2–9.
35. Anthony Grafton and Megan Williams, *Christianity and the Transformation of the Book: Origen, Eusebius, and the Library of Caesarea* (Cambridge, MA: Harvard University Press, 2006).
36. On Origen and the Rabbis, see Nicholas de Lange, *Origen and the Jews: Studies in Jewish-Christian Relations in Third-Century Palestine* (Cambridge: Cambridge University Press, 1976). On Jewish books in late antiquity, see Elizur, *The Book and the Holy* (see note 18), passim.
37. See Chapter 4, p. 69. Furthermore, the early growth of silent reading and that of meditative reading are two unrelated phenomena, despite their synchronicity.
38. Brian Stock, *Bibliothèques intérieures*, (Grenoble: Jérome Lindon, 2005), 107–126, "L'histoire de la lecture: Thérapies de l'âme dans l'Antiquité et au Moyen-Age."

39. See Reinhard Flander, *Der biblische Sprechgesang und seine mündliche Überlieferung in Synagoge und griechische Kirche* (Wilhelmshaven: Noetzel, Heinrichshofen-Bücher, 1988). In both cases, to be sure, the Christians were following the Jews, who had for centuries developed such a dual pattern of reading the Bible, private and public. On reading and readers in Augustine, see Matilde Caltabiano, "Lettura e lettori in Agostino," *Antiquité Tardive* 18 (2010), 151–161.
40. Here too, see William A. Johnson, "Towards a Sociology of Reading in Classical Antiquity," in *The American Journal of Philology*, 121–24 (2000), 593–627.
41. See Claudia Rapp, "Holy Texts, Holy Men, and Holy Scribes: Aspects of Scriptural Holiness in Late Antiquity," in Klingshirn and Safran, eds., *The Early Christian Book*, 194–222. See also, Douglas Burton-Christie, *The Word in the Desert: Scripture and the Quest for Holiness in Early Christian Monasticism* (Oxford: Oxford University Press, 1993), passim.

6. Communities of Knowledge

1. Much has been written on ancient libraries; for a synthetic presentation of the main issues, see for instance, Lionel Casson, *Libraries in the Ancient World* (New Haven, CT: Yale University Press, 2001), as well as Jason König, Katerina Oikonomopoulou, Greg Woolf, eds., *Ancient Libraries* (Cambridge: Cambridge University Press, 2013), although no chapter is devoted to Christian libraries in this last work (See Chapter 1, note 14).
2. See Chapter 3.
3. For Vivarium, see for instance, Cassiodorus, *Institutions of Divine and Secular Learning; On the Soul*, translated by James W. Halporn with an introduction by Mark Vessey (Translated Texts for Historians 42; Liverpool: Liverpool University Press, 2004). For Nisibis, see *Sources for the Study of the School of Nisibis*, Translated with an introduction and notes by Adam H. Becker (Translated Texts for Historians 50; Liverpool: Liverpool University Press, 2008). See also, Adam H. Becker, *Fear of God and the Beginning of Wisdom: The School of Nisibis and Christian Scholastic Culture in Late Antique Mesopotamia* (Philadelphia: University of Pennsylvania Press, 2006). Also see notes 29 to 32 below. On Jewish literacy, there has been no systematic study since Catherine Hezser, *Jewish Literacy in Roman Palestine* (Tübingen: Mohr Siebeck, 2001), to be complemented by her "Crossing Enemy Lines: Network Connections Between Palestinian and Babylonian Sages in Late Antiquity," *Journal for the Study of Judaism* 46 (2015), 224–250.
4. Moreover, while early Christian literature sometimes follows known patterns (such as the Clementine "novel," both in the Greek *Homilies* and in the Latin *Recognitions*), it usually reflects rather original genres, such as Gospels and theological treatises and commentaries, quite different from anything in Latin *Belles Lettres* or philosophical literature.

5. B. Stock, *The Implications of Literacy: Written Language and Models of Interpretation in the Eleventh and Twelfth Centuries* (Princeton, NJ: Princeton University Press, 1983).
6. See Chapter 5.
7. See for instance, Elizabeth A. Clark, *Reading Renunciation: Asceticism and Scripture in Early Christianity* (Princeton, NJ: Princeton University Press, 1999).
8. See Samuel Rubenson, *The Letters of St. Antony: Origenist Theology, Monastic Tradition and the Making of a Saint* (Lund: Lund University Press, 2002). See also, the website of the collective research project on early monasticism and classical *paideia* led by Rubenson and based at Lund University (www.monasticpaideia.org).
9. See Samuel Rubenson, ed., trans., *The Letters of Saint Antony: Monasticism and the Making of a Saint* (Minneapolis: Fortress, 1995).
10. See Chryssi Ktosifou, "Books and Book Production in the Monastic Communities of Byzantine Egypt," in William E. Klingshirn and Linda Safran, eds., *The Early Christian Book* (Washington, D.C.: Catholic University of America Press, 2007), 48–66. For a later period, in the East, see Joel T. Walker, "Ascetic Literacy: Books and Readers in East Syrian Monastic Tradition," in Henning Börm and Josef Wiesehöfer, eds., *Commutatio et Contentio: Studies in Late Roman, Sasanian and Early Islamic Near East* (Reihe Geschichte, 3; Düsseldorf: Wellem Verlag, 2010), 307–345.
11. On Gaza, see Brouria Bitton-Ashkelony and Arieh Kofsky, *The Monastic School of Gaza* (Supplements to *Vigiliae Christianae* 78; Leiden: Brill, 2006).
12. See Bentley Layton, *The Canons of Our Fathers: Monastic Rules of Shenute* (Oxford: Oxford University Press, 2014).
13. Edward J. Watts retains the traditional dichotomy when he argues that different kinds of teachers were active in rhetorical schools and in monasteries. Although the differences between them must have been less rigid than usually perceived, they existed nonetheless. See Samuel Rubenson, "Asceticism and Monasticism, I: Eastern," *Cambridge History of Christianity, II: Constantine to c. 600* (Cambridge: Cambridge University Press, 2007), 637–668.
14. On the *Questions and Answers* literature, see in particular Marie-Pierre Bussières, ed., *La littérature des questions et réponses dans l'antiquité païenne et chrétienne: de l'enseignement à l'exégèse* (Turnhout: Brepols, 2013). Cf. G. G. Stroumsa, "The Scriptural Movement of Late Antiquity and Christian Monasticism," *Journal of Early Christian Studies* 16 (2008), 61–76.
15. Carol Harrison, *The Art of Listening in the Early Church* (Oxford: Oxford University Press, 2013).
16. On monastic spiritual education, see Antoine Guillaumont, "L'enseignement spirituel des moines d'Egypte : la formation d'une tradition," in Michel Meslin, ed., *Maîtres et disciples dans les traditions religieuses* (Paris: Cerf, 1990), 143–154. Guillaumont emphasizes the oral (dialogical) and the silent aspects of monastic education.

17. This has been duly noted by Brian Stock: see Chapter 5, note 38.
18. On Marcus Aurelius, see for instance, R. B. Rutherford, *The Meditations of Marcus Aurelius: A Study* (Oxford: Clarendon Press, 1989).
19. Benedicta Ward, transl., *Apophtegmata Patrum: The Sayings of the Desert Fathers: The Alphabetical Collection* (2nd ed.; Kalamazoo, MI: Cistercian Publications, 1884), 49.
20. On the devotion moderna, see John Van Engen, *Sisters and Brothers of the Common Life: The* Devotio Moderna *and the World of the Late Middle Ages* (Philadelphia: University of Pennsylvania Press, 2008); on Ignatian spirituality, see John W. O'Malley, *The First Jesuits* (Cambridge, MA: Harvard University Press, 1993).
21. On knowledge and religion in general, see for instance, Jacques Duchesne-Guillemin, "Knowledge and Ignorance," in Mircea Eliade, ed., *Encyclopedia of Religion* (New York: Macmillan, 1987), VIII, 343–356. About knowledge in late ancient religion, see in particular Raoul Mortley and Carsten Colpe, "Gnosis (Wissen)," *Reallexikon für Antike und Christentum* 11 (1981), 446–537.
22. For some examples of the cognitive approach to religion, see Pascal Boyer, *Et l'homme créa les dieux: comment expliquer la religion* (Paris: Lafont, 2003), and Robert N. McCauley and E. Thomas Lawson, *Bringing Ritual to Mind: Psychological Foundations of Cultural Forms* (Cambridge: Cambridge University Press, 2002). On religion and knowledge, see especially Harvey Whitehouse, *Modes of Religiosity: A Cognitive Theory of Religious Transmission* (Walnut Creek, CA: Altamira, 2004). Whitehouse seeks to distinguish between doctrinal and imagistic modes of religiosity (the latter being older than the former) involving very different sets of dynamics. See also Chapter 9.
23. The Kantian approach to religion remains deeply anchored in pietistic Christianity, and cannot account for most historical situations, in numerous cultures and societies.
24. See developments in Guy G. Stroumsa, *The End of Sacrifice: Religious Transformations in Late Antiquity* (Chicago: Chicago University Press, 2009), 28–55.
25. *Contra Apionem* II. 165. On this text, see Hubert Cancik, "Theokratie und Priesterherrschaft: Die Mosaische Verfassung bei Flavius Josephus, Contra Apionem 2, 157–198," in Cancik, *Religionsgeschichten, Gesammelte Aufsätze, II* (Tübingen: Mohr Siebeck, 2008). On conceptions of theocracy in late antiquity, see Guy G. Stroumsa, *The Making of the Abrahamic Religions in Late Antiquity* (Oxford Studies in the Abrahamic Religions; Oxford: Oxford University Press, 2015), 123–135.
26. Elias J. Bickerman, "The Historical Foundations of Post-Biblical Judaism," in Louis Finkelstein, ed., *The Jews, Their History* (New York: Schocken, 1970), 111.
27. See Hans-Georg Kippenberg and Guy G. Stroumsa, eds., *Secrecy and Concealment: Studies in the History of Mediterranean and Near Eastern Religions* (Leiden: Brill, 1995).

28. See Guy G. Stroumsa, *Hidden Wisdom: Esoteric Traditions and the Roots of Christian Mysticism* (2nd ed.; Leiden: Brill, 2005), XI–XVI and 1–9.
29. The heuristic usefulness of "Gnosticism" as a concept has been submitted to criticism from various parts, in particular since the publication of Michael A. Williams, *Rethinking "Gnosticism": An Argument for Dismantling a Dubious Category* (Princeton, NJ: Princeton University Press, 1996). See for instance, Karen L. King, *What Is Gnosticism?* (Cambridge, MA: Harvard University Press, 2003); see also, David Brakke, *The Gnostics: Myth, Ritual, and Diversity in Early Christianity* (Cambridge, MA: Harvard University Press, 2010). Notwithstanding such criticism, we retain the need to use a general concept inclusive of the various dualistic proclivities in early Christianity, and Gnosticism is as good as any, provided we remain aware of its limitations.
30. See Guy G. Stroumsa, "Cultural Memory in Early Christianity: Clement of Alexandria and the History of Religions," in S. N. Eisenstadt, J. P. Arnason and B. Wittrock, eds., *Axial Civilizations and World History* (Jerusalem Studies in Religion and Culture 4; Leiden: Brill, 2005), 293–315.
31. See for instance, Vladimir Lossky, *Théologie mystique de l'Eglise d'Orient* (Paris: Aubier, 1944). The origins of this mysticism of darkness can be found in Gregory of Nyssa's *Life of Moses*.
32. See for instance, S. A. Ivanov, *Holy Fools in Byzantium and Beyond* (Oxford: Oxford University Press, 2006), and Michael W. Dols, *Majnūn: The Madman in Medieval Islamic Society* (Oxford: Oxford University Press, 1992). For new horizons on the holy fool in comparative perspective, see Youval Rotman, *Insanity and Sanctity in Byzantium: The Ambiguity of Religious Experience* (Cambridge, MA: Harvard University Press, 2016). My thanks to the author for sending me his manuscript.
33. Hans Blumenberg has studied the development of the concept of *curiositas* from Cicero to Augustine. See his "Augustins Anteil and der Geschichte des Begriffs des theoretischen Neugierde," *Revue des Etudes Augustiniennes* 7 (1961), 35–70.
34. *De praescriptione haereticorum*, VII.
35. On the Christian transformation of Greco-Roman *paideia*, see Werner Jaeger, *Early Christianity and Greek Paideia* (Cambridge, MA.: Harvard University Press, 1961). For Byzantium, see Bernard Flusin, "La culture écrite," in Cécile Morrisson, ed., *Le monde byzantin, I, L'Empire romain d'Orient (330–641)* (Paris: Presses Universitaires de Fance, 2004), 255–276. See also, Stephen Shoemaker, "Gnosis and Paideia: Education and Heresy in Late Ancient Egypt," *Studia Patristica* 31 (Leuven: Peeters, 1997), 535–539.
36. See Polymnia Athanassiadi, *La lutte pour l'orthodoxie dans le platonisme tardif: de Numénius à Damascius* (Paris: Belles Lettres, 2006). Such communities created a world that did not encourage laughter, and where the body was denied rather than cultivated, in opposition to ancient cultural instincts and practices. Porphyry tells us in his *Life of Plotinus* that the founder of Neoplatonism shared this attitude.

37. See Robert Lamberton, *Homer the Theologian: Neoplatonist Allegorical Reading and the Growth of the Epic Tradition* (Berkeley: University of California Press, 1986).
38. See Philippe Hoffman, "Formes de culture, programmes et pensée pédagogique à la fin de l'antiquité," in François Jacquet-Francillon and Denis Kambouchner, ed. *La crise de la culture scolaire: Origines, interprétations, perspectives* (Paris: Presses Universitaires de France, 2005), 15–44. Cf. The *Discourse on the Eighth and the Ninth, Cairoensis Gnosticus* VI. 6.
39. See Isaiah Gafni, *The Jews of Babylonia in the Talmudic Era* (Jerusalem: Magnes Press, 1998) (in Hebrew). See also, Jeffrey L. Rubinstein, *The Culture of the Babylonian Talmud* (Baltimore: Johns Hopkins University Press, 2003), esp. 16–38, with references to the Nestorian Academy at Nisibis (35–38). Detailed study of late Antique Jewish education is still in urgent scholarly desideratum. For some preliminary references, see Marc Hirshman, *The Stabilization of Rabbinic Culture: 100 C.E.–350 C.E.* (Oxford: Oxford University Press, 2009), esp. Appendix 1: "A Survey of Secondary Literature" (121–126). On religious communities in late antiquity, see J. B. Segal, "Mesopotamian Communities from Julian to the Rise of Islam," *Proceedings of the British Academy*, 41 (London: British Academy, 1955; separate reprint: Oxford: Oxford University Press, 1956), John E. Wansbrough, *The Sectarian Milieu: Content and Composition of Islamic Salvation History* (Oxford: Oxford University Press, 1978), and Garth Fowden, "Religious Communities" in Glen W. Bowersock, Peter Brown, Oleg Grabar, eds., *Late Antiquity: a Guide to the Postclassical World* (Cambridge, MA: Harvard University Press, 1999), 82–106.
40. See for instance, Adam H. Becker, *Fear of God and the Beginning of Knowledge: The School of Nisibis and Christian Scholastic Culture* (Philadelphia: University of Pennsylvania Press, 2006), as well as Joel T. Walker, "Ascetic Literacy: Books and Readers in East-Syrian Monastic Tradition," in Henning Börn and Joseph Wiesehöfer, eds., *Commutatio et contentio: Studies in the Late Roman, Sasanian, and Early Islamic Near East, in Memory of Zeev Rubin* (Düsseldorf: Wellem Verlag, 2010), 307–345.
41. Becker, *Fear of God*, IX. On the monastic schools, see ibid., 160–168.
42. Becker, *Fear of God*, 204.
43. For a comparative study of Nisibis and Vivarium, see Hervé Inglebert, "La formation des élites chrétiennes d'Augustin à Cassiodore," in *Studia Patristica* 62 (Leuven: Peeters, 2013), 185–204. Inglebert notes that after 500, the secular patristic educational model disappeared, and that one had then the choice between a secular education or a monastic one. At Vivarium, in contradistinction to the case in the Benedictine monasteries, monks could spend the whole day (and sometimes the night) in the scriptorium. For references to the discussion of the possible links between the two institutions, see Adam Becker, *Sources for the Study of the School of Nisibis* (Translated Texts for Historians 30; Liverpool: Liverpool University Press, 2008), 3, note 8. On Cassiodorus's construction of an "ideal type" of higher education, see

Mark Vessey's introduction to Cassiodorus, *Institutions of Divine and Secular Learning on the Soul* (Translated Texts for Historians 43; Liverpool: Liverpool University Press, 2004), 11.

44. See Françoise Briquel-Chatonnet, "La religion comme enseignement: les écoles dans la tradition historique et culturelle de l'Eglise syro-orientale," *Comptes Rendus des Séances de l'Académie des Inscriptions et Belles Lettres*, janvier 2008 (2010), 59–76. On the Nisibis Academy, see Adam H. Becker, *Fear of God*.

45. See for instance, Sebastian Brock, "Charting the Hellenization of a Literary Culture: The Case of Syriac," *Intellectual History of the Islamicate World* 3 (2015), 98–124.

46. See Chapter 5.

47. The difference between Jewish and Christian attitudes to copying scriptures is striking here. We know precious little about patterns of transmission of the Qur'anic text in the earliest strata of Islam, but it is clear that the oral (and aural) aspect was predominant, and the rules for copying the text were less stringent than they were (and remained) among the Jews.

7. Eastern Wisdoms

1. It is in the framework of interdisciplinary research on the transformations of wisdom from antiquity to the Middle Ages—including Byzantium and the Islamic realm that this text must be interpreted. For a recent collection of studies, see Constanza Cordoni and Matthias Meyer, with Nina Hable, eds., *Barlaam und Joasaph: Neue Pespektiven auf ein europäisches Phänomen* (Berlin: de Gruyter, 2015). An earlier version of this chapter was published as "Eastern Wisdoms in Late Antiquity," in Reka Forai, ed., *Annual of Medieval Studies at Central European University* 14 (2008), 31–40.

2. See Aaron P. Johnson, *Religion and Identity in Porphyry of Tyre: The Limits of Hellenism in Late Antiquity* (Cambridge: Cambridge University Press, 2013).

3. See Kevin Van Bladel, *The Arabic Hermes: From Pagan Sage to Prophet of Science* (Oxford: Oxford University Press, 2009).

4. A. Momigliano, *Alien Wisdom: the Limits of Hellenization* (Cambridge: Cambridge University Press, 1975). The excellent synthesis of Erich S. Gruen, *Rethinking the Other in Antiquity* (Princeton, NJ: Princeton University Press, 2011) does not permit, both in terms of topics and time frame, a focus on the developments in late antiquity.

5. *Contra Celsum*, I.14–16. On *Kulturvölker* and *Naturvölker* in early Christian conceptions, see G. G. Stroumsa, *Barbarian Philosophy: The Religious Revolution of Early Christianity* (Tübingen: Mohr Siebeck, 1999), 57–84.

6. See Chapter 3.

7. A.-J. Festugière, *La révélation d'Hermès Trismégiste, I, L'astrologie et les sciences occultes* (Paris: Gabalda, 1943), 20. See also, Zlatko Pleše, "Platonic Orientalism," in A. Pérez Jiménez and F. Titchener, eds., *Historical and Biographical*

Values of Plutarch's Works: Studies Devoted to Professor Philip A. Stadter (Málaga: International Plutarch Society, 2005), 355–382. For a brief survey of Platonic Orientalism, see Wouter Hanegraaf, *Esotericism and the Academy: Rejected Knowledge in Western Culture* (Cambridge: Cambridge University Press, 2012), 7–12.

8. On the cultural contacts between the cultural traditions of the Near East, many insightful remarks can be found in Garth Fowden, *Empire to Commonwealth: Consequences of Monotheism in Late Antiquity* (Princeton, NJ: Princeton University Press, 1993).

9. On bilingualism in the late antique Near East, see David K. Taylor, "Bilingualism and Diglossia in Late Antique Syria and Mesopotamia," in J. N. Adams, Mark Janse, and Simon Swaine, eds., *Bilingualism in Ancient Society: Language Contact and the Written Word* (Oxford: Oxford University Press, 2002), 298–331. Despite a great number of monographs, the late ancient oriental fad has never received, it seems, a synthetic and sustained study.

10. See in particular, Aaron P. Johnson, *Religion and Identity in Porphyry of Tyre: The Limits of Hellenism in Late Antiquity*. See also, Jeremy M. Schott, *Christianity, Empire, and the Making of Religion in Late Antiquity* (Philadelphia: University of Pennsylvania Press, 2008). For the Stoic background of the interest in Ancient Wisdom as reflected in some foreign cultures—and in particular among the Jews—see G. R. Boys-Stones, *Post-Hellenistic Philosophy: A Study of its Development from the Stoics to Origen* (Oxford: Oxford University Press, 2001).

11. On this question, see for instance, Peter Sarris, *Empires of Faith: The Fall of Rome and the Rise of Islam, 500–700* (The Oxford History of Medieval Europe; Oxford: Oxford University Press, 2011), and G. W. Bowersock, *Empires in Collision in Late Antiquity* (The Jerusalem Menahem Stern Lectures; Waltham, MA: Brandeis University Press, 2012).

12. See Gilbert Dagron, "L'empire romain d'orient au IVe siècle et les traditions politiques de l'hellénisme: le témoignage de Thémistios," *Travaux et Mémoires* 3 (Paris: de Boccard, 1968), 149–186, esp. 156.

13. See for instance his Fragment 1a (des Places), from "On the Good." On Numenius, see "H.-C. Puech, "Numénius d'Apamée et les théologies orientales au second siècle," in Puech, *En quête de la gnose, I* (Paris: Gallimard, 1978), 245–54.

14. This phenomenon was studied by the late Patricia Crone, in a series of memorable workshops held at the Princeton Institute for Advanced Study during the first decade of the century. These workshops employed *shuʿubyya* (an Arabic term originally used to describe movements of cultural and ethnic identity in early Islam) as a generic name referring to this phenomenon.

15. See Harald Fuchs, *Der geistige Wiederstand gegen Rom in der antiken Welt* (Berlin: de Gruyter, 1938).

16. See Peter Struck, *Birth of the Symbol: Ancient Readers and the Limits of their Texts* (Princeton, NJ: Princeton University Press, 2004), 206.

17. See David S. Potter, *Prophets and Emperors: Human and Divine Authority from Augustus to Theodosius* (Cambridge, MA: Harvard University Press, 1994), 183–212 and notes.
18. See Dimitri Gutas, *Greek Thought, Arabic Culture: The Graeco-Arabic Translation Movement in Baghdad and Early 'Abbāsid Society, 2nd–4th/8th–10th Centuries* (New York: Routledge, 1998).
19. See John Matthews, "Hostages, Philosophers, Pilgrims, and the Diffusion of Ideas in the Late Roman Mediterranean and Near East," in F. M. Clovers and R. S. Humphreys, eds., *Tradition and Innovation in Late Antiquity* (Madison: University of Wisconsin Press, 1989), 29–47.
20. See G. G. Stroumsa, "Communautés religieuses, communautés de savoir," in Christian Jacob, ed., *Lieux de savoir*, vol. 1, *Espaces et communautés* (Paris: Albin Michel, 2007), 271–278.
21. On Clement and his perception of Eastern wisdom in general, and Buddhism in particular, see Albrecht Dihle, *Antike und Orient: Gesammelte Aufsätze* (Heidelberg: Winter, 1984), passim, as well as Alain Le Boulluec, "La rencontre de l'hellénisme et de la philosophie barbare selon Clément d'Alexandrie," in his *Alexandrie antique et chrétienne* (Turnhout: Brepols, 2006), 81–93.
22. See H.-C. Puech, *Le manichéisme: son fondateur, sa doctrine* (Paris: Civilisations du Sud, 1948).
23. *de def. orac.* 410 A–B (Plutarch, *Moral Works*, vol. V; Loeb Classical Library; 352–353 trans. F. C. Babbit).
24. See note 7.
25. See Christopher P. Jones, ed., trans., Philostratus, *The Life of Apollonius of Tyana*, Books I–IV (Loeb Classical Library; Cambridge: Harvard University Press, 2005), Introduction, 12–13, and 13, note 7. From the long list of studies devoted to this text, see in particular E. L. Lowie, "Apollonius of Tyana: Tradition and Reality," *Aufstieg und Niedergang der römischen Welt* II.16.2 (1978), 1652–1699.
26. Since Alexander's campaigns, the Indian "naked sages" had enjoyed a high reputation, augmented, in the third century by an embassy to the Emperor Elagabalus (218–222 C.E.) commemorated by Porphyry (*Abst.* 256 Nauck). According to Mark Edwards, this may have been the inspiration for the fictitious visit of Apollonius of Tyana to India. See M. Edwards, trans., Porphyry, *Neoplatonist Saints: The Lives of Plotinus and Proclus by their Students* (Liverpool: Liverpool University Press, 2000), 6 and notes 34 and 35.
27. On docetic thought patterns in the ancient world, see Guy G. Stroumsa, "Christ's Laughter: Docetic Origins Reconsidered," in *Journal of Early Christian Studies*, 12 (2004), Ronnie Goldstein and Guy G. Stroumsa, "The Greek and Jewish Origins of Docetism: A New Proposal," in *Zeitschrift für Antikes Christentum/Journal of Ancient Christianity* 10 (2007), 423–441, as well as Maurizio Bettini, *Je est l'autre? Sur les traces du double dans la culture ancienne* (Paris: Belin, 2012). I hope to work further on this problem and its broader implications in the future.

8. A World Full of Letters

1. Cf. Keith Hopkins, *A World Full of Gods: The Strange Triumph of Christianity* (New York: Plume Books, 2001 [1st ed. 1999]). For a former version of this chapter, see *"The Mystery of the Greek Letters:* A Byzantine Kabbalah?" in *Historia Religionum,* 6 (2014), 35–43.
2. Franz Dornseiff, *Das Alphabet in Mystik und Magie* (Leipzig: Teubner, 1925 [1922]).
3. See Guy G. Stroumsa, *Savoir et Salut* (Paris: Cerf, 1992), 21–84.
4. See for instance, "The Infancy Gospel of Thomas," in Bart D. Ehrman and Zlatko Pleše, *The Apocryphal Gospels* (Oxford: Oxford University Press, 2011), 13–15, and Christoph Markschies and Jens Schroeter, eds., *Antike Apokryphen in deutscher Übersetzung,* I, 2 (Tübingen: Mohr Siebeck, 2012), 930–959.
5. C. Bandt, *Der Traktat "Vom Mysterium der Buchstaben." Kritischer Text mit Einführung, Übersetzung und Anmerkungen* (Berlin: de Gruyter, 2007).
6. A. Hebbelynck, *"Les mystères des lettres grecques.* Texte copte, traduction, notes," *Le Muséon* 19 (1900), 5–36, 105–136. 269–300; 20 (1901), 5–33, 369–414.
7. See C. Bandt, "The Alphabet as "Henotikon." The tract "On the Mystery of the Letters" against the background of the Origenist Controversies of the Fourth and Sixth Centuries," *Historia Religionum* 6 (2014), 45–57.
8. G. G. Stroumsa, "A Zoroastrian Origin to the *Sefirot*?", in S. Shaked, A. Netzer, eds., *Irano-Judaica* 3, 1994 (Jerusalem: Ben Zvi, 1994), 17–33.
9. On this text, see the doctoral thesis of Elianne Katterer, *Otiyyot de-Rabbi Akiva* (Hebrew University of Jerusalem, 2005).
10. For a similar cosmogonic role of the letters of the alphabet, see an important Syriac text from the late sixth century, *The Cause of the Foundation of the Schools,* for which God, "the eternal teacher," arranged the letters of the alphabet in the firmament. I have used Adam H. Becker's translation, in his *Sources for the History of the School of Nisibis* (Liverpool: Liverpool University Press), 118–119. I owe this reference to Tzahi Weiss. See also, Yakir Paz and Tzahi Weiss, "From Encoding to Decoding: The ATBASH of R. Hiyya in Light of a Syriac, Greek and Coptic Cipher," *Journal of Near Eastern Studies, Journal of Near Eastern Studies* 74 (2015), 45–65.
11. See A. P. Hayman, ed., trans., *Sefer Yezira* (Tübingen: Mohr Siebeck, 2004).
12. See S. Pines, "Points of Similarity between the Doctrine of the Sefirot in the "Sefer Yezirah" and the "Pseudo-Clementine Homilies: the Implications of this Resemblance," in *Proceedings of the Israel Academy of Sciences and Humanities,* 1989, esp. 80–81. On the tradition in *Otiot de-Rabbi Akiva,* see Y. Liebes, *"Christian Influences on the 'Zohar,' " Mehkerei Yerushalaim be-Mahshevet Israel* 2, 1983, 43–74 [in Hebrew]; cf. G. Scholem, *Les origines de la Kabbale* (Paris: Aubier-Montaigne, 1966), 164ff.
13. See Pines, "Points of similarity"; cf. G. G. Stroumsa, "A Zoroastrian Origin to the *Sefirot?*"

14. A. Dieterich, *Kleine Schriften* (Berlin: Teubner, 1911), 224–225
15. ". . . quomodo oporteat omnia spiritali Alphabeti elementa cognoscere." *Patrologia Latina* 23, 68, 91–106.
16. *Patrologia Latina* 23, 87.
17. On the symbolic significance of the Greek letter *episemon* and of the Hebrew letter *vav,* see A. Dupont Sommer, *La doctrine gnostique de la lettre "waw" d'après une lamelle araméenne inédite* (Paris: Geuthner, 1946). On Jesus as the *episemon,* see Irenaeus, *Adv. Haer.,* I. 14. 1, and commentary in N. Förster, *Marcus Magus: Kult, Lehre unde Gemeindeleben einer valentinianischen Gnostikergruppe. Sammlung der Quellen und Kommentar* (Tübingen: Mohr Siebeck, 1999), 232. On the symbolic significance of numbers in Gnostic Christianity, and in particular in Marcus's system, see Joel Kalvesmaki, *The Theology of Arithmetic: Number Symbolism in Platonism and Early Christianity* (Hellenic Studies 59; Washington, D.C.: Center for Hellenic Studies, 2013).
18. Same play on *Christos/Chreistos* (pronounced in the same way, due to iotization) the *Sophia of Jesus Christ,* a Coptic text from Nag Hammadi (*Cairoensis Gnosticus* III, 100: 19–20).
19. See further Brouria Bitton-Ashkelony and Arieh Kofsky, *The Monastic School of Gaza* (Leiden: Brill, 2006), Ch. 5: *Counseling through Enigmas,* esp. 107–110, with references to the monks" alphabetic codes and cryptic language, as well as to the "Alphabet of the mind" from the *Apophtegmata Patrum.*
20. Eusebius of Caesarea, *Praeparatio Evangelica* XI. 6,
21. Isidore of Seville, *Etymologies,* I, 3.
22. "Quinque autem esse apud Graecos mysticas litteras"; I,3,8.
23. See E. Lohmeyer, "A und O," *Reallexikon für Antike und Christentum* I (1950), 1–4.
24. *Cairoensis Gnosticus* III. 2, 43:22–44:2.
25. G. G. Stroumsa, "A Nameless God: Judaeo-Christian and Gnostic Theologies of the Name," in *The Image of the Judaeo-Christians in Ancient Jewish and Christian Literature,* P. J. Tomson and D. Lambers-Petry, eds. (Tübingen: Mohr Siebeck, 2003) 230–243.
26. F. Wisse, "Gnosticism and Early Monasticism in Egypt," in B. Aland, ed., *Gnosis. Festschrift für Hans Jonas* (Göttingen: Vandenhoeck & Ruprecht, 1978), 431–440; Id., "Language Mysticism in the Nag Hammadi Texts and in early Coptic Monasticism I: Cryptography," *Enchoria* 9, 1979, 101–120.
27. *Adversus Haereses* I, 13–20. On Marcus, see N. Förster, *Marcus Magus.*
28. Irenaeus, *Adv. Haer.* I,14.3, pp. 216–217 (ed. by Rousseau-Doutreleau).
29. See Hayman's edition and translation in note 11.
30. See Y. Liebes, *The Doctrine of Creation of the Sefer Yezira* (Jerusalem: Schocken, 2000) [in Hebrew].
31. See note 12.
32. Müller does the same with Mani's *Great Gospel,* written in twenty-two chapters arranged according to the letters of the alphabet).

33. See W. Müller, "Mazdak and the Alphabet Mysticism of the East," *History of Religions* 3, 1963, 72–82. See also, Franz Altheim, "Mazdak and Porphyrios," ibid., 1–20. For Altheim, Mazdak's letter speculation is of Greek origin. See Patricia Crone, *The Nativist Prophets of Early Islamic Iran* (Cambridge: Cambridge University Press, 2012), for a sustained argument on the late antique Jewish Christian and Gnostic roots of a number of early Islamic heresies.
34. See George Boas, trans., *The Hieroglyphics of Horapollo* (Princeton, NJ: Princeton University Press, 1993).
35. See for instance *Philebos* 18b–c.
36. Aristotle, *Metaphysics* 985a31.
37. See W. K. C. Guthrie, *A History of Greek Philosophy*, II, 143.
38. Philo, *De Vita Mosis*, I, V, 23 (Loeb Classical Library, Philo, *Works*, VI [Cambridge, MA: Harvard University Press], 286–289).
39. The *Infancy Gospel of Thomas* and other apocryphal texts present the child Jesus being taught the alphabet. Jesus rebukes the teacher Zachaeus, arguing that he should only move to teach the *beta* after showing he knows the true nature of the *alpha*. In most versions, Jesus then expounds the mystical meaning of the alphabet. In this story, the child Jesus seems to be perceived as a *Moses redivivus*. See note 4.
40. See P. Hadot, *Le voile d'Isis. Essai sur l'histoire de l'idée de nature* (Paris: Gallimard, 2004).

9. Scriptural and Personal Authority

1. See Wilfred C. Smith, *What Is Scripture? A Comparative Approach* (Minneapolis: Fortress, 1993). Cf. also the Introduction. Another version of this chapter was published as "Modes of Scriptural and Personal Authority in Late Antique Religion," in Andrea Ercolani and Manuela Giordano, eds., *Submerged Literature in Ancient Greek Culture: The Comparative Perspective* (Berlin: De Gruyter, 2016), 169–182.
2. For a detailed study of the term "Bible" and its origins, see Jan Bremmer, "From Holy Books to Holy Bible: An Itinerary from Ancient Greece to Modern Islam via Second Temple Judaism and Early Christianity," in Mladen Popović, ed., *Authoritative Scriptures in Ancient Judaism* (Leiden: Brill, 2010), 327–360.
3. See Guy G. Stroumsa, *Hidden Wisdom: Esoteric Traditions and the Roots of Christian Mysticism* (Studies in the History of Religions 70; Leiden: Brill, 2005 [2nd ed.]), chapter 4, 79–91.
4. On this, see the seminal work of William Marx, *Le tombeau d'Oedipe: pour une tragédie sans tragique* (Paris: Minuit, 2012).
5. This is the scholarly consensus. See for instance A. T. Welch, "al-Kur'ān," in *Encyclopedia of Islam* [2nd ed.] V (1986), 400–420. For a solitary voice, according to which the text of the Qur'an was written from the start, see

John Burton, *The Collection of the Qur'ān* (Cambridge: Cambridge University Press, 1977).
6. Similar attitudes existed with regard to medical texts.
7. Eric R. Dodds, *Pagan and Christian in an Age of Anxiety: Some Aspects of Religious Experience from Marcus Aurelius to Constantine* (Cambridge: Cambridge University Press, 1965), 114.
8. See Shaul Shaked, James Nathan Ford, and Siam Bhayro, *Aramaic Bowl Spells: Jewish Babylonian Aramaic Bowls*, I (Leiden: Brill, 2014), Introduction, 1–26. For a striking argument about a Manichaean parallel of sorts to the oral law of the Mishna, see also, Timothy Pettipiece, "Coptic Answers to Manichaean Questions: The Erotapokritic Nature of the *Kephalaia*," in Marie-Pierre Bussières, ed., *La littérature des questions et réponses dans l'antiquité profane et chrétienne: de l'enseignement à l'exégèse* (Instrumenta Patristica et Medievalia 64; Turnhout: Brepols, 2013), 51–61.
9. See in particular Harvey Whitehouse, "Modes of Religiosity: Towards a Cognitive Explanation of the Sociopolitical Dynamics of Religion," in *Method and Theory in the Study of Religion* 14 (2002), 293–315. See also, Harvey Whitehouse and James Laidlaw, eds., *Ritual and Memory: Towards a Comparative Anthropology of Religion* (Walnut Creek, CA: Alta Mira, 2004). Cf. Chapter 6, note 22.
10. For an attempt to use Weber's and Whitehouse's concepts in order to understand religious trends in late antiquity, see Guy G. Stroumsa, *The Making of the Abrahamic Religions in Late Antiquity* (Oxford: Oxford University Press, 2015), 43–55 (chapter 2: "Patterns of Rationalization").
11. See esp. Tertullian, *De pudic.* II.10; *Adv. Prax.* XI.9; *Apol.* 19.1; cf. Aug., *Civ. Dei* XII.11). The concept of *regula fidei* appears in Tertullian, *Adv. Marc.* IV.12.3.
12. Tertullian, *De Praescr. Haer.* XXI.4.
13. Cyprian, *Ep.* LIX.4.13.
14. Cyprian, *Ep.* LXVI.8.3.
15. See for instance, Jack Goody, *The Power of the Written Tradition* (Washington, D.C.: Smithsonian Institution Press, 2000).
16. See William V. Harris, *Ancient Literacy* (Cambridge, MA: Harvard University Press, 1989). As we have seen in previous chapters, this is not true of Jewish society, as many young Jewish males received some kind of literate education. See for instance, Catherine Hezser, *Jewish Literacy in Roman Palestine* (Tübingen: Mohr Siebeck, 2001).
17. Peter Brown, "The Rise and Function of the Holy Man in Late Antiquity," in his *Society and the Holy in Late Antiquity* (Berkeley: University of California Press, 1982), 103–152 [first publication 1971]; as well as P. Brown, "The Rise and Function of the Holy Man in Late Antiquity, 1971–1997," *Journal of Early Christian Studies* 6 (1998), 353–376. See also, P. Brown, *Authority and the Sacred: Aspects of the Christianization of the Roman World* (Cambridge: Cambridge University Press, 1995), esp. chapter 3.

18. See Yun Lee Too, *The Idea of the Library in the Ancient World* (Oxford: Oxford University Press, 2010), chapter 3.
19. In a doctoral thesis on "The Crucified Book" submitted to the University of Michigan in 2014, Ann Starr Kreps called attention to the passage in the *Gospel of Truth* (CG I, 20: 10–21: 7) describing the crucified Jesus wrapped in a scroll (of Scriptures), as well as to parallel early Christian and Jewish texts.
20. Claudia Rapp, "Holy Texts, Holy Men, and Holy Scribes: Aspects of Scriptural Holiness in Late Antiquity," in William E. Klingshirn and Linda Safran, eds., *The Early Christian Book* (Washington, D.C.: Catholic University of America Press, 2007), 194–222, here 222. See also, Claudia Rapp, "Author, Audience, Text and Saint: Two Modes of Early Byzantine Hagiography," (Lennard Rydén Memorial Lecture, Uppsala, 2014), *Scandinavian Journal of Byzantine and Modern Greek Studies* 1 (2015), 111–129.
21. See Derek Krueger, *Writing and Holiness: The Practice of Authorship in the Early Christian East* (Philadelphia: University of Pennsylvania Press, 2004).
22. See for instance, Brian Stock, *Augustine the Reader* (Cambridge, MA: Harvard University Press, 1996).
23. On the Foucauldian concept "Program of truth," see for instance, Paul Veyne, *Les grecs ont-ils cru à leurs mythes? Essai sur l'imagination constituante* (Paris: Seuil, 1983).
24. "ḥakham 'adif mi-navi" (the sage is superior to the prophet), Babylonian Talmud, Tractate *Baba Batra* 12a.
25. Michael Berger, *Rabbinic Authority* (Oxford: Oxford University Press, 1998), 131. Florence Dupont has shown that in Rome, the *auctor* of a book was he who paid for it. See for instance F. Dupont, "Comment devenir à Rome un poète bucolique? Corydon, Tityre, Virgile et Pollion," in Roger Chartier et Claude Calame, eds., *Identités d'auteur dans l'Antiquité et la tradition européenne* (Grenoble: Million, 2004), 171–189. In the Hebrew tradition, the sole, or ultimate *auctor* is, of course, God.
26. See Babylonian Talmud, Tractate *Menaḥot* 29b, where Moses does not recognize "his" Torah as taught in Rabbi Aqiba's school. For another conception of authorless authority in nonliterate societies, see Carlo Severi, "Autorités sans auteur: Formes de l'autorité dans les traditions orales," in Antoine Compagnon, ed., *De l'autorité: Colloque annuel du Collège de France* (Paris: Odile Jacob, 2008), 93–123.
27. In *Before and After Muhammad: The First Millennium Refocused* (Princeton, NJ: Princeton University Press, 2014), Garth Fowden has mentioned prophecy, scripture and exegesis as three successive stages in the development of the Abrahamic religions (p. 56). It might be more accurate to see them, instead, as simultaneous forms of religious expression.

Conclusion

1. Averil Cameron, *Late Antiquity on the Eve of Islam* (Farnham: Ashgate, 2013), xxviii. Cf. Joel Walker, "Ascetic Literacy: Books and Readers in the East-Syrian Monastic Tradition," (2010), 311–216.
2. On the end of late antiquity, see the excellent survey of Averil Cameron, "What Exit from Antiquity?" in Shady Hekmat Nasser and Nadia al-Baghdadi, eds., *The Arab Muslim World in Universal History: Forms of Authority, Power and Transformations* (Leiden: Brill, in press).
3. See Luciano Canfora, *The Vanished Library* (London: Vintage, 1991 [First Italian edition 1987]), chapter XVI, 83–106.
4. For a study of the changing attitudes to translation practice announcing the Abbbasid translation movement, see Sebastian Brock, "Charting the Hellenization of a Literary Culture: the Case of Syriac," *Intellectual History of the Islamicate World* 3 (2015), 98–124.
5. See for instance Rachel Stroumsa, *People and Identities in Nessana* (Ph.D. Thesis, Duke University, 2005).
6. See Peter Brown, "Late Antiquity and Islam: Contrasts and Parallels," in B. D. Metcalf, ed., *Moral Conduct and Authority: The Place of Adab in South Asian Islam* (Berkeley: University of California Press, 1984), 23–37.
7. On this seemingly arcane topic, a violent polemic has stirred the French academic world, following the publication of Sylvain Gougenheim, *Aristote au Mont Saint Michel: Les racines grecques de l'Europe chrétienne* (Paris: Seuil, 2008), which argued for a major impact of Christian medieval translators. See for instance, Philippe Büttgen, Alain de Libera, Marwan Rashed, Irène Rosier-Catach, *Les Grecs, les Arabes et nous: Enquête sur l'islamophobie savante* (Paris: Fayard, 2009).
8. See Sidney H. Griffith, *The Bible in Arabic: The Scriptures of the "People of the Book" in the Language of Islam* (Princeton, NJ: Princeton University Press, 2013). Dimitri Gutas, *Greek Thought, Arabic Culture: The Graeco-Arabic Translation Movement in Baghdad and Early Abbasid Society (2nd–4th/8th–10th centuries)* (New York: Routledge, 1998) tends to minimize the Christian import on the translation movement.
9. See Dāwūd ibn Marwān al-Muqammas, *Twenty Chapters* (Sarah Stroumsa, ed., trans.) (Provo: Brigham Young University Press, 2016). Cf. Garth Fowden, *Before and After Muhammad: The First Millennium Refocused* (Princeton, NJ: Princeton University Press, 2015), 179, for situating Muqammas within the movement of scriptural exegesis in the ninth century.
10. See Yonatan Moss, "Fish Eats Lion Eats Man: Saadia Gaon, Syriac Christianity and the Resurrection of the Dead," *Jewish Quarterly Review* 106 (2016, in press).
11. See Averil Cameron, *Dialoguing in Late Antiquity* (Cambridge, MA: Center for Hellenic Studies, Harvard University, 2014). See also, Yannis Papadogiannakis, "Didacticism, Exegesis, and Polemics in pseudo-Kaisarios's

erotapokriseis," in Marie-Pierre Bussières, ed., *La littérature des questions et réponses dans l'antiquité profane et chrétienne: de l'enseignement à l'exégèse* (Instrumenta patristica et medievalia 64; Turnhout: Brepols, 2013), 271–289.

12. Michael Cook, "The Origins of Kalam," *Bulletin of the School of Oriental and African Studies* 43 (1980), 32–43.

13. John Wansbrough, *The Sectarian Milieu: Content and Composition of Islamic Salvation History* (London Oriental Series 34; Oxford: Oxford University Press, 1978).

ACKNOWLEDGMENTS

The gestation period of this book has been particularly long. I started working on the themes of some of its chapters in 2000, at the Institute of Advanced Studies at the Hebrew University of Jerusalem (now the Israel Institute of Advanced Studies). There, my classicist colleague and friend from Tel Aviv University Margalit Finkelberg and I coordinated a research group called "Mechanisms of Canon-Making in Ancient Societies."

The invitation of Lord Rees, then Master of Trinity College, Cambridge, to deliver the Birkbeck Lectures for 2011 provided the incentive for a preliminary attempt at a synthetic presentation of my views. I wish to express my deep thanks to Lord Rees and to the Fellows of Trinity College for their generous hosting during my stay in Cambridge. I have learned much from the discussion that followed each of my four lectures.

Preliminary versions of most chapters have been read before learned audiences in various places: Toulouse, Erfurt, Eisenach, Heidelberg, Berlin, Budapest, Amsterdam, Rome, Paris, Cambridge (U.K.), Princeton, Saint Louis, and New York. I am most grateful to a great number of colleagues for their remarks on those occasions. I could not possibly name them all, but I must mention at least the late Simon Price, who welcomed me so kindly to Lady Margaret Hall in 2009, and the late Evelyne Patlagean, who offered to me and to my family, for so many years, a very warm and close friendship in Paris.

I wish to thank as well my hosts Richard Serjeantson and Simon Goldhill (in Cambridge), Robert Lamberton (in Saint Louis), AnneMarie Luijendijk (in Princeton), Manuela Giordano (in Rome), Jörg Rüpke (in Erfurt and Eisenach), Bas ter Haar Romeny (in Amsterdam), Michael Welker (in Heidelberg and New York), Corinne Bonnet (in Toulouse), István Perczel and György Geréby (in Budapest), as well as Isabella Sandwell and Josef Lössl. At Oxford, Averil

Cameron, Sebastian Brock, Mark Edwards, Robin Lane Fox, Martin Goodman, Robert Parker, Beate Dignas, John Ma, Jas Elsner, Neil McLynn, Johannes Zachhuber, and Fergus Millar were the best possible guides to the world of pagan, Christian, and Jewish antiquities. Some of the topics of this book also provided the material for a seminar I taught together with Christoph Markschies at Humboldt University in Berlin, during the winter semester of 2014. My appreciation goes to him and to our students for their patience with my halting German.

Charles Stang, Eduard Iricinschi, Moshe Blidstein, Yonatan Moss, and in particular Brian Stock generously offered to read chapters and provided very helpful comments. For many years, conversations with Hildegard Cancik-Lindemaier and Hubert Cancik, in Tübingen and Berlin, with Jan Assmann and Winrich Löhr in Heidelberg, with Charles Malamoud, Evelyne Scheid-Tissinier, John Scheid, and Nicole Belayche in Paris, and with Glen Bowersock and Peter Brown in Princeton, have helped me sharpen my ideas on pagans and Christians in antiquity (and in the present). The friendship and generosity of Lorenzo Perrone, in Bologna and Jerusalem, has done much to educate me, over the years, in Origeniana, and much more. Ideas from most of these presentations were, or will eventually be, published (publication details are duly acknowledged in the first endnote of each chapter); all have undergone various, significant changes resulting in their present form. Some of the final revisions were made in Ann Arbor during my tenure as a Fellow at the Frankel Institute for Judaic Studies of the University of Michigan in the fall semester of 2015. In Ann Arbor, I was able to discuss chapters of this book with a number of people, in particular Ellen Muehlberger and Michail Kitsos.

I am deeply grateful to Sara Tropper for her absolutely splendid editing of my text. My thanks go to Rami Schwartz, who prepared the index. I am also profoundly beholden to Sharmila Sen, from Harvard University Press, for her support and careful reading at various stages of the preparation of the manuscript. The two anonymous readers of my manuscript for the Press have put me very much in their debt, and I have sought to take their many helpful remarks into due consideration.

Last in line but first in thought, Sarah Stroumsa, to whom I owe what can never be repaid.

INDEX

"Abrahamic triangle," 8–9, 135–136
Abu Qurra, Theodore, 135
aletheia (Truth), 116
Alexander the Great, 106
Amesha Spenta, 110
Ammonius Saccas, 105
Anthony, letters of, 58
apocryphal texts, 11–12, 19
Apollonius of Tyana, 104–107
Aristotelian, school, 63
Aristotle, works of, 134
Athanasius, 123, 128
Athanassiadi, Polymnia, 24
Augustine, 14, 26, 51, 125; on the Bible, 67; on books and reading, 66–70; on canonical writings, 59; *Confessions*, 69; *De Doctrina Christiana*, 62, 68; library, 83; perception of the individual, 73–74
Avesta, 20, 123

Bagnall, Roger, 78–79
Bandt, Cordula, 109–110
"barbarian philosophies," 101–102
Bardaisan, 102
Barlaam and Joasaph, 98
Basil of Caesarea, 26, 59
Beard, Mary, 13
Benedict XVI (Pope), 71–72
Bible: attitude of Church Fathers toward the Hebrew Bible, 63; ritual role, 78; role in education, 63; text of, 128; traditions of, 2, 35

Bickerman, Elias, 27, 53
"Body of Truth," 109
Book of Aḥiqar, 117
"Book of the Heart," 82
books: in ancient religion, 76–77, as cult, 15–16; in early Christianity, 77–78; oral, 123–124; in Roman society, 12–14, 67
Books of Mysteries, 21
Borgeaud, Philippe, 41
Bowersock, Glen, 52
Bowman, Alan, 57
Brague, Rémi, 4
Brahmins, 99, 101
Brown, Peter, 42, 51–52
Buddhism, 104

Cadmus, 111
Caesarea (Palestine), 80
Cameron, Averil, 133
canonization, 19–20, 29, 65–66, 87, 122–124, 125
Cappadocian Fathers, 52
Cassian, 85
Cassiodorus, 14, 27, 83, 93
Cavallo, Guglielmo, 14
Celsus, 103
Chaldean Oracles, 24, 92, 104
Christianization: of Greco-Roman culture, 64–65; of Roman Empire, 45–47, 54
Clark, Gillian, 78

Clementine literature (Pseudo-Clementine), 80, 112, 117
Clement of Alexandria, 58, 61–62, 90–91, 102, 104
codex, 3–4, 12, 14; Christian adaptation of, 77, 78–80
Cologne Mani Codex, 79
Constantine, 101
culture, Greco-Roman: Christian appropriation of, 3–5, 42–43, 45; transmission to medieval world, 42
Cumont, Franz, 46, 100
Cyprian, 126
Cyril of Jerusalem, 77

Damis, 106
dār al-ḥikma (House of Wisdom), 103
Didaskalia Apostolorum, 61
Dieterich, Albrecht, 113
Dodds, E. R., 123
Dornseiff, Franz, 109

education: Byzantine, 52; in early Christianity, 26–27, 42, 43, 70; monastic, 51–52; in Roman empire, 41; Syriac, 93–94. See also *paideia*
Epictetus, 85
Epiphanius, 91
epistēmē, 94–95
Epistle to Diognetes, 52, 75
esoteric tradition, 89–90, 102–103, 115, 119
Essenes, 72
ethics, 50–51
ethos: in Roman empire, 46, 48, 54; societal, 44–45
Eucharist, 37
Euchytes, 85
Eusebius, 56, 61, 80, 114
Evagrius Ponticus, 58

Festugière, André-Jean, 46, 100, 105
Foucault, Michel, 50, 73
Fox, Robin Lane, 51, 57, 78
Freud, Sigmund, 38
Fuchs, Harald, 102

Gamble, Harry, Jr., 77
Garden of Eden, 111
Garnsey, Peter, 45
Gelasius (Pope), 126
Gennadius of Marseille, 113

gnōsis, 90–91, 94–95
Gnostics, 21, 89–90, 109, 104
Goody, Jack, 33
Gospel of the Egyptians, 115
Gospel of Thomas, 89
Gospel of Truth, 17
Grafton, Anthony, 80
Greek Anthology, 114
Gregory of Nyssa, 91, 128

Hadot, Pierre, 45, 73
Halbertal, Moshe, 57
Halbwachs, Maurice, 30–32
Harris, William, 13
Harrison, Carol, 84
Hebbelinck, A., 109
Hebrew language, 18, 111
Hegel, Georg Wilhelm Friedrich, 89
Herford, Robert Travers, 66
hermeneutics: of canon, 9; Christian, 35, 57–58, 16, 56–57; Greek, 26–27, 60, 80, 92, 102–103, "hermeneutic communities," 16, 56–57; hermeneutic literature, 4, 11; "hermeneutic triangle," 136; Rabbinic, 37–38, 80–81; of scripture, 2, 5, 15–22, 65–66, 80–81, 87
Herodotus, 90, 99, 101, 117
Hervieu-Léger, Danièle, 32
Hilarion, Abba, 85
"holy man," 17, 105, 127–128
Homer, works of, 3, 26–27, 52, 60, 63, 64, 88, 124
Hopkins, Keith, 13, 56, 78
Horapollo, 118
Humfress, Caroline, 45

Iamblichus of Chalcis, 48, 102, 104
Iarchas, 106
Ibn al-Kiftī, 133–134
identity: collective, 75–76; religion as, 86–87
imago Dei, 74
imitatio Christi, 63, 73, 82, 131
Infancy Gospel of Thomas, 109
Inglebert, Hervé, 44
Irenaeus of Lyon, 90, 122
Isidore of Seville, 114–115
Islam, 69, 134

Jaspers, Karl, 6
Jerome, 40, 59, 113–114
Jesuits, 86

INDEX

Jesus, 122
John Chrysostom, 68
John of Damascus, 135
Johnson, William, 13
Josephus Flavius, 88, 129
Julian, 18, 24, 44, 45, 47, 52
Justinian, 104
Justinian Codex, 123
Justin Martyr, 49, 61

Kandel, Eric, 38
Krueger, Derek, 127–128

Lactantius, 58
Langer, Susanne, 45
Layton, Bentley, 84
literacy: among ancient Jews, 56; in early Christianity, 16, 78; in Roman society, 12–14, 26, 78
Lucian, 56, 90

MacMullen, Ramsey, 45
madrasa (pl. *madāris*) (religious schools), 87
Mani, 20, 49, 57, 69, 105, 122
Manichaean myth, 104
Manichaeans, 8, 11, 21, 25, 57, 91
Marcellinus, Ammianus, 99
Marcus Aurelius, 85, 122
Mark the Gnostic, 109
Marrou, Henri-Irénée, 42, 43, 67–68
Mazdak, 117
McLuhan, Marshall, 11, 22
Megasthenes, 101
memory: in Christianity, 34–38; "communicative memory," 32, 36; cultural, 32, 34–35; in Rabbinic Judaism, 36–38; theories of, 30–34
Messalians. *See* Euchytes
Midrash, 128, 130
"midrashic communities," 56, 135–136
Mishna, 65, 80, 122
Momigliano, Arnaldo, 99, 102
monks, 5–6, 35, 94, 113, 127, 129; monastic movement, 71–73, 84–87, 104
monotheism, 87–88; "pagan monotheism," 49
Muhammad, 122
Müller, Max, 25
Müller, Werner, 117
Murray, Gilbert, 100
al-Muqammas, Dāwūd ibn Marwān, 135
mystical traditions, 21, 109–110, 112–114

Nagarjuna, 106–107
Nag Hammadi codices, 115
Neoplatonic philosophy, 85, 87, 89, 92, 104
New Testament, 17, 65, 122
Newton, Isaac, 120
Nisibis Academy, 27, 83, 93–94, 104
Numenius of Apamea, 48, 49, 101, 104

On the Mystery of the Greek Letters, 109–115
oral traditions, 22–23, 36, 123, 130; of Mani, 20; in Rabbinic Judaism, 23, 80–81
Origen, 43, 47, 61, 66, 80, 99
original sin, 74
Orpheus, 92
Ottiyot de-Rabbi Akiva (Letters of Rabbi Akiva), 111

Pachomian Rule, 85, 86
Pachomius, 113
pagan literature: Patristic attitudes toward, 60–63, 87; translation of, 103, 134–135
paideia, 4–5, 34, 26–28, 42–44, 47, 92; Arabization of, 134; attitude of Church Fathers toward, 61; Christian adaptation of, 59–63, 84, 93; monastic objection to, 72. *See also* education
"People of the Book." *See* "religion of the Book"
Philo of Alexandria, 47, 60, 88, 119, 129
Philostratus, 102, 104, 105–107
Pines, Shlomo, 117
Plato, works of, 63, 89, 92, 101, 112, 118, 123
Platonic philosophy, 74, 85, 104–105, 123
Porphyry, 48, 99, 102, 105
pseudepigrapha, 129
Pseudo-Dionysius, 91
Pythagoras, works of, 63, 72, 89, 92, 99, 118

Questions and Answers literature, 84, 135
Qur'an, 2, 24–25, 39, 56, 67, 87, 123, 134

Rapp, Claudia, 127
reading, 35–36, 81–82, 85–86
redaction: of Manichaean literature, 87; of Patristic literature, 37; of Rabbinic literature, 37, 87

Reitzenstein, Richard, 46
"religion of the Book," 10–11, 24–25, 55–56, 69
religious plurality, 16–17
"rites of passage," 95
Roberts, Colin H., 14
Romanos the Melodist, 128
Rubenson, Samuel, 84

Sa'adia Gaon, 135
Sabbath, 111, 112
sacrifice, end of, 72
Sasanian Empire, 70, 100, 103–104, 124, 135
Scaliger, Joseph Julius, 41, 129
scholasticism, 92
scholē, 53, 94
scripture: "scriptural movement," 2, 22–24, 56, 76, 122–124, 127; translation of, 20–21, 70, 102, 122. *See also* hermeneutics
Sefer Yezira (Book of Creation), 112, 116–117
Sefirot, 110
Shaked, Shaul, 20, 123
Shenute, 51
Shi'ur Qoma (cosmic body of God), 109, 116
Skeat, T. C., 14
slavery, 51
Smith, Wilfred Cantwell, 56
Stock, Brian, 16, 67
Stoic philosophy, 50, 63, 122
Subrahmanyam, Sanjay, 6, 22

Tacitus, 90
Talmud, 66, 116, 123, 130
Talmud Torah (Torah study), 27, 53, 56, 88–89
Tatian, 43, 61–62, 102
Teaching of Addai, 128
Tertullian, 61, 74, 91–92, 126
Tetragrammaton, 115, 116
Themistius, 101
Theodoret of Cyrrhus, 53, 128
Theodosian Codex, 66, 75, 123
theology, 88
Trinity, 110

Umayyad Caliphate, 134
Universalism, Christian, 49

Varro, 90
verus Israel, 35, 38, 57
Veyne, Paul, 49–51

Wansbrough, John, 56, 136
Weber, Max, 124
Werner, Jaeger, 47–48
Whitehouse, Harvey, 32–33, 37, 125
Whitmarsh, Tim, 63
Williams, Megan, 80
Wisdom, conceptions of, 98–100
Woolf, Greg, 57

yeshivot (religious schools), 87, 93, 104

Zoroaster, 99
Zoroastrianism, 11, 21, 23, 57, 89, 92, 124

www.ingramcontent.com/pod-product-compliance
Lightning Source LLC
Chambersburg PA
CBHW021829090426
42811CB00032B/2083/J